THE GREAT TIBETAN
STONEWALL OF CHINA

THE STATUS OF TIBET IN INTERNATIONAL LAW AND INTERNATIONAL POLICY ON TIBET

(including Supplement containing
constitutional documents
and basic treaties)

To Agnieszka

and the people of Tibet

THE GREAT TIBETAN STONEWALL OF CHINA

THE STATUS OF TIBET IN INTERNATIONAL LAW AND INTERNATIONAL POLICY ON TIBET

(including Supplement containing constitutional documents and basic treaties)

by

MARTYN BERKIN

Barry Rose Law Publishers Limited
Chichester, West Sussex
England

© 2000 Martyn Berkin and Barry Rose Law Publishers Limited

ISBN 1 902681 11 8

All rights reserved. No part of this publication may be reproduced, stored in a retrieval system, or transmitted, in any form or by any means, electronic, mechanical, photocopying, recording or otherwise, without prior written permission of the author and publisher.

Published by
Barry Rose Law Publishers Limited
Little London, Chichester
West Sussex

CONTENTS

Tibetan Chronology	vii
Introduction	xv
Tibet and its People	1
Historical Perspective	5
Tibet Appeals to the United Nations	21
The 17-Point Agreement	28
Back to the United Nations	53
Revolt	72
Weasel Words	75
Is Tibet Part of China	83
Tibet's Status	88
Independence and Recognition in International Law	93
Self-Determination	104
China and Human Rights	114
Mongolia	142

Constitution of the People's Republic of China and Law on Regional National Autonomy	145
The Status of Hong Kong	161
British Quiet Diplomacy	167
United States Policy on Tibet	177
The Role of the European Union	187
A New Start	193
Envoy	206
Index to Documents	209
Documents	211
Index	387

TIBETAN CHRONOLOGY
(Recorded dates)

630	28th king, Songten Gampo ascends Tibetan throne at the age of 13 and marries a Nepalese princess.
633	Foundation of Lhasa.
640	China defeated by Songten Gampo who unifies Tibet.
641	Songten Gampo takes Chinese Buddhist princess as second consort.
775	First Tibetan monastery built at Samye.
7th/8th century	Sino-Tibetan war.
8th century	Trade relations established between Tibet and the Muslim world.
783	Treaty of Ching-Shui establishes boundaries between Tibet and China.
842 -1247	Collapse of Tibetan kingdom and period of decentralized control.
1252	Kublai Khan overruns eastern Tibet but embraces Lamaism and confers Tibetan sovereignty on high priest of the Sakya sect.
1368	Collapse of Mongol Yuan dynasty and start of Ming rulers in China (1368-1644). Tibet regains independence under Chang Chub Gyaltsen (1302-1364).

1391	Gedun Truppa (1391-1474) 1st Dalai Lama born at Shabtod in Tsang.
1617	Birth of Ngawang Lozang Gyatso, Great 5th Dalai Lama in whose reign Tibet was re-unified.
1644-1911	Q'ing dynasty in China (Manchu rulers).
1682	Death of 5th Dalai Lama.
1720	China invades Tibet and occupies Lhasa.
1728	China stations Amban in Tibet ("Amban" means a resident in Chinese).
1850 onwards	Chinese power in Tibet declines.
1854	Gurkhas of Nepal repulsed from Tibet.
1856	Treaty between Tibet and Nepal.
1876	Anglo Chinese Treaty.
1886	Tibet refuses to recognize Anglo Chinese Treaty of 1876.
17 March 1890	Convention between Great Britain and China relating to Sikkim signed.
5 December 1893	"Regulations regarding Trade, Communications and Pasturage" between Great Britain and China appended to Convention.

Tibetan Chronology

1894-5	China defeated in war against Japan.
1900	Boxer Rebellion in China.
11 December 1903	Great Britain invades Tibet ("Younghusband Expedition").
1 August 1904	Younghusband Expedition reaches Lhasa.
7 September 1904	Lhasa Convention between Great Britain and Tibet signed.
1905	Chinese army under Chao Erh-feng invades Tibet.
27 April 1906	Convention between Great Britain and China signed.
31 August 1907	Convention between Great Britain and Russia relating to Persia, Afganistan and Tibet.
20 April 1908	Agreement between Great Britain, China and Tibet amending 1893 Regulations signed.
1910	Chinese occupy Lhasa.
1911	Fall of Manchu Empire. Period of Nationalist rule 1912-1949.
December 1912	All Chinese troops finally expelled from Tibet.
1913	13th Dalai Lama returns from exile. Tibet and Mongolia issue proclamations of independence.

3 July 1914	(1) Convention between Great Britain, Tibet and China (which China refused to ratify) (2) Anglo Tibetan Trade Regulations (also unratified).
10 October 1918	Supplemental Agreement between China and Tibet.
1928	Invitation of Kuomintang Government to join the Chinese Republic declined by Tibet.
1931	Kuomintang Government declares Tibet to be part of China.
1931-32	Chinese forces repulsed from Tibet.
December 1933	Death of 13th Dalai Lama.
1934	"Long March".
6 June 1935	Tenzin Gyatso, 14th Dalai Lama born at Amdo, eastern Tibet.
1936	Great Britain establishes a permanent Mission in Lhasa.
1938	Fourteenth incarnation of Dalai Lama revealed.
1947	Indian Independence. India assumes Britain's treaty obligations to Tibet and takes over British Lhasa mission.

Tibetan Chronology

1 October 1949	Communists gain complete control of mainland China. Chinese People's Republic proclaimed under Chairman Mao Zedong.
6 January 1950	British Government announces *de facto* recognition of People's Republic of China.
1 May 1950	Radio Beijing May Day message announcing: "The tasks of the People's Liberation Army for 1950 are the liberation of Formosa and Tibet".
June 1950	Start of Korean War.
7 October 1950	People's Liberation Army invades Tibet.
17 November 1950	At the age of 15 the 14th Dalai Lama assumes full ruling power from the 75 year old regent Taktra who had been in power since 1941.
24 November 1950	Tibet's appeal to the United Nations adjourned.
23 May 1951	Agreement on Measures for the Peaceful Liberation of Tibet (17-point Agreement).
9 September 1951	People's Liberation Army reaches Lhasa.
March 1956	Revolt against the Chinese in eastern Tibet.
1958-60	"Great Leap Forward" in which 20/30 million die.
8 March 1959	Beginning of Tibetan national uprising.

17 March 1959	Dalai Lama flees. Tibetan Government in exile established in India.
20 June 1959	Dalai Lama publicly repudiates 17-point Agreement on the grounds of forgery and coercion.
21 October 1959	UN General Assembly adopts Resolution 1353 calling for respect of human rights of Tibetan people and their distinct cultural and religious life.
20 December 1961	UN General Assembly adopts Resolution 1723 expressing grave concerns "at the continuation of events in Tibet including the violation of fundamental rights of the Tibetan people ... considering that these events violate fundamental human rights and freedoms ... including the principles of self-determination of peoples".
18 December 1965	UN General Assembly adopts Resolution 2079 deploring the continued violation of the fundamental rights and freedoms of the people of Tibet".
1965	Outer Tibet declared an "Autonomous Region of China" by China.
1966-76	Cultural Revolution.
16 December 1966	(1) International Covenant on Civil and Political Rights and (2) International Covenant

	on Economic, Social and Cultural Rights adopted by UN General Assembly.
25 October 1971	People's Republic of China replaces Nationalist China in United Nations and takes its seat as permanent member of the Security Council.
January 1976	Death of Zhou Enlai.
September 1976	Death of Mao Zedong (end of "Cultural Revolution").
4 December 1982	Fourth Constitution of the People's Republic of China adopted. (Deng Xaioping Constitution)
1984	Law of the People's Republic of China on Regional National Autonomy adopted.
1986	Tibet opened to independent foreign travellers.
1988	Access to Tibet limited to group travellers.
1988	Dalai Lama's Strasbourg address calling for genuine Tibetan autonomy.
7 March 1989	Martial law declared in Tibet.
3-4 June 1989	Tienanmen Square Massacre.
5 December 1989	Dalai Lama awarded Nobel Peace Prize.

April 1990	China expels who it considers to be politically suspect monks and nuns from Tibetan monasteries.
1 May 1990	Martial law lifted.
1994	United States Congress passes Tibet Act.
May 1995	The 11th Panchen Lama and his parents kidnapped by the Chinese Government. Their whereabouts are unknown.
1997	United States Foreign Relations Committee hears testimony concerning Tibet.
18 September 1997	Deng Xiaoping Theory incorporated into Chinese Communist Party Constitution.
27 October 1997	China Signs International Covenant on Economic Social and Cultural Rights as a preliminary to ratification.
February 1998	Zhu Rongji appointed China's new Premier. Jiang Zemin elected as President. Li Peng retires as premier to become Chairman of National People's Congress.
1-10 May 1998	Ineffective visit to Tibet by EU Troika of Ambassadors.
5 October 1998	International Covenant on Civil and Political Rights signed by China as a preliminary to ratification.

INTRODUCTION

"Suffering is written in the valleys and in the mountains and in the villages and monasteries of Tibet. It will continue until the day Tibet is free." - Palden Gyatso (64 year old Tibetan monk who spent 33 years in Chinese prisons and labour camps in Tibet)

This book is about a lost state. It is about the position of Tibet in international law and the factors that caused Tibet to be swallowed up by China, namely: Britain's imperial policy in the past; Tibet's careless history of self-imposed isolation; the annexation of Tibet by China in 1950 after the defeat of the Kuomintang without real opposition from the international community; the violation of human rights by China; the failure of the United Nations to enforce its resolutions and covenants broken by China; the failure of weak western governments to support Tibet or say anything that might offend China; how the lure of the growing new markets of China has clouded the moral judgment of politicians and big business.

But the question of Tibet is not just about legal, historical and human rights issues. It is about a clash of values; between western democracy and oriental absolutism. It is about world stability. It is about what is to be done and that requires understanding how China is run; how China's communist government which rules 20% of the world's population maintains absolute power and why China denies self- determination to minority nationalities whose lands it clings to and colonizes, in not only Tibet but also the Autonomous Regions of Xingjiang (East Turkestan) and Inner Mongolia.

The ultimate question in this book is whether Tibet is a portent of China's wider aggressive intent and whether the campaign for Tibetan freedom involves universal moral issues concerning what can we learn from the peaceful message of Tibetan Buddhism; whether we accept or ignore that China is one of the worst repressive regimes the world has ever known; whether we, through our governments, want to profit unconditionally from China's economic growth, kidding ourselves into thinking that working with China will somehow eventually change things; or whether we demand that all democratic states and international institutions use all their diplomatic skill, economic clout and determination to tackle China on human rights and democracy to bring about Tibetan self-determination.

Because Deng Xiaoping's economic reforms have taken China from an impoverished centrally controlled Maoist state to a thriving market driven communist dictatorship, engaged in world trade, trade has elevated China to the status of a world super power and brought about an improvement in living conditions in China. But the benefits of China's economic progress are not without a price; China still illegally occupies Tibet and China is still a hard line communist dictatorship. China, one of the five permanent members of the Security Council, will not tolerate any discussion of its occupation of Tibet or record on human rights and will block any resolution which it interprets as intervention in a state's internal affairs. So that when the G8 powers discussed a proposed United Nations Security Council resolution for Kosovo, a bargain had to be struck with China, respecting Serbia's sovereignty over Kosovo to

Introduction

prevent the use of its veto.

But whilst China's Government tries to convince the world that they are really nice people working towards genuine reform, and for Chinese in the fast growing coastal zones living standards have dramatically risen, the reality for the majority in China, especially those living in the backward interior provinces and the minority nationalities, is repression and low living standards. On 18 December 1998 President Jiang Zemin boasted that China would never tread the path of democracy adding a few days later that China would crush any challenge to the communist monopoly on power.

The most commonly asked question in a study of Tibetan affairs is, "what is Tibet's status?" The Tibet question is complex but there is an answer. Tibet is an occupied country. In 1960 the International Commission of Jurists found that before 1950 Tibet was at least a *de facto* state. They say before 1950 Tibet was self-governing and that it also possessed the criteria of statehood according to the norms of international law. But that status is disputed by China, who says that Tibet has always been part of the "Motherland". In 1961 the United Nations General Assembly passed Resolution 1723 calling for the right of the Tibetan people to their fundamental rights and freedoms, including the right to self-determination. Resolution 1723 is not accepted by China.

Neither has an independent Tibet ever been on the agenda of the British Government. In the second half of the nineteenth century Britain developed a forward policy for the expediency of preventing Czarist Russia threatening British India. To block Russia, and to pursue its own self-interest, Britain borrowed inappropriate terminology from the European concept of weak Turkish suzerainty over its rebellious Balkan domains and, in a series of treaties which it attempted to force on China and Tibet, nominated China as the "suzerain" power in Tibet in exchange for China undertaking not to permit foreign interference in Tibet. But unlike the Turkish vassal states, Tibet had always had strong self-government and co-existed with China whose leaders at the time had no idea what suzerainty meant. In reality the relationship between China and Tibet had always been like a binary star system in which two generally associated but independent parts move around a common centre of gravity in conjunction, the parts being more or less equal or sometimes very unequal. That Tibet was never under the suzerainty of China is rarely something upon which China and Tibet agree.

In 1950 Tibet was invaded and forcibly overrun by the People's Liberation Army of the People's Republic of China. "Autonomy" was granted to Tibet by the Chinese in the Tibet Autonomous Region, but it was autonomy in name only. The Tibetans suffered terrible persecution and ceased to be a self-governing people. Half of Tibet (what the British called "Inner Tibet") Kham and Ando was incorporated directly into the Chinese provinces of Qinghai, Gansu, Yunnan and Sichuan and heavily populated by Han Chinese settlers. Although Britain had extensively meddled in Tibetan affairs during the Indian Empire, once it handed-over its treaty obligations on Tibet to the newly independent government of India in 1947, Britain effectively washed its hands of Tibet and, for example, when El Salvador in 1950 attempted to raise the invasion of Tibet in the United Nations General

Assembly, Ernest Bevin's Foreign Office (which had already recognized Communist China) pusillanimously professed ignorance of what was happening in Tibet and declared the legal position of Tibet uncertain, and despite events in Korea, said that the invasion was not a threat to world peace, thereby thwarting a debate on the Tibet situation in the United Nations General Assembly at the critical time of the invasion.

Despite massive popular worldwide sympathy for Tibet, the enthusiasm of western governments to cash in on China's burgeoning economy seems to enervate any positive political action. The policy on Tibet of most western governments, including Britain, has looked to prospective trade and commerce with China while professing quietly to press the Chinese Government on respecting human rights and genuine Tibetan autonomy but not independence. Britain has never officially recognized the existence of Tibet, even as a *de facto* state, and the current British Government will only say that Tibet is autonomous while recognizing the special position of China there. But self-rule will never be allowed by China's communist regime. The reliance on Chinese nationalism in China's constitutional set up is such that China will never allow genuine autonomy to minority nationalities.

Between 1949-1976 the world trod warily of Mao's China: war involving China included the Chinese Civil War, Korean War, Vietnam and Cambodian Wars. No one was prepared to stand up for a remote Himalayan state. Nothing was done, Tibet was quietly left to its fate, a threat to world peace was cynically averted and Tibet became a marginal issue of human rights. So within increased political dialogue today, the European Union Commission now says it too will practice quiet diplomacy and says: "As it attaches great importance to the respect for the cultural, linguistic and religious identity of ethnic minorities, the EU will continue to raise issues relating to these matters in Tibet within the bilateral dialogue on human rights": EU Communication "Building a Comprehensive Partnership with China", 1997. Similarly the British Government whose foreign policy in the past has singulary failed to stand up to China says that in the context of a broad co-operative new relationship with China it will be able to address human rights issues directly and work with China to bring about concrete improvements on the ground: see House of Commons statement Derek Fatchett, Minister of State, Foreign and Commonwealth Office (See Appendix, document 19).

As we shall see, United Nations resolutions and human rights covenants and general condemnation of China in report after report by leading international lawyers and non-governmental organisations exposing human rights abuses by China and supporting the Tibetan people's right to self-determination* have met with defiant response from the Chinese Government. Among the leading nations of the world, only the United States strongly challenges China's actions. The United States Department of State which publishes country by country annual reports on human rights practices is particularly condemnatory of China. There have also been important pro-Tibet measures in Congress, including recognition of the Dalai Lama as leader of the Tibetan Government in exile and the appointment of a United

Introduction

States Special Envoy for Tibet with the personal rank of ambassador (see Appendix, document 18). But apart from the United States no other government in the world recognizes the Tibetan Government in exile. Successive British Governments simply allow token debates on Tibet in Parliament and make meaningless or, worse, misleading statements on the status of Tibet despite the consensus of leading international lawyers and non-governmental organisations in the field of human rights which is that:

(1) between 1913 and 1951 Tibet was at very least a *de facto* state and the Chinese claim that it has always been part of China is not true;

(2) the Chinese invasion of Tibet in 1950 was contrary to international law;

(3) the Agreement on Measures for the Peaceful Liberation of Tibet of 23 May 1951 (the so called "17-point Agreement" between Tibet and China whereby Tibet signed away her independence) is void on the ground that it was obtained by China under fraud and duress;

(4) the continued occupation of Tibet by the People's Republic of China is unlawful;

(5) China has committed gross human rights abuses in Tibet, to the extent of genocide and that China's human rights record in Tibet is the concern of all nations;

(6) Tibet does not enjoy true autonomy;

(7) the Tibetan people are entitled to exercise the right of self-determination as defined in the United

Nations Charter, its declarations and covenants and as called for in United Nations Resolution 1723.

Respect for human rights everywhere is the concern of all civilized states. It is also the concern of all states that China should be a stable world power. But the solution of China's communist leaders to the problem of keeping themselves in power and China together is the invention of capitalist dictatorship structured around the artificial concept of greater China ("the Motherland") incorporating minority nationalities, including Tibet. No government with these aims is worth supporting and, as happened in the former Soviet Union and Federal Yugoslavia, eventually China's communism will collapse because totalitarian regimes do not last long and minority nationalities who never asked to be part of China will break away. In the end freedom always prevails over tyranny.

Paradoxically, although there are comprehensive universal covenants on human rights, including universal recognition that human rights and aggression by one country against another is the concern of all responsible states and recognition in international law of the right to self-determination, China, the world's largest state, says that what it does within its own domestic jurisdiction is its business and not the concern of other states. We only need to read China's constitutional documents to see what China is up to.

But there is no uniform system of international enforcement, although sometimes states legitimately, with the collective authority of the United Nations, take action against aggressors, for example during the Korean War and the Iraqi invasion of Kuwait. Since 1990 there have been nearly 100 conflicts in the world causing five million deaths. But there are no international policemen and, for example, when Indonesia invaded East Timor, in December 1975, despite ten United Nations resolutions calling for Indonesia to withdraw nothing was done to implement them until the tragic events of 1999; nobody intervened in Rwanda in 1994 to stop the slaughter of an estimated half million people.

Hitherto a distinction had to be noted in international law between the use of international force to restrain an aggressor and a situation where the ultimate right of self-determination, secession, was involved. Thirty years ago U Thant, Secretary-General of the United Nations (1962-1972) said: "As far as the question of secession is concerned, the United Nations has never accepted and does not accept a principle of secession on the part of its member states": Secretary-General's Press Conference, 7 UN Monthly Chronicle, February 1970, p. 36. But NATO intervention in Kosovo has changed the rules. Kosovo is part of Serbia and, in the former Republic of Yugoslavia at least, Europe has reverted to the gunboat diplomacy of the nineteenth century.

The proponents of air strikes against Serbia argue that NATO action is a humanitarian intervention that is justified in international law and in an interim ruling the International Court of Justice refused Serbia's call to halt the bombs. In comparison the North Korean invasion of South Korea and the Iraqi invasion of Kuwait were cases of aggression against neighbour states. The humanitarian case for international intervention in Tibet is compelling. Tibetans have suffered as much if not more than Albanian Kosovans. It can be achieved peaceably and can be done without getting bogged down in the question whether Tibet is historically part of China. It is all about self-determination and human rights. It requires international organisations, the United Nations, the World Bank, World Trade Organisation, G8 and individual governments including the European Union to acquire a new mind-set in dealing with China and to stop trying to accommodate China. At the time of writing this book, despite the e-mail protests of over two million people, the World Bank is proposing to lend China $81 million to do some ethnic cleansing in a squalid project re-settling 57,775 Chinese farmers in part of Tibet incorporated by China into Qinghai province. Of the EU members only Britain supports this.

China ignores its human rights obligations because it knows it can get away with it. Its Constitution in Chapter II purports to contain a list of meaningless fundamental rights. It proclaims it to be "a socialist state under the people's democratic dictatorship led by the working class and based on the alliance of workers and peasants". It now aims to sustain communism through its form of capitalism without democratic reform. The sustaining ethos of Chinese communism is rigid control state control over personal freedom. Chinese nationalism is paramount and that is why China cannot show respect for universal human rights in Tibet or anywhere else. Western politicians do seem to have not learnt the lessons of appeasing dictators in the 1930s and China's leaders are led to think they can do as they please. It falls to Wei Jingsheng, one of China's leading pro-democracy campaigners, who in a letter to the late Deng

Xiaoping written in 1992 expresses what our leader should be saying to China: "It was your one-sided propaganda that has resulted in this national discrimination against the Tibetans" and "you will be laughed at and condemned by history" for your Tibetan policies ... "You have all along advocated anti-colonialism and national independence. In fact, you do not understand what anti-colonialism and national independence are. You have only taken it as a convenient tool and do not really want to understand it or genuinely believe in it. This is exactly the root cause of your leftism."

* * * * *

* See in particular:

"The Question of Tibet and the Rule of Law" (International Commission of Jurists), 1959.

"Tibet and the Chinese People's Republic, A Report to the International Commission of Jurists by its Legal Inquiry Committee in Tibet, (International Commission of Jurists),1960.

"Human Rights in Tibet" An Asia Watch Report, February-1988.

"Tibet in China" An International Alert Report, August-1988.

International Convention on Tibet and Peace in South Asia (1989).

Report of International Hearings on Tibet and Human Rights, Bonn (1989).

Nobel Peace Prize Citation of Dalai Lama (1989).

"The Chinese and Human Rights in Tibet". A Report to the British Parliamentary Human Rights Group by WP Ledger.

Secretary-Generals Report on Situation in Tibet, UN, ENOSOC, DocE/CN4/Sub2/L19, 1991.

"Tibet: The Position in International Law", (Report of the Conference of International Lawyers on Issues relating to Self-Determination and Independence for Tibet, London 6-10 January 1993, Serindia, London:

"Resistance and Reform in Tibet", Indiana University Press, 1994

Delhi Convention of Parliamentarians Resolution (1994).

Second World Parliamentarians Resolution on Tibet (1995).

International Parliamentarians Union's 12+ Group Memorandum on Tibet (1996).

The World Conservation Congress (IUCN) Resolution (1966).

"China - No One is Safe: Political repression and abuse of power in the 1990's", Amnesty International, 1996.

(Also see Amnesty International publications: "People's Republic of China - Gross Human Rights Violations Continue", February 1996; "China State Secrets: A Pretext for Repression", May 1966; "People's Republic of China: Torture and Ill-Treatment on China's Second Periodic Report to the UN Committee Against Torture", April 1996; "People's Republic of China - Women in China: Detained, Victimized but Mobilized", July 1996. "China Action for Writers and Journalists: Appeal Cases", March 1996; "People's Republic of China - Religious Repression in China", July 1996).

"Tibet: Human Rights and the Rule of Law" (International Commission of Jurists), December 1997;

" A Poisoned Arrow - The Secret Report of the 10th Panchen Lama", Tibet Information Network, 1997.

"China's Tibet-The World's Largest Colony (Report of a Fact-Finding Mission and Analyses of Colonialism and Chinese Rule in Tibet" (UNPO in co-operation with Tibet Support Group Nederland, International Campaign for Tibet, January 1998.

"Annual Report 1998: Human Rights Violations in Tibet," 1999, Tibetan Centre for Human Rights and Democracy.

U.S. State Department, China Country Report on Human Rights Practices for 1998. (Released 26 February 1999).

TIBET AND ITS PEOPLE

"The true paradises are paradises we have lost" - Marcel Proust
1871-1922

Just like geophysics which tells us that Tibet was once under the sea before the Indian tectonic plate smashed against the Asian mainland pushing the Tibetan mountain ranges to their present dizzying loftiness, Tibetan legend says that Tibet was once covered by ocean.

A land of furious winds, blue sky, brilliant sunshine, extremes of temperature (from severe cold to sweltering heat in the course of a single day); barren landscapes are the feature of Tibet. The highest country in the world and equal to the size of western Europe, the majority of its inhabitants live at altitudes between 7,000 feet and 12,000 feet and in the north of the country up to 16,000 feet. Covering an area of just under 500,000 square miles Tibet is largely a high plateau surrounded by mountains, the Himalayas on Tibet's southern border; on the western border by the Karakoram range and in the north the Altyn Tagh mountains bordering on Xinjiang (East Turkestan). Mount Everest (Chomolongma), 29,002 feet in height as everyone knows is the highest mountain in the world and stands on its southern border with Nepal. Common to its border with Nepal and Sikkim is Kanchenjunga. Between Bhutan and Tibet lies Mount Chomolhati. Tibet is divided into three geographical regions; the arid central plateau; the great river system valleys in the southwest and southeast and the fertile lower region of eastern Tibet which China claims is part of China proper. The largest lakes in Tibet are Tso Mapham in the west, Namtso Chukmo in the northwest, Yardok Yutso in central Tibet and Tso Trishor Gyalmo in the northeast. Many of the world's mighty rivers rise in Tibet. The Sengye Khabab becomes the Indus in Pakistan; the Langchen Hhabab becomes the Sutlej in western India; the Mapcha Khabab becomes the Ganges and the Tachok Khabab flowing east becomes the Brahmaputra. The Ngochu River rises in central Tibet and eventually flows into Burma as the Salween; two rivers in the north, the Ngomchu and the Zachu merge and enter Laos and Thailand as the Mekon; the Drichu River flows through Kham and into China as the Yangtse. The Manchu River rises in eastern Tibet and eventually becomes the Yellow River of China.

Most Tibetans live in the countryside, herding mountain oxen, yaks, sheep and horses. Before the Chinese invasion about a fifth of the population were Buddhist monks and nuns living in monasteries and nunneries. A million Tibetans (600,000 of them monks and nuns) were massacred, tortured, worked to death or simply disappeared between 1950 and 1970.

The staple crops of Tibet are barley, wheat and black peas. But at lower altitudes a variety of vegetables and fruit grows in abundance. Lhasa the capital (11,000 feet) had a population of 35/40, 000 before the Chinese invaded in 1950. But during festivals the population would more than double as the people flooded into Lhasa. Near the Tashilhunpo monastery (the former residence of the Panchen Lama) is Shigatse, the second largest town with a pre-invasion population of 13/20,000. Chamdo in eastern Tibet had a population of

9/12,000. The fourth largest town is Gyantse where the fifteenth century Stupa of Gyantse is one of the chief wonders of the Buddhist world. The population of Tibet in May 1951 according to the New China News Agency was 3.75 million. The Chinese census for June 1953 gave a figure of 1.27 million for the "Tibet region and the Chamdo area" and 2.77 million Tibetans in the "whole of China". Over 125,000 Tibetans now live in exile mostly in India (centred around the Dalai Lama's Government in exile in Dharamsala) and Nepal.

The climate of Tibet varies according to the altitude, for example Lhasa can be hot and dusty in the summer; but in winter the night temperature in the mountains can dip to 30 degrees below freezing. The lower regions are less arid with moderate rainfall and more equable year round temperatures. The Tibetans although related to the Mongols are a distinct racial group with their own language, culture and religion, Tibetan Mahayana Buddhism combining aspects of an earlier Tibetan Bon belief with Buddhism introduced from India in the seventh century. Research shows that the Tibetan people have inhabited high altitudes for longer than South American Indians, as they have developed a unique genetic factor which allows them to utilize oxygen more effectively than any other high altitude dwellers: Nature Vol.287 p.486. Han Chinese (the majority nationality in China) on the other hand are a separate race constitutionally unsuited to high altitudes.

Much of old Tibet has been destroyed by China. They have destroyed most of the temples and monasteries but develop major sites for the benefit of a lucrative tourist trade. They have suppressed the Tibetan Buddhist religion and the

Tibetan language. It is estimated that two million Han Chinese have settled in Tibet (which is denied by China who says that there are only 30,000 settlers and the rest are military or technical personnel). The truth is that Tibetans are being replaced in their own country by Han Chinese settlers and every year thousands of Tibetans risk their lives escaping to neighbouring countries. As China exploits Tibetan resources, Tibetans are becoming a second class remnant people in their own country.

HISTORICAL PERSPECTIVE

"Those who have turned their attention to the affairs of men, must have perceived that there are tides in them; tides very irregular in their duration, strength and direction and seldom to be found to run twice exactly in the same manner or measure" - The Federalist No.64, John Jay 1788

All that is known of Tibet's remote history is that it comprised a number of petty kingdoms. According to Tibet legend the earliest kings descended from ropes suspended from the sky. United for the first time by the great 28th king, Songtsen Gampo, who ruled Tibet from 620 to 650 CE, his marriages to a Nepalese princess and as second consort, a Chinese princess, brought Buddhism into Tibet. In his reign, upper Burma and western China were conquered. During the reign of Thisong Detsen (742-797) China annually paid tribute to more powerful Tibet. In 779 King Tirsong Detsen invited the Buddhist masters Santarakshita and Padmasambhava from India to establish the first Buddhist monastery at Samye. During the second half of the eighth century and the first half of the ninth, Tibet continued to expand into Chinese territory. After 850 Tibet declined and Buddhist-Bon rivalries split Tibet into warring small kingdoms. But the eleventh century saw the re-introduction of Buddhism and the development of monastic life.

In 1252 Kublai Khan, the Mongol Emperor of China, conquered eastern Tibet, but embraced Lamaism and conferred sovereignty of Tibet on the high priest of the Sakya sect. The period of Sakya rule lasted about a hundred years until shortly before the collapse of the Mongol Yuan dynasty in 1368 when Tibet regained independence under its secular leader, Chang Chub Gyaltsen (1302-1364). From then on until the early eighteenth century Tibet functioned again as an independent state and in the fifteenth century its theocracy was developed further by the introduction of the system of Dalai Lama incarnations, the first of whom, recognized retrospectively, was Gedun Truppa (1391-1474). But it was actually upon the third Dalai Lama, Sonam Gyatso that the title Dalai Lama was bestowed by Altankhan of the Tumat Mongols, "Dalai" in Mongolian signifying the word "ocean", as a compliment to the depth of the Dalai Lama's spiritual knowledge. Re-unified under the great fifth Dalai Lama, Ngawang Lozang Gyatso, (1617-1682), Tibet was recognized by China as an independent sovereign state. In 1645, the building of the Potola Palace was started and about this time the fifth Dalai Lama declared his tutor Choki Gyaltsen (1570-1662) to be an incarnation of the Buddha Amitabha and installed him as Panchen Lama which means "Great Teacher". After the murder of the sixth Dalai Lama, China took advantage of political dissent and turbulence in Tibet and in 1720 despatched an army which reached Lhasa in 1728. For the first time China appointed two Chinese "Ambans" (the word amban in Chinese meaning a "resident") who were stationed in Lhasa until the expulsion of the Chinese in 1911.

By the middle of the nineteenth century Chinese influence on Tibet had already declined to nominal. But just as Tibet began to re-assert its independence at the end of the nineteenth century Tibet was increasingly brought into conflict with the British in India who regarded Tibet as within its sphere of influence.

Fearful of a Russian invasion of India through Tibet as the influence of China in Tibet dwindled, Lord Curzon (who was Viceroy of India between 1898-1905) thought it time to teach the Tibetans a lesson. But relations between Tibet and Britain had hitherto been cordial. In 1774 Warren Hastings had despatched a mission into Tibet under a Scot called George Bogle who married the sister of the Panchen Lama by whom he had two daughters who were educated and settled in Scotland. Bogle's mission went to Shigatse and established friendly relations between Tibet and Bengal so much so that a second mission was sent in 1784 under Captain Samuel Turner and Tibet agreed to grant free admission to all merchants and natives of India. In contrast to Tibet's friendly independent foreign policy a diplomatic expedition sent to Beijing in 1793 under Lord Macartney was contemptuously dismissed by Emperor Quianlong. But when the Gurkhas invaded Tibet in 1854 the relationship between Tibet and Britain soured as Tibet believed that Britain had encouraged the Gurkha invasion. Tibet's hostility to foreigners at that time was also attributable to the influence of conservative lamas who wanted Tibet to be totally isolated from the outside world. The death of the twelfth Dalai Lama in 1875 left a power vacuum until the thirteenth Dalai Lama dispensed with the Regent and assumed rule in 1894.

Disputed Tibetan borders with Sikkim, Nepal and Bhutan which the Britain had been endeavouring to settle for years without conspicuous success ought to have been no more than a minor irritant to the British Government, but events at times verging on the farcical became a *casus belli*. In 1888 a small British expedition repulsed without difficulty Tibetan soldiers from an eighteen mile strip in the Chumbi valley. But without consulting Tibet, a"Convention between Great Britain and China relating to Sikkim and Tibet" was signed in Calcutta on 17 March 1890 to which "Regulations regarding Trade, Communications and Pasturage", 5 December 1893 were appended (see Appendix, documents 1. and 2.). Under the Convention the boundary between Sikkim and Tibet was agreed and China recognized a British protectorate over Sikkim. The question of providing increased trade across the Sikkim-Tibet frontier was left open for discussions between Britain and China. Since party to neither, the Tibetans, who detested the Amban, ignored the Convention and the Regulations; grazing rights were infringed by the Tibetans, free trade was obstructed by heavy duty imposed by the Tibetan Government on goods coming from India, and boundary pillars were torn down. British attempts to negotiate with the Tibetan Government met with intransigence because the Tibetans just refused to negotiate with the British Government and in 1894 at the age of eighteen the thirteenth Dalai Lama, over the protests of the Amban, was enthroned in Lhasa.

China's already weak influence in Tibet was further weakened by a disastrous war against Japan (1894-1895) following a Moslem rebellion in the north west. "Whatever be Russia's designs on India", Curzon wrote in 1889, "whether they be serious and inimical or imaginary and fantastical, I hold that the first duty of English Statesmen is to render any hostile actions futile". Politically astute, the thirteenth Dalai Lama took advantage of the decline of the

Manchu empire by asserting Tibetan independence. Deciding that direct communication with Tibet was essential, Lord Curzon wrote to the Dalai Lama on 11 August 1900. In firm but courteous terms he urged the Dalai Lama to use his authority to secure settlement of disputed issues. A letter was taken by a British officer to Garrok in northwest Tibet for onward transmission to Lhasa, but because the Garrok Governor apparently dared not forward it to Lhasa it was returned to the Viceroy with the seals intact six months later. A second letter was entrusted to a fantastical Burmese trader called Vgajen Kazi who was setting off to Lhasa with a consignment of animals (two elephants, two peacocks and a leopard) for the Dalai Lama's private zoo. Four months later Kazi returned with this letter also intact probably having made no attempt to deliver it.

One of the criteria of statehood is the capacity to engage in formal relations with other states. If China, as it claims, had sovereignty over Tibet it is difficult to see why diplomatically correct Britain insisted that it dealt in external matters directly with the Dalai Lama and not through China. Thus the attributes of an independent sovereign Tibetan state can already be seen in Lord Curzon's time if not in the eighteenth century when friendly relations between Warren Hastings' envoys and the Tibetan Government already existed.

Believing that he had been personally insulted and that peaceful negotiations were futile, Lord Curzon sent a mission of 500 troops in June 1903 for the purpose of opening up trade negotiations and discussing British relations with Tibet. But this mission was a failure. Two Tibetan officials arrived at Nadong with instructions from the Dalai Lama to hold talks only on the border and not on Tibetan territory. After three months of stalemate limited to talks about the venue of talks, the British force was suddenly ordered by Lord Curzon to withdraw to Sikkim. Interpreting Tibet's refusal to talk as a Tibetan affront to the whole of British power in Northern India, under the pretext of alleged yak rustling by the Tibetans on the frontier with Nepal and wild rumours of Russians in Lhasa, Colonel Francis Younghusband (who had led the abortive earlier mission) was appointed Commissioner for Tibetan Frontier Matters by Lord Curzon with nebulous orders to advance to Gyantse "for the sole purpose of obtaining satisfaction".

But the British Government's obsession with Russian designs on Tibet lacked understanding that many Russian subjects were Buddhist (the Tibetan Abbott Dorjieff was a Russian citizen from the mainly Buddhist Russian state of Buryatia) and that the Czar and Czarina's interest in Tibet was purely spiritual. A meeting between Dorjieff and the Czar and Czarinna at the Yalta summer palace in September 1900 took place and an exchange of letters and presents was interpreted by British intelligence as further evidence of Russian designs on Tibet.

On 11 December 1903, ignoring Chinese and Russian protests, a British expeditionary force under Colonel Younghusband, with a substantial military escort under the command of an obnoxious Brigadier-General, James Macdonld, crossed the Jelap La Pass leading from Sikkim at 14,390 feet above sea level and entered Tibet. Younghusband's ill-defined diplomatic objectives were to persuade the Tibetan Government to accept the Anglo-Chinese Convention and Regulations of 1890 and 1893 defining the border and to recognize Chinese "suzerainty" over Tibet which, according to British forward strategy, would thereby create a buffer state and check a Russian threat to India through Tibet. Balfour told King Edward VII on 6 November 1903:" The Cabinet are apprehensive that the Viceroy entertains schemes of territorial expansion detrimental to Indian interests and to international relations of the Empire."

With thousands of Indian and Sikh troops led by British officers, possessing a maxim gun and heavy artillery the imperial gunfire easily cut to pieces the courageous Tibetans armed only with spears, swords and ancient matchlock rifles in a series of fierce pitched battles (Guru, Red Idol Gorge, Karo Pass and Gyantse) in which over 3,000 Tibetans died (against only 40 British expeditionary force casualties). The invasion lasted eight months and ended when the British with fixed bayonets marched noisily into Lhasa on 1 August 1904 to the accompaniment of a brass band (ignorant that the hand clapping of the Tibetan crowd was a token of abuse and not a sign of welcome) only to find that the Dalai Lama had fled to Mongolia leaving the seals of office with an extremely able Regent (the Ganden Tri Rimpoche, Lozang Gyaltsen Lannosha) who was authorized to sign a Treaty with the British.

By 4 September 1904 Younghusband reached agreement with the remnant Tibetan Government. Under the Lhasa Convention (see Appendix, document 3) the Tibetan Government agreed that it would not without the previous consent of the British Government grant concessions or give up any Tibetan land to any foreign power, permit no such power to intervene in Tibetan affairs and admit no representative of any foreign power to Tibet. Trade marts at Gyantse and Gartok were to be opened up and the Tibetans agreed to respect the 1890 Anglo-Chinese Convention and pay an indemnity of 7.5 million rupees (about £500,000) which the Tibetans were generously given 75 years to pay. But exceeding his authority Younghusband added provision for the stationing of an agent in Gyantse with rights to visit Lhasa if necessary and the British occupation of the Chumbi valley as security until the indemnity expired.

The Convention was signed on 7 September 1904 in the Potala Palace with British heavy guns trained on its walls in case of trouble. After the signing ceremony the British troops celebrated with football, held a horse race meeting and within a week were gone.

Almost as soon as the ink was dry, the British Government vetoed the Lhasa Convention. This was taken as an acute rebuff by Curzon which he expressed in such vehement language that the Cabinet decided not to re-appoint him when his leave expired. It decided to get out of Tibet completely. The article giving the British access to Lhasa was torn up. The indemnity was reduced to 2.5 million rupees payable over three years and the Chumbi valley was to be vacated by 1908 (see Appendix, document 4). In the 1906 Convention between Great Britain and China, the British agreed to keep out of Tibet and deal only with the Tibetans through China. As Valentine Chirol of *The Times* prophetically wrote in a private letter at the time: "The end of it will be that China has climbed back into Lhasa on Younghusband's shoulders".

It is difficult to see what the invasion achieved. Britain

retreated as soon as it could and the treaty was promptly torn up by Britain. As a result of the invasion and Britain's undertakings in the 1906 Convention China must have considered it the open season for invading Tibet. Successive British Governments had played the "Great Game" (the spying game between Russia and Britain in the Asiatic deserts) and now Britain was stupidly encouraging China as part of that strategy to think of Tibet as its back yard. But there were no Russians in Tibet and Tibet did not recognize any Chinese rights over Tibet. Only the Dalai Lama emerges with credit having steered between the Scylla of foreign powers and the Charybdis of conservative lamas (who he later claimed, prevented him establishing friendly relations with Great Britain before 1904). He survived the British invasion and was the architect of Tibetan independence that lasted until 1950.

But in 1906, again without consulting the Tibetan Government, Great Britain signed an agreement with China the "Convention between Great Britain and China respecting Tibet" at Beijing, 27 April 1906 (See Appendix, document 5) whereby Britain and China confirmed the amended Lhasa Treaty and Britain engaged not to annex Tibetan territory or interfere in the administration of Tibet, China undertaking not to permit any other foreign state to interfere with the territory or internal administration of Tibet. In the following year without informing Tibet, Persia, Afganistan or China, Britain signed a further set of ill thought-out agreements with Tzarist Russia concerning Persia, Afghanistan and Tibet, the "Convention between Great Britain and Russia relating to Persia, Afghanistan and Tibet", 31 August 1907 appending to the latter the Declaration of the Viceroy varying the Lhasa

Treaty of 1904 (see Appendix, document 5) which was to land the twentieth century with three major areas of conflict. Persia was divided into two spheres of influence with a neutral zone. In Afghanistan Russia undertook to have no political relations with the Afghan Government except through Britain and Britain undertook not to change the political state of that country. Concerning Tibet, Britain and Russia admitted China's "suzerainty" over Tibet (the first appearance of the word in treaty) and agreed not to send representatives to Lhasa or negotiate with Tibet except through the intermediary of the Chinese Government. To consolidate this piecemeal and chaotic treaty-making the Britain arranged the tripartite 1908 Agreement between the governments of Britain, China and Tibet amending the 1893 Trade Regulations.

In 1914, with China in turmoil, Britain attempted to re-negotiate with a further treaty and trade agreement with Tibet and the new Republic of China. This agreement says in Article 2: "The governments of Tibet and China recognizing that Tibet is under the suzerainty of China and recognizing the autonomy of Outer Tibet, engage to respect the territorial integrity of the country, and to abstain from interference in the administration of Outer Tibet (including the selection and installation of the Dalai Lama which shall remain in the hands of the Tibetan Government at Lhasa)". China undertook not to turn Tibet into a Chinese province and Great Britain undertook not to annex Tibet or any portion of it. Obscurely Clause 5 says: "... Great Britain agrees to relinquish her rights of extra-territoriality in Tibet, whenever such rights are relinquished in China ..."

But the Chinese had been carrying systematic incursions into Tibetan territory since 1896. They came back in 1906 under the ferocious Chinese commander, Chao Erh-feng (nick-named "Butcher Chao" for his reputation for wholesale executions), killing and looting. Chao was appointed Imperial Resident with instructions to turn Tibet into a Chinese province. The Dalai Lama returned to Lhasa in December 1909 but his stay was short-lived and within a few months he fled again, this time south seeking the protection of the British in Darjeeling just as Butcher Chao's soldiers closed in on Lhasa, firing on the Potola. When the Chinese discovered that the Dalai Lama had fled, they sent two hundred soldiers in pursuit and put a price on his head.

On 14 March 1910 the Dalai Lama, treated by the British as head of state, met Lord Minto, the new Viceroy in Calcutta at Hastings House. The Dalai Lama invoked the 1904 and 1906 Conventions for assistance from the British to drive out the Chinese but Britain refused to intervene and Tibet's salvation only came in October 1911 when a revolution led by Sun Yat-sen overthrew the Manchu Dynasty in China. As news of the revolution reached Tibet the Chinese soldiers stationed in Lhasa mutinied. They attacked the Amban's house and called for other Army units to join them for the march back to China. The Amban and Chao Erh-feng fled. In 1912 Chao Erh-feng was executed by his own people. The Tibetans rose against the Chinese attacking them at Shigatse and Gyantse. Meanwhile in November 1911 the Chinese returned to Lhasa which was divided and contested in street fighting between the two zones; the north occupied by the Tibetans, the south by the Chinese. But the occupying Chinese were short of food and supplies. In 1912 the Dalai

Lama returned to Tibet and a Chinese surrender was negotiated. A surrender agreement was signed on 12 August 1912 stipulating that the Chinese would lay down their arms and that troops and officials would return to China within 15 days (see Appendix, document 7) and a further agreement 14 December 1912 between the Chinese and Tibetan Governments (see Appendix, document 8) agreed the Chinese withdrawal from Lhasa through India.

Shortly after his return to Lhasa in 1913 the Dalai Lama issued the proclamation which is regarded by Tibetans as Tibet's Declaration of Independence, declaring Tibet to be a, "small, religious and independent nation", stressing the need "to safeguard and maintain the independence of Tibet", (see Appendix, document 9). Thus by 1913 the Chinese had been expelled from all Tibet. But in another muddled attempt to clarify Tibet's status, the British Government again interfered and arranged talks with Tibet and China leading to the unratified "Convention between Great Britain, China and Tibet-1914" and the new "Anglo-Tibetan Trade Regulations-1914" between Great Britain and Tibet (see Appendix, documents 10 and 11). But although the Chinese participated fully in the talks and the Convention was initialled by the Chinese Plenipotentiary, the Convention was neither signed nor ratified by the revolutionary Chinese Government. Nevertheless the British and Tibetan Governments subsequently went through the meaningless exercise of agreeing to adhere to the Convention between themselves, but so far as China was concerned the Convention was repudiated.

On 19 August 1917 and 10 October 1918 the Chinese and

Tibetan Governments entered into a Supplementary Agreement concerning the withdrawal of the defeated Chinese troops (see Appendix, documents 12 and 13) "pending the receipt of the decisions of the President of the Republic and the Dalai Lama regarding the Chiamdo negotiations". In 1919 China submitted draft proposals to Britain to renegotiate the Simla Convention but no alteration was ever agreed. In 1936 regarding itself no longer bound by the treaties with China, Britain established a Mission in Lhasa.

Once India obtained its independence in 1947 Great Britain relinquished all rights and responsibilities in Tibet as set out in the treaties with China and Tibet, and the new government of India assumed those rights and responsibilities, (see s.7 of the Indian Independence Act 1947). After Indian independence, until the Chinese invasion the Indian Government treated Tibet as an independent state just as the British had done, for example, taking over the British Mission and continuing to employ the former British representative Hugh Richardson as its representative. It invited Tibet to send delegates to the Asia Relations Conference in 1947 where Tibet was seated along with the other delegates of other states and had its flag on the table. But in 1950 Britain and India failed to support Tibet in the United Nations General Assembly thereby seriously damaging the Tibetan cause.

With the expulsion of the Chinese in 1913, Tibet became less isolated. Younghusband's army in 1904 had been the first Europeans openly to enter Lhasa. During his two years in exile (1910-1912) the Dalai Lama struck up a friendship with Charles Bell, a Tibetan-speaking English political officer, who had been assigned to look after him. After his restoration to

Lhasa the Dalai Lama invited Bell in 1920 to visit him and when the British Cabinet decided that the Bolshevik Revolution had rendered null and void Britain's commitment to the 1907 Anglo-Russian Convention which prohibited such visits pressed Bell to accept the invitation. There were also visits to Lhasa by Colonel Bailey, then Political Officer in Sikkim and in 1930 by Bailey's successor Colonel Weir. Weir met the Dalai Lama for a second time in 1932 to advise on China. Harry Williamson, the next Political Officer, also visited Lhasa twice for talks but lucklessly became ill on his second visit, died and is buried at Gyantse alongside Younghusband's troops who fell in Tibet. Following the death of the thirteenth Dalai Lama in December 1933, Basil Gould the new political officer in Sikkim came to Lhasa at the Tibetans invitation leaving behind a young Tibetan speaking official Hugh Richardson as head of a small British mission in Lhasa.

After 1913 the Tibetan Government attempted to modernize Tibet. Paper currency was introduced (banknotes were issued in denominations of 5, 10, 15, 25 and 50 tamkas (later a 100 sang note was introduced)). Postage stamps were also introduced and silver coins minted. Four Tibetan boys were sent to English public school. One of the boys was trained as an electrical engineer after leaving Rugby and he eventually began the electrification of Lhasa. The Tibetan Army was reformed and modelled on British lines and the Dalai Lama fostered friendly relations with Great Britain until his death in December 1933.

On 22 February 1940 the 4 year old boy, Tenzin Gyatso was enthroned as fourteenth Dalai Lama. In 1941 after an internecine struggle Regent Rating resigned and was superseded by Regent Taktra Rimpoche. But Tibet unwisely withdrew from world events and remained strictly neutral in World War II finding to its cost that, unlike its sister state Mongolia, it had no international support at the end of World War II. Thus Mongolia with Soviet backing but not neutral Tibet was included in the great powers' plans for world peace at Yalta in 1944.

Hugh Richardson points out in his book "Red Star over Tibet" (Delhi 1959) p.8:"When the Manchu dynasty collapsed in 1911, Tibet completely severed that link and until the Communist invasion in 1950 there was no Chinese Government in Tibet and Tibet enjoyed full *de facto* independence from Chinese control".

Although between 1913 and 1950 successive Chinese Governments made sporadic claims that Tibet was part of China, during this period Tibet was completely self-governing, and despite occasional border skirmishes between Tibetan and Chinese troops, China made no effective encroachment on Tibetan territory and had no influence in Tibet. Within weeks of the proclamation of the Chinese Republic in 1912, however, Sun Yat-sen, the revolutionary who had been elected China's first president was replaced by a powerful military figure from the old order, Yuan Shih-K'ai. By 1914 he was virtual dictator. After Yuan's death in 1916 China was divided up between war lords and civil war raged in China in the 1920s, causing millions of deaths; only the Treaty Ports under foreign protection remained safe. In 1923 Sun Yat-sen's revolutionary party re-organized the Nationalist Kuomintang Party and formed an alliance with the Communists. But Sun Yat-sen died in 1925 and by 1926

Chiang Kai-shek had succeeded in unifying the nation and crushing the war lords. Soon, however, the Communists rose against the Kuomintang only to be defeated and in 1934 the Communists began the "Long March" to the north west where Mao Zedong took charge. After World War II, in which only the Kuomintang fought the Japanese, full scale civil war broke out between the Kuomintang Government under Chiang Kai-shek and the Communist Government under Mao Zedong and by 1949 the Communists were in control of all mainland China.

The Permanent Court of International Justice stated in *Legal Status of Eastern Greenland* (1933), Series A/B, No.53 (cited with approval in the *Western Sahara Case*, 1975 ICJ 12), a claim to sovereignty based upon continued display of authority involves "two elements each of which must be shown to exist: the intention and will to act as sovereign, and some actual exercise or display of such authority". Before 1913, Tibet had never been under direct Chinese rule. It had enjoyed self-government with only very weak links with China. Britain had called it "suzerainty". But by 1913 Tibet had driven out the Chinese and declared independence. Tibet was truly self-governing until 1950 and even the one-sided 17-point Agreement impliedly concedes in point 14 that Tibet had hitherto been responsible for its own external affairs. Moreover as the former colonies in post-colonial South East Asia, (India, Pakistan and Burma (which Britain had annexed in 1852)) lined up for independence Tibet did not figure in any discussions to become independent because it already possessed *de facto* independent status.

TIBET APPEALS TO THE UNITED NATIONS

"The Pope! How many divisions has he got?" - Joseph Stalin 1879-1953

By the autumn of 1949 the People's Liberation Army gained complete control of the Chinese mainland, and the Nationalist forces of Chiang Kai-shek fled to Taiwan. On 1 October 1949, the Chinese People's Republic was proclaimed under Chairman Mao Zedong. In October 1949 Radio Beijing rhetorically proclaimed that Tibet was part of China and that the People's Liberation Army would march into Tibet to liberate the Tibetans from foreign imperialists. Actually there were six westerners in the whole of Tibet at the time. Fearing the worst the Tibetans sent a mission to engage in talks with the Chinese to try to save their independence. Talks were held in New Delhi on 5 September 1950 but little headway was made and China suggested an adjournment to Beijing. In the meantime on 25 October 1950 (the invasion having began on 7 October 1950) the People's Republic of China announced that: "People's army units have been ordered to advance into Tibet to free three million Tibetans from imperialist oppression and to consolidate national defences on the western borders of China". India who had all along been advising that the Sino-Tibetan dispute should be settled peaceably, could only express its "deep regret that the Chinese Government should have decided to seek a solution to the problem of their relations with Tibet by force". In reply to the government of

India, the People's Republic of China replied: "Tibet is an integral part of China and the problem of Tibet is entirely a domestic problem of China. The Chinese People's Liberation Army must enter Tibet, liberate the Tibetan people and defend the frontiers of China". The government of India in a Note of 31 October 1950 repudiated China's charges and suggested a solution on the basis of Tibetan autonomy under Chinese suzerainty. It stated that "Tibetan autonomy is a fact" and described military operations against Tibet as unprovoked and unjustifiable. Yet China simply restated its position over Tibet and accused India of trying to prevent China exercising its sovereignty over Tibet.

Within a matters of days, despite stiff resistance, the hopelessly outnumbered poorly armed Tibetan Army suffered a decisive defeat. On 19 October 1950, Chamdo in eastern Tibet fell to the Chinese. At Chamdo, the invasion halted whilst China waited to see what the world would do.

On 11 November 1950, Tibet made a desperate appeal to the United Nations begging "the nations of the world to intercede ... and restrain Chinese aggression". Tibet said it disputed the Chinese claim that Tibet was part of China. Tibet said China's claim conflicted radically with the facts and Tibetan opinion and invited China if it thought it had claims on Tibet to use civilized methods open to it not involving the use of force or coercion. "The armed invasion of Tibet for the incorporation of Tibet into Communist China through sheer physical force" it declared was "a clear case of aggression". So long as the people of Tibet were compelled by force to become part of China against their will and consent, it continued, " the present invasion of Tibet will be the grossest instance of the violation of the weak by the strong", adding "Tibet will not go down without a fight, though there is little hope that a nation dedicated to peace will be able to resist the brutal effort of men trained to war, but we understand that the United Nations has decided to stop aggression wherever it takes place."

Articles 1(1); 2(3); 2(4); 2(6) of the United Nations Charter enshrine the principle prohibiting the use of force in international relations. In international law the Charter obliges members of the United Nations and non-members alike, to settle their disputes by peaceful means and to abstain in their relations with other states from the threat or use of force. Article 2(6) says that the United Nations must ensure that "states which are not Members of the United Nations act in accordance with these Principles so far as may be necessary for the maintenance of international peace and security". Thus within the norms of international law an unrecognized state or territory has the right to respect for its fundamental rights by other states including the right to respect for its territorial integrity and independence. These are rights which can not be violated with impunity; see Ti-Chiang Chen, "The International Law of Recognition: With Special Reference to Practice in Great Britain and the United States", LC Green, ed (London 1951) n.22, p.33 and H.W. Briggs, *The Law of Nations: Cases, Documents and Notes* (New York, NY, 1952), pp.114-115. Whatever Tibet's status may have been before being invaded by China in 1950, the use of force by China, even though neither of them was a member of the United Nations, was contrary to international law.

In fact until 25 October 1971, Nationalist China held

China's United Nations membership and Nationalist China was one of the five permanent members of the Security Council, the others being, the United States of America, Great Britain, the Soviet Union and France. It was not until UN Resolution 2758 [XXIV] of 1971 that the General Assembly decided: "to restore all its rights to the People's Republic of China and to recognize the representatives of its government as the only legitimate representative of China to the United Nations and to expel forthwith the representative of Chiang Kai-shek from the place they unlawfully occupied at the United Nations and in all the organizations related to it".

Although primary responsibility for the maintenance of peace lies with the Security Council, the General Assembly which comprises all United Nations member states can discuss any question or matter within the scope of the Charter, including the maintenance of international peace and security and can make recommendations to United Nations members provided the Security Council is not itself dealing with the same matter: see Articles 10, 11, and 12 of the United Nations Charter. Similarly under Article 14 of the United Nations Charter, the General Assembly may "recommend measures for the peaceful adjustment of any situation regardless of origin, which it deems likely to impair the general welfare or friendly relations among nations" and although resolutions and declarations of the General Assembly are not binding in practice they have, however, covered a wide range of matters which have become part of international law, including colonial disputes, violations of human rights and the need for justice in international economic affairs, so much so that at the height of the Cold

War in response to fears in the General Assembly that the exercise of the Security Council veto might render the United Nations powerless to take effective measures, "The Uniting for Peace Resolution", (General Assembly Resolution 377[V]) was adopted by the General Assembly in 1950. It provides that where the Security Council because of lack of unanimity among the permanent Members fails to exercise its responsibility upon the occurrence of a threat to the peace, a breach of the peace or act of aggression, the General Assembly was to consider the matter at once with a view to making appropriate recommendations to members for collective measures, including the use of force when necessary in the case of a breach of the peace or act of aggression. (If not in session the General Assembly can meet within twenty-four hours in emergency special session). Thus, in 1956 the General Assembly created the United Nations Emergency Force to supervise a cease-fire in the Suez crisis and in 1960 the United Nations Congo Force attempted to restore order in the former Belgian colony. The Uniting for Peace procedure has also been used for example with regard to the 1956 Hungarian crisis, conflict in the Lebanon and Jordan in 1958, the war between Israel and its Arab neighbours in 1967, the East Pakistan/Bangladesh question in 1971, Afghanistan in 1980, Namibia in 1981 and the Palestine question in 1980/82.

The unprovoked aggression of the Peoples's Republic of China against Tibet was raised in the United Nations by El Salvador in November 1950 under Article 35 of the UN Charter. Reminding the United Nations of its primary role to maintain international peace and security, El Salvador's delegate said: "It is true that Tibet is not a member of the United Nations, but it is also a clear fact that the responsibilities of this organization are not limited to the maintenance of international peace among members, but, on the contrary, that they extend to the whole world."

When El Salvador's motion that the Tibetan appeal should be put on the agenda of the General Assembly (Item: "Invasion of Tibet by Foreign Forces" [A/1453]) came before the General Committee of the General Assembly, El Salvador begged the members of the United Nations not to dismiss the Tibetan case unheard. The British delegate Sir Gladwyn Jebb, professing ignorance of what was happening in Tibet and declaring that the legal position was uncertain, expressed the hope that the dispute would be settled amicably and proposed that the matter should be adjourned. The Indian Government, supporting the British proposal, pointed out that the Chinese forces had ceased to advance after the fall of Chamdo, a town some 270 miles from Lhasa. Arguing for postponement of the issue, the Indian delegate said that, "The Indian Government was certain that the Tibetan question could still be settled by peaceful means, and that such a settlement could safeguard the autonomy which Tibet had enjoyed for several decades while maintaining its historical association with China". The Soviet Union and the Chinese Nationalists also opposed the discussion on the ground that Tibet was an integral part of China. The United States later admitted it agreed to an adjournment solely because the government of India (politically and geographically the most closely affected state) had suggested that the question could be settled peaceably and honourably. On 24 November 1950, thanks to lack of support, the General Committee unanimously decided to postpone consideration of the item indefinitely on the ground that the information available was insufficient.

Shocked by the failure of the United Nations to do anything, the Tibetans sent a telegram to the United Nations on 8 December 1950 expressing concern and dismay at the indifferent treatment meted out to "the peace appeal of the weak and peace-loving people ... beleaguered by their powerful neighbours". They requested the United Nations to send a fact-finding Commission to carry out investigation in Tibet but to its shame the United Nations took no action.

THE 17-POINT AGREEMENT

"God pardon all oaths that are broke to me" - Richard II, William Shakespeare 1564-1616

In the absence of any positive reaction from the international community it did not take China long to consolidate its position. By the end of November 1950 Chinese forces were strongly entrenched in western Tibet. On 21 November 1950, the Dalai Lama (who had assumed full powers at the age of 15) and leading officials of his government, left Lhasa, reaching the Chumbi Valley near the Indian border intending to negotiate with the Chinese invaders at arms length or seek asylum in India. An exchange of messages followed between the Tibetan and the Chinese Governments whose troops were entrenched in camps at lower altitudes to escape the freezing Tibetan winter.

In April 1951, the beleaguered Tibetans sent a delegation to Beijing to "negotiate" an agreement between Tibet and China and the so-called 17-point Agreement, (see Appendix, document 14) was signed on 23 May 1951. Written in the mind-set of Marxism-Leninism the recitals of the 17-point Agreement declare that Tibet has always been part of China. "... Over the last 100 years or more" "... imperialist forces", it prates, "penetrated into China and in consequence also penetrated into the Tibet region and carried out all kinds of deceptions and provocations. Like previous reactionary governments the Kuomintang reactionary government continued to carry out a policy of oppression and sowing dissention among the nationalities, causing division and disunity among the Tibetan people. The local government of Tibet did not oppose the imperialist deception and provocation and adopted an unpatriotic attitude towards the great Motherland. Under such conditions the Tibetan nationality and people were plunged into the depths of enslavement and suffering".

Declaring that all nationalities in China are equal, China pledged the Tibetans, "freedom to develop their own spoken and written languages and to preserve or reform their customs, habits and religious beliefs ...". Under points (1) and (2) the Tibetans undertook" to unite and drive out imperialist aggressive forces from Tibet and return to "the big family of the Motherland - The People's Republic of China" and actively assist the People's Liberation Army to enter Tibet and consolidate national defences. China agreed in point (3) to afford the Tibetan people the right of exercising national regional autonomy and under points (4) and (5) China promised not to alter the existing political system in Tibet or the established status, function and powers of the Dalai Lama and Panchen Lama (qualified in point (6) by the statement that that meant their status function and powers "when they were in friendly and amicable relations with each other"). Under point (7) China promised to maintain a "policy of freedom of religious belief"and declared that: "The religious beliefs, customs and habits of the Tibetan people shall be respected and lama monasteries shall be protected". Point (8) says that the Tibetan army was to be incorporated into the People's Liberation Army. Point (9) contains the vague statement that the Tibetan language "shall be developed step by step in accordance with the actual condition in Tibet"and point (10) contains a similar statement with regard to Tibetan agriculture. Point (11) promises that in matters relating to reforms "there will be no compulsion on the part of the central authorities" and further stipulates that "The local government of Tibet should carry out reforms of its own accord, and, when the people raise demands for reform, they shall be settled by means of consultation with the leading personnel of Tibet". Point (12) says that former imperialist and pro-Kuomintang can continue to hold office provided they do not engage in sabotage or resistance. Point (13) contains a picaresque statement that the People's Liberation Army will abide by the agreement "and shall also be fair in all buying and selling and shall not arbitrarily take a needle or thread from the people". Responsibility for all external affairs is taken away from the Tibetan Government under point (14) and it declares there will be peaceful co-existence with the neighbouring countries. Point (15) establishes a Military and Administrative Committee and a Military HQ in Tibet which it says should include local Tibetan personnel. Point (16) makes it clear that funds needed by the Committee and HQ are to be provided by the People's Republic of China and goes on to say that the local government will assist the People's Liberation Army "in the purchase and transport of food, fodder and other daily necessities". Point 17 states that the agreement is to come "into force immediately after signatures and seals are affixed to it" (in other words the agreement was expressed to be effective immediately without ratification by the Tibetan Government).

Tsepon W. D. Shakabpa (a leading figure in the Tibetan Government of the time) in his book "Tibet A Political

History", 1984, p.304, gives this account of what happened when the 17-point Agreement was signed.

> "Once in Chinese hands, the Tibetan delegation had no alternative but to fall prey to Chinese pressure and to serve as an instrument for the construction of the so-called 'Agreement on Measures for the Peaceful Liberation of Tibet', commonly referred to as the 17 Article agreement of 23 May 1951. It is to be noted that the Tibetan delegation was not allowed to refer to the Dalai Lama or the Tibetan Government for additional instructions. On top of this contempt and disregard for the generally accepted rules of international law and practices, the Chinese forged duplicate Tibetan seals in Peking, and forced our delegation to seal documents with them."

In international law as in domestic contract law where a breach of an agreement is material, the injured party may treat the agreement as discharged and void. A void treaty has no legal force: see Article 69(1) Vienna Convention on the Law of Treaties. Coercion, fraud and the threat or actual use of force are generally regarded as vitiating *ab initio* the validity of international agreements under the norms of international law and in violation of the United Nations Charter. Under Article 52 of the Vienna Convention on the Law of Treaties a treaty is void if its conclusion has been procured by the threat or use of force in violation of international law. As was said by the International Court of Justice in the *Namibia* case: "One of the fundamental principles governing the international relationship thus established is that a party which disowns or does not fulfil its obligations cannot be recognized as retaining those rights which it claims from the relationship ... The rules laid down by the 1969 Vienna Convention on the Law of Treaties concerning termination of a treaty relationship on account of breach (adopted without a dissenting vote) may in many respects be considered as a codification of existing customary law on the subject ...": *Namibia (SW Africa) (Advisory Opinion)* ICJ Reports 1971 pp.16, 47; 49 ILR pp.2, 37.

In the *Nuclear Test Cases* ICJ Reports 1974, 253, 268;57 ILR 398, 413, the Court added: "One of the basic principles governing the creation and performance of legal obligations, whatever their source, is the principal of good faith. Trust and confidence are inherent in international co-operation, in particular in an age when this co-operation in many fields is becoming increasingly essential. "

The International Law Commission was established by UN General Assembly Resolution 174[II] of 21 November 1947 to promote the progressive development of international law and its codification. It drafted the 1969 Vienna Convention on the Law of Treaties (which was adopted unanimously and came into force in 1980) laying down a number of principles reflecting the existing norms of international law. The International Law Commission's Commentary in The Vienna Convention says: "That an obligation of good faith to refrain from acts calculated to frustrate the object of the treaty attaches to a state which has signed a treaty subject to ratification appears to be generally accepted." *Pacta sunt servanda* - the rule that treaties are binding on the parties and must be performed in good faith - is the fundamental principle of the law of treaties. There is much authority in the jurisprudence of international tribunals for the proposition that in the present context the principle of good faith is a legal principle which forms an integral part of the rule *pacta sunt servanda*. Thus, speaking of certain valuations to be made under Articles 95 and 96 in the Act of Algeciras, the International Court of Justice said in *Case concerning Rights of Nationals of the United States of America in Morocco*, Judgment 27 August 1952, (ICJ Rep. 1952, p.212): "The power of making the valuation rests with the Customs authorities, but it is a power which must be exercised reasonably and in good faith". Similarly, the Permanent Court of International Justice, in applying treaty clauses prohibiting discrimination against minorities, has insisted in a number of cases, that treaty clauses must be so applied as to ensure the absence of discrimination in fact as well as law; in other words, the obligation must not be evaded by a merely literal application of the clauses. Numerous precedents can also be found in the reports of arbitral tribunals. To give only one example, the *North Atlantic Coast Fisheries Arbitration*, the Tribunal, dealing with Great Britain's right to regulate fisheries in Canadian waters in which she had granted certain fishing rights to United States nationals by the Treaty of Ghent, said: "... the Treaty results in an obligatory relation whereby the right of Great Britain to exercise its right of sovereignty by making regulations is limited to such regulations as are made in good faith, and are not in violation of the Treaty."

That Tibet was entitled to repudiate the 17-point Agreement is beyond question. Articles 26, 42, 45, 46, 48, 49, 51, 52, 53, 60, 61, 62, 64, 65, 69, 70, 71, 72 of the Vienna

Convention spells out that:

> "Every treaty in force is binding upon the parties to it and must be performed by them in good faith": Article 26

> "The validity of a treaty or of the consent of a state to be bound by a treaty may be impeached only through the application of the present Convention": Article 42(1)

> "A right of a party, provided for in a treaty or arising under Article 56, to denounce, withdraw from or suspend the operation of the treaty may be exercised only with respect to the whole treaty unless the treaty otherwise provides or the parties otherwise agree.

> A ground for invalidating, terminating, withdrawing from or suspending the operation of a treaty recognized in the present Convention may be invoked only with respect to the whole treaty except as provided in the following paragraphs or in Article 60.

> If the ground relates solely to particular clauses, it may be invoked only with respect to those clauses where:

> (a) the said clauses are separable from the remainder of the treaty with regard to their application;
> (b) it appears from the treaty or is otherwise established that acceptance of those clauses was not an essential basis of the consent of the other party or parties to be bound by the treaty as a whole; and

(c) continued performance of the remainder of the treaty would not be unjust.

In cases falling under Articles 49 and 50 the state entitled to invoke the fraud or corruption may do so with respect either to the whole treaty or, subject to paragraph 3, to the particular clauses alone.

In cases falling under Articles 51, 52 and 53, no separation of the provision of the treaty is permitted": Article 44(1)(2)(3)(4)(5).

"A state may no longer invoke a ground for invalidating, terminating, withdrawing from or suspending the operation of a treaty under Articles 46 to 50 or Articles 60 to 62 if, after becoming aware of the facts:

(a) it shall have expressly agreed that the treaty is valid or remains in force or continues in operation , as the case may be; or
(b) it must have by reason of its conduct be considered as having acquiesced in the validity of the treaty or its maintenance in force or in operation, as the case may be": Article 45.

"A state may not invoke the fact that its consent to be bound by a treaty has been expressed in violation of a provision of its internal law regarding competence to conclude treaties as invalidating its consent unless that violation was manifest and concerned a rule of its internal law of fundamental importance.

A violation is manifest if it would be objectively evident to any state conducting itself in the matter in accordance with normal practice and in good faith": Article 46(1)(2).

"A state may invoke an error in a treaty as invalidating its consent to be bound by the treaty if the error relates to a fact or situation which was assumed by that state to exist at the time when the treaty was concluded and formed an essential basis of its consent to be bound by the treaty.

Paragraph 1 shall not apply if the state in question contributed by its own conduct to the error or if the circumstances were such as to put that state on notice of a possible error.

An error relating only to the wording of the text of a treaty does not affect its validity; Article 79 then applies": Article 48(1)(2)(3).

"If a state has been induced to conclude a treaty by the fraudulent conduct of another negotiating state, the state may invoke fraud as invalidating its consent to be bound by the treaty": Article 49.

"If the expression of a state's consent to be bound by a treaty has been procured through the corruption of its representative directly or indirectly by another negotiating state, the state may invoke such corruption as invalidating its consent to be bound by the treaty". Article 50.

"The expression of a state's consent to be bound by a treaty which has been procured by the coercion of its representative through acts or threats directed against him shall be without any legal effect": Article 51.

"A treaty is void if its conclusion has been procured by the threat or use of force in violation of the principles of international law embodied in the Charter of the United Nations": Article 52.

"A treaty is void, if, at the time of its conclusion, it conflicts with a peremptory norm of general international law. For the purposes of the present Convention, a peremptory norm of general international law is a norm accepted and recognized by the international community of states as a whole as a norm from which no derogation is permitted and which can be modified only by a subsequent norm of general international law having the same character": Article 53.

"A material breach of a bilateral treaty by one of the parties entitles the other to invoke the breach as a ground for terminating the treaty or suspending its operation in whole or in part.

A material breach of a multilateral treaty by one of the parties entitles :

(a) the other party by unanimous agreement to suspend the operation of the treaty in whole or in part or to terminate it either:

    (i) in the relations between themselves and the defaulting state or
    (ii) as between all parties;

(b) a party specially affected by the breach to invoke it as a ground for suspending the operation of the treaty in whole or in part in the relations between itself and the defaulting state;

(c) any party other than the defaulting state to invoke the breach as a ground for suspending the operation of the treaty in whole or in part with respect to itself if the treaty is of such a character that a material breach of its provisions by one party radically changes the position of every party with respect to the further performance of its obligations under the treaty.

A material breach of a treaty , for the purposes of this article, consists in:

(a) a repudiation of the treaty not sanctioned by the present Convention; or
(b) the violation of a provision essential to the accomplishment of the object or purpose of the treaty.

The foregoing paragraphs are without prejudice to any provision in the treaty applicable in the event of a breach.

Paragraphs 1 to 3 do not apply to provisions relating to the protection of the human person contained in treaties of a humanitarian character, in particular to provisions prohibiting any form of reprisals against persons protected by such treaties": Article 60(1)(2)(3)(4)(5).

"A party may invoke the impossibility of performing a treaty as a ground for terminating or withdrawing from it if the impossibility results from the permanent disappearance or destruction of an object indispensable for the execution of the treaty. If the impossibility is temporary, it may be invoked only as a ground for suspending the operation of the treaty.

Impossibility of performance may not be invoked by a party as a ground for terminating, withdrawing from or suspending the operation of a treaty if the impossibility, is the result of a breach by that party either of an obligation under the treaty or of any other international obligation owed to any other party to the treaty": Article 61(1)(2).

"A fundamental change of circumstances which has occurred with regard to those existing at the time of the conclusion of a treaty, and which was not foreseen by the parties , may not be invoked as a ground for terminating or withdrawing from the treaty unless;

(a) the existence of those circumstances constituted an essential basis of the consent of the parties to be bound by the treaty; and
(b) the effect of the change is radically to transform the extent of the obligation still to be performed under the treaty.

A fundamental change of circumstances may not be invoked as a ground for terminating or withdrawing from a treaty:

(a) if the treaty establishes a boundary; or
(b) if the fundamental change is the result of a breach by the party invoking it either of an obligation under the treaty or of any other international obligation owed to any other party to the treaty.

If, under the foregoing paragraphs, a party may invoke a fundamental change of circumstances as a ground for terminating or withdrawing from a treaty it may also invoke the change as a ground for suspending the operation of the treaty": Article 62(1)(2)(3).

"If a new peremptory norm of general international law emerges , any existing treaty which is in conflict with that norm becomes void and terminates": Article 64.

"A party which, under the provisions of the present Convention, invokes either a defect in its consent to be bound by a treaty or a ground for impeaching the validity of a treaty, terminating it, withdrawing from it or suspending its operation, must notify the other parties of its claim. The notification shall indicate the measure proposed to be taken with respect to the treaty and the reasons therefor.

If, after the expiry of a period which , except in cases of special urgency, shall be not less than three months after the receipt of the notification, no party has raised any objection, the party making the notification may carry out in the manner provided in Article 67 the measure which it has proposed.

If, however objection has been raised by any other party, the parties shall seek a solution through the means indicated in Article 33 of the Charter of the United Nations": Article 65(1)(2)(3).

"A treaty the invalidity of which is established under the present Convention is void. The provisions of a void treaty has no legal force.

If acts have nevertheless been performed in reliance on such a treaty:

(a) each party may require any other party to establish as far as possible in their mutual relations the position that would have existed if the acts had not been performed;
(b) acts performed in good faith before the invalidity

was invoked are not rendered unlawful by reason only of the invalidity of the treaty.

In cases falling under Articles 49, 50, 51, 52, paragraph 2 does not apply with respect to the party to which the fraud, the act of corruption or the coercion is imputable.

In the case of the invalidity of a particular state's consent to be bound by multilateral treaty, the foregoing rules apply in the relations between that state and the parties to the treaty": Article 69(1)(2)(3)(4).

"Unless the treaty otherwise provides or the parties otherwise agree, the termination of a treaty under its provisions or in accordance with the present Convention:

(a) releases the parties from any obligation further to perform the treaty;
(b) does not affect any right, obligation or legal situation of the parties created through the execution of the treaty prior to its termination.

If a state denounces or withdraws from a multilateral treaty, paragraph 1 applies in the relations between that state and each of the other parties to the treaty from the date when such denunciation or withdrawal takes effect": Article 70(1)(2).

"In the case of a treaty which is void under Article 53 the parties shall:

(a) eliminate as far as possible the consequences of any act performed in reliance on any provision which conflicts with the peremptory norm of general international law; and
(b) bring their mutual relations into conformity with the peremptory norms of general international law.

In the case of a treaty which become void and terminates under Article 64, the termination of the treaty:

(a) releases the parties from any obligation further to perform the treaty;
(b) does not affect any right, obligation or legal situation of the parties created through the execution of the treaty prior to its termination; provided that those rights, obligations or situations may thereafter be maintained only to the extent that their maintenance is not itself in conflict with the new peremptory norm of general international law": Article 71(1)(2).

"Unless the treaty otherwise provides or the parties otherwise agree, the suspension of the operation of a treaty under its provisions or in accordance with the present Convention:

(a) releases the parties between which the operation of the treaty is suspended from the obligation to perform the treaty in their mutual relations during the period of the suspension;
(b) does not otherwise affect the legal relations between

the parties established by the treaty.

During the period of the suspension the parties shall refrain from acts tending to obstruct the resumption of the operation of the treaty": Article 72(1)(2).

The International Commission of Jurists in two reports, "The Question of Tibet and the Rule of Law" (1959) and "Tibet and the Chinese People" (1960) considered the validity of the 17-point Agreement, the status of Tibet and her relationship to China, and the application to the Tibet question of the United Nations Universal Declaration of Human Rights and the Genocide Convention of 1948. The Legal Inquiry Committee on Tibet in its 1960 report found the evidence against China damning. It concluded that China had broken the 17-point Agreement. It concluded that genocide had been committed in Tibet by China in an attempt to destroy the Tibetans as a religious group and that such acts were acts of genocide independently of any obligation imposed by any international Conventions. The Committee found the detailed evidence that it had considered established four principal facts in relation to genocide:

"(a) that the Chinese will not permit adherence to and practice of Buddhism in Tibet;
(b) that they have systematically set out to eradicate this religious belief in Tibet;
(c) that in pursuit of this design they have killed religious figures because their religious belief and

practice was an encouragement and example to others;
(d) that they have forcibly transferred large numbers of Tibetan children to a Chinese materialist environment in order to prevent them from having a religious upbringing".

The Committee found China's allegations that the Tibetans enjoyed no human rights before the entry of China were based on distorted and exaggerated accounts of life in Tibet. The Committee examined evidence in relation to human rights within the framework of the United Nations Universal Declaration of Human Rights and found that the Chinese authorities in Tibet were guilty of breaches of the following articles:

Article 3: The right to life, liberty and security of person had been violated by acts of murder, rape and arbitrary imprisonment.

Article 5: Torture and cruel inhuman and degrading treatment had been inflicted on the Tibetans on a large scale.

Article 9: Arbitrary arrests and detention had been carried out.

Article 12: Rights of privacy, of home and family life had been persistently violated by the forcible transfer of members of the family and by indoctrination turning children against their parents. Children from infancy upwards had been removed contrary to the wishes of the parents.

Article 13: Freedom of movement within, to and from Tibet was denied by large-scale deportations.

Article 16: The voluntary nature of marriage was denied by forcing monks and lamas to marry.

Article 17: The right not to be arbitrarily deprived of private property was violated by the confiscation and compulsory acquisition of private property otherwise than on payment of just compensation and in accordance with the freely expressed wish of the Tibetan people.

Article 18: Freedom of thought, conscience and religion were denied by acts of genocide against Buddhists in Tibet and by other systematic acts designed to eradicate religious belief in Tibet.

Article 19: Freedom of expression and opinion was denied by the destruction of scriptures, the imprisonment of members of the Mimang group and the cruel punishments inflicted on critics of the Communist regime.

Article 20: The right of free assembly and association was violated by the suppression of the Mimang movement and the prohibition of meetings other than those called by the Chinese.

Article 21: The right to democratic government was denied by the imposition outside of rule by and under the Chinese Communist Party.

Article 22: The economic, social and cultural rights indispensable for the dignity and free development of the personality of man were denied. The economic resources of Tibet were being used to meet the needs of the Chinese. Social changes were adverse to the interests of the majority of the Tibetan people. The old culture of Tibet, including its religion, was being attacked in an attempt to eradicate it.

Article 24: The right to reasonable working conditions was violated by the extraction of labour under harsh and ill-paid conditions.

Article 25: A reasonable standard of living was denied by the use of the Tibetan economy to meet the needs of the Chinese settling in Tibet.

Article 26: The right to liberal education primarily in accordance with the choice of parents was denied by compulsory indoctrination, sometimes after deportation, in communist philosophy.

Article 27: The Tibetans are not allowed to participate in the cultural life of their own community, a culture which China has set out to destroy.

On the status of Tibet the Committee found that: "Tibet was at the very least a *de facto* independent state when the 17-point Agreement was signed in 1951 and the repudiation of this agreement by the Tibetan Government in 1959 was fully justified. In examining the evidence, the Committee took into account events in Tibet as related in authoritative accounts by officials and scholars familiar at first hand with the recent history of Tibet and official documents which have been published showing that Tibet demonstrated from 1913 to 1950 the conditions of statehood as generally accepted in international law, namely that in 1950 there was a people and a territory, and a government which functioned in that territory, conducting its own domestic affairs free from any outside authority. From 1913-1950 foreign relations of Tibet were conducted exclusively by the government of Tibet and countries with whom Tibet had foreign relations are shown by official documents to have treated Tibet in practice as an independent state until Tibet surrendered her independence by signing in 1951 the 17-point Agreement. Under that agreement the Central People's Government of the Chinese People's Republic gave a number of undertakings, among them: promises to maintain the existing political system of Tibet, to maintain the status and functions of the Dalai Lama and the Panchem Lama, to protect freedom of religion and the monasteries and to refrain from compulsion in the matter of reforms in Tibet. The Committee found that these and other undertakings had been violated by the Chinese People's Republic, and that the government of Tibet was entitled to repudiate the agreement as it did on March 11, 1959. "

But even in 1951 within months of the 17-point Agreement,

one of the joint Tibetan Prime Ministers, Lukhangwa had already accused the Chinese of bringing the Tibetan people to the point of starvation by violating the 17-point Agreement and forcing it on the Tibetans by unjust extortion of Tibetan food and resources for its Army and armed repression. He openly demanded the withdrawal of the Chinese forces which had illegally occupied Tibet, and the Dalai Lama was subsequently obliged by Beijing to sack both Prime Ministers.

In response to appeals from the lamas, the Dalai Lama returned to Lhasa on 17 August 1951. But on 9 September 1951 a first wave of 3,000 elite Chinese troops stormed Lhasa quickly to be followed by another 20,000 soldiers, and under the Chinese jackboot the Dalai Lama ratified the 17-point Agreement. He explained later, "we were expected to hand ourselves and our country over to China and cease to exist as a nation ..." "We were helpless. Without friends, there was nothing we could do but acquiesce, submit to the Chinese dictates in spite of our strong opposition and swallow our resentment. We could only hope that the Chinese would keep their side of this forced, one-sided bargain." Eight years later after fleeing Tibet, the Dalai Lama and his government repudiated the 17-point Agreement on the grounds of forgery and coercion.

From Mussoorie, India, 20 June 1959, the Dalai Lama later declared:

> "... It is recognized by every independent observer that Tibet had virtually been independent by enjoying and exercising all rights of sovereignty whether internal or external. This has also been implicitly admitted by the

Communist Government of China for the very structure, terms and conditions of the so-called agreement of 1951 conclusively show that it was an agreement between two independent and sovereign states. The agreement which followed the invasion of Tibet was also thrust upon its people and government by the threat of arms. It was never accepted by them of their own free will. The consent of the government was secured under duress and at the point of the bayonet.

"My representatives were compelled to sign the agreement under the threat of further military operations against Tibet by the invading armies of China leading to utter ravage and ruin of the country. Even the Tibetan seal which was affixed to the agreement was not the seal of my representatives but a seal copied and fabricated by the Chinese authorities in Peking and kept in their possession ever since.

"While I and my government did not voluntarily accept the agreement we were obliged to acquiesce in it and decided to abide by the terms and conditions to save my people and country from the danger of total destruction. It was, however, clear from the very beginning that the Chinese had no intentions of carrying out the agreement.

"Although they had solemnly undertaken to maintain my status and power as the Dalai Lama they did not lose any opportunity to undermine my authority and sow dissentions among my people. In fact, they compelled me, situate as I was , to dismiss my Prime Ministers under threat of their execution without trial, because they had in all honesty and sincerity resisted the unjustified usurpations of power by representatives of the Chinese Government in Tibet.

"Far from carrying out the agreement they began deliberately to pursue a course of policy which was diametrically opposed to the terms and conditions which they themselves had laid down. Thus commenced a reign of terror which finds few parallels in the history of Tibet. Forced labour and compulsory exactions, a systematic persecution of the people, plunder and confiscation of property belonging to individuals and monasteries and execution of certain leading men in Tibet, these are the glorious achievements of the Chinese rule in Tibet ..."

History recalls a similar event, Berlin, March 1939, when President Hacha of Czechoslovakia and M. Chvalkovsky were forced to sign a treaty with Nazi Germany establishing a German Protectorate over Bohemia and Moravia. According to the French Ambassador: "The German Ministers were pitiless. (Goering and Ribbentrop) literally hunted Dr Hacha and M. Chvalkovsky round the table on which the documents were lying, thrusting them continuously before them, pushing pens into their hands, increasingly repeating that if they continued in their refusal, half of Prague would lie in ruins from bombing within two hours and that this would only be the beginning".

Soviet writers on international law (see "International Law", ed. Kozhevnikov 1961, p.248) cite the Munich Agreement of 1938 by which France, Italy and Great Britain agreed to the cession of Sudeten German territory in Czechoslovakia to Germany and the Anglo-Egyptian Treaty of Alliance of 1936 as support for a doctrine of "unequal treaties" arguing that treaties which have been obtained by force or which are unequal in character (that is to say lacking equality of the parties) or which violate the elementary sovereign rights of the people, are not legally binding. This view is now supported by "the Declaration on the Prohibition of Military, Political or Economic Coercion in the Conclusion of Treaties" adopted at the conclusion of the Vienna Treaty Conference condemning:

> "... the threat or use of pressure in any form, whether military, political or economic, by any state in order to coerce another state to perform any act relating to the conclusion of a treaty in violation of the principles of the sovereign equality of states and freedom of contract."

Apart from the fact that it was signed when Tibet was being invaded by China, the 17-point Agreement as we have seen has been violated by China. Religious beliefs, customs and culture of the Tibetan people have been savagely suppressed and there has been gross interference in the continuation of the existing political system in Tibet and established status functions and powers of the Dalai Lama and the Panchen Lama. China turned Tibet into a colony and gave Tibet sham autonomy. If the 17-point Agreement was valid in the first place , it was repudiated by the Tibetan Government with every possible justification. In fact every stipulation and pledge made by China in the 17-point Agreement has been broken.

BACK TO THE UNITED NATIONS

"What the United Nations needs is not resolutions but resolution"
- Sir Carl Berendsen, New Zealand representative to the United Nations 1947

1959

The Dalai Lama returned to Tibet in 1951 and endeavoured to work with the Chinese. There were anti-China riots in autumn 1956. But on 8 March 1959, fearing a Chinese coup against The Dalai Lama, the people of Tibet rose up against China. Their protest was brutally suppressed. Thousands of Tibetans were killed by the Chinese and on 17 March 1959 the Dalai Lama fled Tibet and established the Tibetan Government in exile in India.

In a speech made in Delhi (5 September 1959) the Dalai Lama announced that Tibet had decided to appeal again to the United Nations. In a message to the Secretary-General he said: "the area of aggression has been substantially extended" since the United Nations left the question of Tibet adjourned in 1950, "with the result that practically the whole of Tibet is under the occupation of the Chinese forces" and urged the United Nations to intervene at once "in view of the inhumane treatment and crimes against humanity and religion to which the people of Tibet are being subjected", emphasising that "Tibet was a sovereign state at the time when her territorial integrity was violated by the Chinese armies in 1950". Enumerating widespread acts of persecution and genocide being committed against his people he appealed to the United Nations to do something so that, "this wanton and ruthless murder of my people should be immediately brought to an end". The Federation of Malaya and the Republic of Ireland secured the inclusion of the Tibetan case on the agenda of the fourteenth session of the United Nations and on 9 October 1959 against strong opposition from the communist bloc, the General Committee of the United Nations decided that the Tibet question should be discussed in the General Assembly. Without specific reference to the People's Republic of China or its invasion and occupation of Tibet, the following resolution was finally passed on 21 October 1959 (Resolution 1353 [XIV] by a majority of 45 to 9 (Nationalist China voting in favour of the resolution and Britain, France and India to their shame being three notable abstentions out of the 26 states abstaining):

" The General Assembly:
"Recalling the principles regarding fundamental human rights and freedoms set out in the Charter of the United Nations and in the Universal Declaration of Human Rights adopted by the General Assembly on 10 December 1948,
　"Considering that the fundamental human rights and freedoms to which the Tibetan people, like all others, are entitled include the right to civil and religious liberty for all without distinction,
　"Mindful also of the distinctive cultural and religious heritage of the people of Tibet and of the autonomy which they have traditionally enjoyed, gravely concerned at the reports, including the official statements of His Holiness the Dalai Lama to the effect that the fundamental human rights and freedoms of the people of Tibet have been

forcibly denied them,

"Deploring the effect of these events in increasing international tension and in embittering the relations between peoples at a time when earnest and positive efforts are being made by responsible leaders to reduce tension and improve international relations,

"1. Affirms its belief that respect for the principles of the Charter of the United Nations and of the Universal Declaration of Human Rights is essential for the evolution of a peaceful world based on the rule of law,

"2. Calls for respect for the fundamental human rights of the Tibetan people and for their distinctive cultural and religious life."

(*In favour*: Argentina, Australia, Austria, Bolivia, Brazil, Canada, Chile, Nationalist China, Columbia, Cuba, Denmark, Ecuador, El Salvador, Federation of Malaya, Greece, Guatemala, Haiti, Honduras, Iceland, Iran, Ireland, Israel, Italy, Japan, Jordan, Laos, Liberia, Luxembourg, Mexico, Netherlands, New Zealand, Nicaragua, Norway, Pakistan, Panama, Paraguay, Peru, Philippines, Sweden, Thailand, Tunisia, Turkey, United States, Uruguay, Venezuela.

Against: Albania, Bulgaria, Byelorussian SSR, Czechoslovakia, Hungary, Poland, Romania, Ukrainian SSR, USSR,

Abstaining: Afghanistan, Belgium, Burma, Cambodia, Ceylon, Dominican Republic, Ethiopia, Finland, France, Ghana, India,

Indonesia, Iraq, Lebanon, Libya, Morocco, Nepal, Portugal, Saudi Arabia, Spain, Sudan, Union of South Africa, United Arab Republic, United Kingdom, Yemen, Yugoslavia).

1960

In 1960 the Dalai Lama made a third appeal to the United Nations. In a letter to the Secretary-General (29 September 1960) the Dalai Lama reasserted Tibet's claim to be an independent state and begged the United Nations to "take measures to get China to vacate its aggression".

On 19 August 1960 " The question of Tibet" was raised by Thailand and Malaya for further consideration by the General Assembly in the fifteenth session. In an accompanying explanatory memorandum Thailand and Malaya pointed out that the fundamental human rights of the Tibetan people continued to be disregarded and the situation in Tibet remained a source of grave concern, despite the appeal made by General Assembly Resolution (1353 [XIV]) of 21 October 1959. The United Nations, therefore, had an obligation and duty to address itself once again to the Tibetan question for there was a continuing attempt to destroy the Tibetan people's traditional and distinctive way of life and cultural autonomy.

On 10 October 1960 the General Assembly decided to accept the recommendation of its General Committee to include the item in its agenda and to consider it at a plenary meeting without prior reference to one of its main committees. But opposition to this decision was expressed by the representatives of Indonesia, Romania and the Soviet Union who argued that Tibet was part of the People's Republic of China, which was unrepresented in the United Nations. Issues involving Communist China, said the Indonesian representative, could not therefore be settled by the United Nations in China's absence. The Soviet Union citing Article 2(7) of the United Nations Charter (which precludes United Nations intervention in matters falling essentially within the domestic jurisdiction of any state) contended that discussion of the item would mean interference in the domestic affairs of the People's Republic of China of which Tibet was an integral part when at the same time China's membership of the United Nations was being obstructed. Further the Soviet Union said that those who wanted the General Assembly to discuss the Tibet question (despite its lack of competence to do so) sought to impair the growing solidarity of Afro-Asian countries and to complicate relations of the People's Republic of China with other Asian countries and draw Asian countries into the cold war. The Romanian representative argued that serfdom was the traditional way of life in Tibet and attempts to destroy that traditional way of life in Tibet were not contrary to Universal Declaration of Human Rights. The representatives of El Salvador, Ireland and New Zealand arguing in favour of placing the item on the General Assembly's agenda pointing out that if the United Nations should not concern itself because the question of Tibet was a domestic matter, the General Assembly would never have taken up the question of Algeria or Hungary or of race discrimination in South Africa. They said the plight of the Tibetan people remained tragic and the Tibet question involved a violation of human rights and the General Assembly had a compelling obligation not to ignore the flagrant oppression or denial of human rights in any part of the world. The representative of Ireland said that the General Assembly was not debarred from considering the question of Tibet on the ground that the People's Republic of China was not represented because the violation of human rights of the Tibetan people was a legitimate matter for consideration regardless of the status of the regime violating those rights. With regard to the argument that Tibet could not show a history continuously independent of China, the Irish delegate said that most of the countries in the General Assembly including his own would not be there if they had to prove they had never been dominated by another state.

Overruling objections, the General Assembly decided by 49 to 13 (35 states abstaining) to consider the question of Tibet but it was not until the following year that the matter came before the General Assembly.

1961

On 10 April 1961 the Federation of Malaya, Ireland and Thailand circulated a joint draft resolution asking the General Assembly to note with grave concern the continuation of events in Tibet, including the violation of fundamental human rights, suppression of cultural and religious life and denial of the traditional autonomy of the Tibetan people, resulting in a large-scale exodus of refugees. It also pointed out that these events were against the observance of fundamental human rights and freedoms and had the effect of raising international tension and embittering relations between people. By the operative part of the proposed resolution the General Assembly was asked: (1) to re-affirm its conviction that respect for the principles of the United Nations Charter and the Universal Declaration of Human Rights was essential for the evolution of a peaceful world order based on the rule of law; (2) solemnly to renew its call for the cessation of practices which deprived the Tibetan people of their fundamental human rights and freedoms and (3) to appeal to member states to use their good offices and best endeavours as appropriate to achieve the purposes of the resolution. But pressure of work delayed the debate to the sixteenth session.

On 25 September 1961 the General Assembly on the recommendation of its General Committee decided by 48 to 14 (with 35 abstentions) to place the item on its agenda and on 27 September 1961 it decided to consider the matter at plenary meetings without prior reference to one of its main committees. The item was discussed again at two plenary meetings held on 19 and 20 December 1961. On 12 December 1961 El Salvador, the Federation of Malaya, Ireland and Thailand submitted a joint draft resolution asking the General Assembly (1) to re-affirm its conviction that respect for the principles of the United Nations Charter and the Universal Declaration of Human Rights was essential for the evolution of a peaceful world order based on the rule of law; (2) solemnly to renew its call for the cessation of practices depriving the Tibetan people of their fundamental human rights and freedoms, including the right of self-determination; (3) expressing the hope that United Nations member states would make all possible efforts as appropriate towards achieving the purposes of the present resolution. Those speaking in favour of the draft resolution (now backed by the representatives of the United States, Great Britain, New Zealand and Nationalist China) pointed out that the situation in Tibet had not improved since the General Assembly had adopted resolution 1353 on 21 October 1959.

Supporters of the resolution said that the situation had become much graver as the repression of the Tibetan people continued relentlessly and that no less that 45, 000 Tibetans had sought refuge in India, Nepal, Sikkim and Bhutan, and reports from Tibetan refugees spoke of conscription for forced labour, children forcibly separated from their families and deported to China for indoctrination; that religious institutions and beliefs were being suppressed and that well over a thousand monasteries had been destroyed. As we have seen it was pointed out that in August 1960 the Legal Inquiry Committee appointed by the International Commission of Jurists had published a study confirming these reports listing sixteen separate articles of the Universal Declaration of Human Rights which were being violated by the Chinese in Tibet. Further, they argued that in adopting its Declaration of Independence to Colonial Countries and Peoples, the Assembly had declared that the subjection of people to alien subjugation constituted a denial of fundamental human rights, that the Tibetans had for a long time suffered a forcible deprivation of their fundamental human rights under China and that the General Assembly would not be true to its policies if it failed to take a similar stand on Tibet as it had done on other issues involving colonialism, self-determination and fundamental human rights.

Albania, Bulgaria, Czechoslovakia and the Soviet Union again opposed the General Assembly even considering the question of Tibet. They maintained Tibet had always been an integral part of China and that discussion of the question of Tibet was a gross violation of Article 2(7) of the UN Charter. They asserted that the failure of the rebellion of feudal and reactionary elements in 1959 and the full support given by the majority of Tibetan people to China had caused fury and disappointment among the allies of the Tibetan feudalists who wished to bring about a return of the feudalists and reactionaries who for centuries had kept Tibet in subjugation and poverty. The Soviet bloc delegates alleged the democratic process and the people of Tibet had made enormous progress since the liquidation of the rebellion of reactionaries in 1959 and could not be halted; they said democratic freedoms and the rights of the population had been restored, the feudal regime of exploitation and suppression had been eradicated from the monasteries. Tibet's economy, the Soviets said, was being developed in all fields; progress was being made in the ending of illiteracy and in developing education and there was full religious freedom.

Sponsors of the resolution, however, maintained that the General Assembly was fully justified in discussing the Tibetan question, just as it had in the past considered questions involving colonialism, self-determination and the observance of human rights. The General Assembly, the sponsors said, had on many occasions overruled submissions of domestic jurisdiction and affirmed its right to discuss such questions. Violations of human rights on the scale that had occurred in Tibet they said could not be ignored by the United Nations.

On 20 December 1961 the General Assembly adopted a watered down resolution (Resolution 1723 [XVI] by 56 votes to 11 (29 abstaining) in these terms :

"The General Assembly,

"Recalling its resolution 1353[XIV] of 21 October 1959 on the question of Tibet,

"Gravely concerned at the continuation of events in Tibet, including the violation of the fundamental human rights of the Tibetan people and the suppression of the distinctive cultural and religious life which they have traditionally enjoyed,

"Noting with deep anxiety the severe hardships which these events have inflicted on the Tibetan people, as evidenced by the large-scale exodus of the Tibetan refugees to the neighbouring countries,

"Considering that these events violate fundamental human rights and freedoms set out in the Charter of the United Nations and the Universal Declaration of Human Rights, including the principles of self-determination of peoples and nations, and have the deplorable effect of increasing international tension and embittering relations between peoples,

"1. Reaffirms its conviction that respect for the principles of the Charter of the United Nations and of the Universal Declaration of Human Right is essential for the evolution of a peaceful world order based on the rule of law;

"2. Solemnly renews its call for the cessation of practices which deprive the Tibetan people of their fundamental rights and freedoms, including their right to self-determination;

"3. Express the hope that member states will make all possible efforts as appropriate, towards achieving the purposes of the present resolution."

(*In favour*: Argentina, Australia, Austria, Belgium, Bolivia, Brazil, Cameroon, Canada, Central African Republic, Chile, Nationalist China, Colombia, Congo (Leopoldville), Costa Rica, Cyprus, Dahomey, Denmark, Dominican Republic, El Salvador, Federation of Malaya, Gabon, Greece, Guatemala, Haiti, Iceland, Iran, Ireland, Israel, Italy, Ivory Coast, Japan, Jordan, Laos, Liberia, Luxembourg, Madagascar, Mauritania, Netherlands, New Zealand, Nicaragua, Niger, Norway, Panama, Paraguay, Peru, Philippines, Senegal, Sierra Leone, Sweden, Thailand, Turkey, United Kingdom, United States, Upper Volta, Uruguay, Venezuela.

Against: Albania, Bulgaria, Byelorussian SSR, Cuba, Czechoslovakia, Hungary, Mongolia, Poland, Rumania, Ukrainian SSR, Soviet Union.

Abstaining: Afghanistan, Burma, Cambodia, Ceylon, Ethiopia,

Finland, France, Ghana, Guinea, India, Indonesia, Iraq, Lebanon, Libya, Mali, Morocco, Nepal, Nigeria, Pakistan, Saudi Arabia, Somalia, South Africa, Sudan, Syria, Togo, Tunisia, United Arab Republic, Yemen, Yugoslavia).

1964

On 30 October 1964 El Salvador, Nicaragua and the Philippines requested that an item "Question of Tibet" be included in the General Assembly's nineteenth session pointing out in an attached memorandum that human rights and freedoms were still being forcibly denied in Tibet, the religious and civil liberties of the Tibetan people were still being suppressed and the situation in Tibet remained a source of grave concern to the member states representing the international community.

1965

On 22 September 1965, the General Committee decided by 10 votes to 3 (11 abstaining) to recommend to the General Assembly the inclusion of this item on the agenda. Again, opposition to this decision was expressed in the General Committee by Hungary, Poland and the USSR on the grounds that Tibet was part of the People's Republic of China and consideration of that question would be a violation of Article 2 (7) of the United Nations Charter. The Soviet block further said, that the previous discussion of this item had been politically motivated and that the matter had been raised at this session to create a hostile atmosphere on the question of the restoration of the legitimate rights of the People's Republic of China in the United Nations. But Nationalist China, Guatemala, Malaysia and the United States urging the General Committee to put the item on the agenda said that it involved questions relating to human rights and on that basis Article 2(7) could not be invoked to bar its inclusion since the General Assembly itself had established the necessary human rights precedents. On 24 September 1965, the General Assembly by a majority of 41 to 26, with 46 abstentions, adopted the recommendation of the General Committee for inclusion of the item on the agenda, the representatives of Albania, Cambodia and Guinea speaking against and those of Malaysia, the Philippines and Thailand speaking in favour of inclusion.

The General Assembly considered the question on 14, 17, and 18 December 1965. It had before it a draft resolution co-sponsored by El Salvador, Ireland, Malaysia, Malta, Nicaragua, the Philippines and Thailand. Also circulated to members was a message to the Secretary-General from the Dalai Lama concerning recent developments in Tibet. Those speaking in support of the joint draft resolution in the debate included the seven co-sponsors and Australia, Nationalist China, Costa Rica, Guatemala, India (which had abandoned its former neutrality on the question of Tibet), New Zealand, Norway and the United States.

The co-sponsors maintained that the hopes engendered by the earlier resolutions had not been fulfilled, that the findings of inquiries by the International Commission of

Jurists in 1959 and 1960 had shown that the Chinese authorities were committing acts of genocide and more recently that the Tibetan people were being subjected to brutal suppression of their religious life and to persecution designed to obliterate the Tibetan people as a distinctive ethnic group. The delegate for the Philippines said that the General Assembly with its history of struggle against apartheid could not turn a deaf ear to the appeals of the Tibetan people. Other delegates referred to United Nations documents on human rights and to the Assembly's 1960 Declaration on the Granting of Independence to Colonial Countries and Peoples.

The constitutional relationship between Tibet and the People's Republic of China, the sponsors said, was not at issue; Articles 55 and 56 of the Charter were applicable. Only by exerting moral pressure could the United Nations induce the People's Republic of China to reconsider its policies. The representative of India pointed out that in 1950 his country had opposed the discussion of Tibet by virtue of assurances made by the People's Republic of China that it was anxious to settle the problem by peaceful means. However the futility of India's expectations, he acknowledged was evidenced by the presence in India of the Dalai Lama along with some 50,000 Tibetan refugees. India maintained that the autonomy guaranteed in the 1951 17-point Agreement was a dead letter and that the autonomous character of Tibet had been obliterated. Similarly the delegate of Nationalist China expressed respect for the traditions of Tibet and its right to self-determination.

The United States delegate asserted that the term

"autonomy" referred to in the instruments governing the relationship between Tibet and the People's Republic of China was meaningless because there was no freedom of action for the Tibetans, no freedom to reject directives from the Chinese Government, no freedom from the armed aggression of Chinese communist military forces.

Albania, Bulgaria, the Congo (Brazzaville), Cuba, Czechoslovakia, Guinea, Hungary, Poland, Romania and the Soviet Union opposing the resolution said that Tibet was an integral part of the People's Republic of China. They said that the United Nations lacked competence to deal with the matter since intervention was precluded by Article 2(7) and claimed that submission of the item was merely intended to postpone the imminent restoration of the rights of the People's Republic of China in the United Nations. They also stressed the economic and social progress of the Tibetan people under China which they said constituted a great advance over the feudal system hitherto prevailing in Tibet. Especially noteworthy they said were achievements recorded in the fields of education, communications and transport. Further, the communist bloc said the human rights issue was merely a hypocritical subterfuge to divert attention from United States aggression in Viet-Nam and the Dominican Republic, and that certain counties which had supported the 1959 rebellion in Tibet wished to use Tibet as a strategic base for aggression.

However, the General Assembly passed the resolution as amended (the sponsors having watered down a request that states "take all measures" to an appeal to states "to use their best endeavours to achieve the purposes of the present resolution") by 43 votes to 26, with 22 abstentions. The full text of Resolution 2079[XX] is:

"The General Assembly,
"Bearing in mind the principles relating to human rights and fundamental freedoms set forth in the Charter of the United Nations and proclaimed in the Universal Declaration of Human Rights,
"Reaffirming its resolutions 1353[XIV] of 21 October 1959 and 1723[XVI] of 20 December 1961 on the question of Tibet,
"Gravely concerned at the continued violation of the fundamental rights and freedoms of the people of Tibet and the continued suppression of their distinctive cultural and religious life, as evidenced by the exodus of refugees to the neighbouring countries,

"1. Deplores the continued violation of the fundamental rights and freedoms of the people of Tibet;

"2. Reaffirms that respect for the principles of the Charter of the United Nations and of the Universal Declaration of Human Rights is essential for the evolution of a peaceful world order based on the rule of law;

"3. Declares its conviction that the violation of human rights and fundamental freedoms in Tibet, and the suppression of the distinctive cultural and religious life of its people increased international tension and embittered relations between peoples;

"4. Solemnly renews its call for the cessation of all practices which deprive the Tibetan people of the human rights and fundamental freedoms which they have always enjoyed;

"5. Appeals to all states to use their best endeavours to achieve the purposes of the present resolution."

(*In favour*: Argentina, Australia, Belgium, Bolivia, Brazil, Canada, Chile, Nationalist China, Columbia, Costa Rica, Dominican Republic, El Salvador, Guatemala, Haiti, Honduras, Iceland, India, Ireland, Israel, Italy, Japan, Jordan, Liberia, Luxembourg, Madagascar, Malaysia, Malta, Netherlands, New Zealand, Nicaragua, Norway, Panama, Paraguay, Peru, Philippines, Spain, Thailand, Togo, United Kingdom, United States, Upper Volta, Uruguay, Venezuela.

Against: Albania, Algeria, Bulgaria, Burma, Byelorussian SSR, Congo (Brazzaville), Cuba, Czechoslovakia, Ethiopia, Guinea, Hungary, Iraq, Mali, Mongolia, Morocco, Nepal, Pakistan, Poland, Rumania, Sudan, Syria, Ukrainian SSR, Soviet Union, United Arab Republic, Tanzania, Yugoslavia.

Abstaining: Afghanistan, Austria, Ceylon, Dahomey, Denmark, Finland, France, Ghana, Iran, Ivory Coast, Jamaica, Kuwait, Lebanon, Maldive Islands, Mexico, Portugal, Saudi Arabia, Senegal, Sierra Leone, Singapore, Sweden, Tunisia).

1991

On 23 August 1991 the Human Rights Commission through its Sub-Commission on the Prevention and Discrimination and Protection of Minorities, by a secret ballot of 9-7 with 4 abstentions called on the People's Republic of China "to respect the fundamental human rights and freedoms of the Tibetan people", and asked the Secretary-General to transmit to the Commission on Human Rights information on the situation in Tibet provided by China and other reliable sources: see Situation in Tibet, UN. ECOSOC, Doc. E/CN4./Sub2./L19 .

1992

In January 1992 the Secretary-General submitted to the Commission on Human Rights a report on the situation in Tibet containing a reply by China to a note verbal he had sent in December 1991. Annexed to the report were attachments to China's reply and information received from NGOs on human rights violations in Tibet. On 4 March 1992 the Commission by a roll call vote of 27 to 15 with 10 abstentions decided to take no decision on a draft resolution concerning the situation in Tibet.

1993

On 20 August the Sub-Commission by a secret ballot of 17-6

with two abstentions decided to take no action on a draft resolution concerning the situation in Tibet urging China to facilitate access to all parts of Tibet by the Special Rapporteur of the Commission and asking the Secretary-General to report to the Commission in 1994 on the situation in Tibet.

Since adopting the three Tibet resolutions in 1959, 1961 and 1965 there has been no further discussion of the Tibetan question in the Security Council or General Assembly and in recent years the UN Human Rights Commission annual meeting in Geneva has repeatedly failed to pass resolutions condemning the People's Republic of China for human rights violations against Tibetans and other minorities. The 1999 resolution proposed by the United States was defeated; the European Union and Britain refusing to act as sponsors. Since the Gulf War there has been a crippling of United Nations authority. The People's Republic of China, one of the five permanent Security Council members since 1971, has steadfastly ignored all United Nations resolutions on Tibet.

REVOLT

"... those people who gathered together to chant scriptures because of their Buddhist religion and for the happiness of mankind were also regarded as counter-revolutionaries, suppressed and attacked" - the Secret Report of the 10th Panchen Lama, 1962

The Tibetans have never accepted their Chinese masters. News of events in Tibet are hard to come by. These are a few examples. The Tibetans rose up against China in the autumn of 1956. In March 1959 there was a major uprising. In September and October 1987 and again in March 1988 there were demonstrations in Lhasa for independence from China. Initially the cause was summary executions of Tibetan dissidents. In the September demonstrations a group of monks and their supporters made three circuits of the Bar-Khor (central circumambulation and market area around the Jokhang Temple) shouting slogans for independence. They were promptly arrested and tortured by members of the Public Security Bureau. On 1 October 1987 a group of about 60 Tibetans were arrested with considerable violence for taking part in a demonstration. Monks were beaten with shovels and electric stun-guns. Following their arrest a crowd of about three thousand gathered in front of the Public Security Bureau demanding the release of detainees. The demonstrators realising that they were being photographed by the Public Security Bureau agents threw stones at the photographers and tried to force their way into the building, resulting in Public Security Bureau forces shooting at the demonstrators killing thirteen Tibetans and injuring many others.

On 6 October 1987 as a group of monks demonstrated, the police showed considerable brutality breaking up the demonstration and in making arrests.

The next major disturbance took place during the Monlam festival in March 1988. The monks had refused to hold the festivals without the release of those arrested in September and October but the Chinese insisted that the festival be held; and ultimately it was held under a heavy presence of Chinese army and police. At the end of the festivities monks shouting slogans for the release of those in detention and for the granting of independence, were immediately arrested. According to reports, stones were thrown by demonstrators, and in response Chinese soldiers stormed Tibet's holiest temple, the Jokhang, participating in the premeditated massacre of at least sixteen monks and the maiming of numerous others inside the temple. There is an account of what happened in the Jokhang in, "Tibet, the Facts", 1990 p.90, citing *Observer* 8 May 1988, "Tibet: Murder in the Temple", by Jonathan Mirsky: "... the Chinese police were waiting inside and once the monks had entered, the gates were closed and the police began beating them. However, as the monks out-numbered the police at this stage more police reinforcements were sent in by ladder over the walls. The police and soldiers who attacked the monks used clubs with nails and knives attached and this explains the severed hands and fingers that were later found near the entrance to the Jokhang. At this point a nun was reported by an eyewitness as saying "Don't you know they are killing monks in there."

According to witnesses after beating the Jokhang monks,

the police snatched wrist watches and other personal possessions and some young monks who were found hidden in cupboards were beaten and thrown to their deaths through the windows. People going to the Jokhang the next day found every nook and cranny spattered with blood. They also found lumps of human flesh and items of bloodstained clothing. The Jokhang massacre sparked off a violent uprising of the Tibetan people, which continued until midnight leaving some monks dead and many more wounded. Following the riots a large number of Tibetans were arrested and tortured.

On 7 March 1989 in response to the deteriorating situation China declared martial law in Tibet. All demonstrations, petitions and public meetings were outlawed and all foreigners and journalists were expelled from Tibet. The martial law edict was lifted on 1 May 1990 having been in force for 14 months.

WEASEL WORDS

"What is truth? said jesting Pilate; and would not stay for an answer" - Francis Bacon 1561-1626

Suzerainty

Suzerainty is a concept of nineteenth century international law applied by the British to Tibet at the beginning of the twentieth century without regard for the true relationship between Tibet and China. The *Oxford English Dictionary* definition of "a suzerain"is :"A feudal overlord, in recent use, a sovereign or a state having supremacy over another state which possess its own ruler but cannot act as an independent power". "Suzerainty" is defined as: "The position rank or power of a suzerain". In international law each case of suzerain-vassal relationship had to be examined on the merits. In 1906 Professor John Bassett Moore wrote, the "extent of the authority or subordination comprehended by this term is not determined by general rules, but by the facts of a particular case": "*Digest of International Law*", Vol.I, p.27. There is apparently no equivalent Tibetan or Chinese word for suzerainty. The Tibetan and Chinese leaders at the turn of the century almost certainly had no idea what suzerainty meant.

Suzerainty originally applied to the feudal relationship between a vassal and his overlord, the vassal paying the latter tribute, giving him military support in return for protection. But in the nineteenth century this type of suzerainty began to be replaced by a kind of international guardianship, the vassal state retaining internal sovereignty which the liege state was under a duty to respect. Participation in international relations by the vassal state generally being accepted by international lawyers as the attainment of *de facto* independence.

As Oppenheim's *International Law* (9th edn. Vol.I, para.81) points out: "An arrangement may be entered into whereby one state, while retaining to some extent its separate identity as a state, is subject to a kind of guardianship by another state. The circumstances in which this occurs and the consequences which result vary from case to case, and depend upon the particular provisions of the arrangements between the two states concerned. Formerly one category of such states were the so-called "vassal states", being states under the suzerainty of another state. These terms are now seldom used, although they are not wholly defunct. Thus Tibet is still sometimes said to be under the suzerainty of China. Vassal states, although retaining internal independence, normally had no separate international position".

The word "suzerainty" was also used by the British in India to describe its relationship with Indian principalities, for example, s.7(1)(b) of the Indian Independence Act 1947 refers to lapsing of "the suzerainty of His Majesty over the Indian States" and until the 1970s the British Foreign Office opinion on the status of Tibet was that Tibet was "autonomous under the suzerainty of China". But now the Foreign Office prefers to say that the British Government regards Tibet as "autonomous while recognizing the special position of China there", quietly dropping thereby reference to suzerainty.

Reference in any treaty to "suzerain rights of China in Tibet" appeared for the first time in the Convention between Britain and Russia, 1907 (see Appendix, document 5). Made without consulting Tibet or China, Britain and Russia in a diplomatic fudge admitted the principle of suzerainty of China over Tibet. Hitherto the Lhasa Convention 1904 and the 1906 Convention between Great Britain and China said nothing about suzerainty. But Article 2 of the ineffective Simla Convention, 1914 (which China negotiated, initialled but refused to ratify) says: "The government of Great Britain and China recognizing that Tibet is under the suzerainty of China, and recognizing also the autonomy of Outer Tibet, engage to respect the territorial autonomy of the country, and to abstain from interference in the administration of Outer Tibet (including the selection and installation of the Dalai Lama), which shall remain in the hands of the Tibetan Government at Lhasa". It goes on to say **"The Government of China engages not to convert Tibet into a Chinese province. The Government of Great Britain engages not to annex Tibet or any portion of it"** (author's emphasis).

Under the Simla Convention, Outer Tibet was considered by the British Government to have "territorial autonomy" and all Tibet was said to be under the suzerainty of China. Under it China undertook not to incorporate Tibet into a Chinese province. It comes as no surprise that China says that suzerainty is a western concept introduced by the British. It says Tibet has always been part of China. Similarly the Tibetan Government in exile regards the concept of suzerainty as inappropriate and unhelpful: see Report, Tibet Society of the UK Third Ennals Memorial Lecture given by

Lodi Gyari, Special Envoy of His Holiness the Dalai Lama, 1 October 1998.

Autonomy

"Autonomy" is an abused word. It means the exercise of independent self-government which connotes personal freedom and freedom of the will. Since the 1960s the Foreign Office says it regards Tibet as autonomous (see BRITISH FOREIGN POLICY, *post*) whilst recognizing the special position of China there. The Law of the People's Republic of China on Regional National Autonomy (see Appendix, document 16) refers to important freedoms and rights of independent administration in National Autonomous Areas but the harshness of Chinese rule over Tibet leaves no doubt that Tibet's designation as an autonomous region is a joke, superficial and far removed from the autonomy promised in point 3 of the 17-point Agreement. Under point 4, China also made the broken promise that "The central authorities will not alter the existing political system in Tibet" but today the Tibetans have no political freedom, no freedom to challenge Beijing and no respite from Chinese repression.

Under the Sino-British Joint Declaration on the Question of Hong Kong, Hong Kong is promised "a high degree of autonomy" which seems to show that China differentiates the lesser form of autonomy enjoyed in the Tibet Autonomous Region. Any future agreement with China over Tibet must carefully define what autonomy means and what genuine autonomous rights the Tibetans are to be given, but, in reality, the Chinese Government will never grant Tibet or any autonomous region true autonomy because, unlike Hong Kong, where Chinese nationalism is strong, any expression of Tibetan national identity and culture is regarded as splittist and intolerable to China's Government.

Democracy

Article 1 of China's Constitution says that China is: "a socialist state under the people's democratic dictatorship". Article 3 says that the state organs of the People's Republic of China apply "the principles of democratic centralism".

The word "democracy" has always had an ambiguity. To people living in the free world it means as Theodore Parker defined it in his speech in 1850 to the Boston Anti-Slavery Convention: "A government of all the people, by the people - for all the people, of course, a government after the principles of eternal justice, the unchanging law of God; for shortness sake, I will call it the idea of freedom."

The second meaning of democracy used by communist governments is a social condition or a form of government. Writing of democracy in 1850 the French aristocrat de Tocqueville said democracy often means a special condition of society in which there exists a general equality of rights; a similarity of conditions, of thoughts, of sentiments, and of ideas.

In the latter sense democracy is used by communist regimes to express opposition to class privilege and, as de Tocqueville points out, in this sense is compatible with despotism. Thus in China's Constitution, democratic socialism is described as the "people's democratic dictatorship".

Splittism

"Splittism" is a term invented by China. It applies to any group or persons who advocate independence or secession from China. Under China's criminal code any expression of splittism is a serious crime carrying seven years' imprisonment. As applied in China, splittism includes any criticism of China's leadership and policies. That has included, shouting "Free Tibet", keeping photographs of the Dalai Lama or any of his teachings, translating the United Nations Declaration of Human Rights into Tibetan or putting up a poster. The Dalai Lama and his supporters are vehemently branded by China as splittist.

The Motherland

Emotive expression used by China to appeal to the Chinese nationalism describing the territory of the People's Republic of China and all the territories it has laid claim to in the past including Taiwan, Mongolia, border regions of India and elsewhere in south east Asia.

Cadres

According to the *Oxford English Dictionary* a cadre is "The permanent establishment forming the framework of a regiment". Chapter VI of China's Communist Party Constitution deals with party cadres (see Appendix, document 17). Article 33 says: "Party cadres are the backbone of the party's cause and public servants of the people". Article 34(4) says they must be "fervently dedicated to the revolutionary cause". Chapter VII deals with Party discipline.

The cadres are the unpleasant face of political and religious repression in Tibet. Above the law, working closely with police and state security officials it is the cadres who descend on monasteries, forcing out monks and nuns, making them renounce the Dalai Lama. Cadres also manage China's birth control policy through "target management responsibility contracts", parents facing penalties for failing to keep within quotas.

Article 18 of the Law on Regional National Autonomy provides that cadres in the departments under the organs of self-government should, wherever possible, be chosen from among citizens of the nationality exercising regional autonomy and of the other minority nationalities in the area. If China can be believed, in 1986, out of a total number of 52,311 cadres in Tibet, 31,567 were Tibetans and 23,268 were other Party members: Data for the History of CCP Organizations. Tibetan cadres seem to possess little education. They are employed by the Party. The work is salaried.

Elections

The National People's Congress is composed of 1,500 deputies elected for five years by the provinces, autonomous regions and municipalities directly under the Central Government and by the armed forces: see Article 59. Lists of candidates are selected by Communist Party local leaders.

Elections are held from the lists but no one opposed to the government or Communist Party can stand. A similar system operates in local elections. The Chinese Democracy Party is banned from putting up alternative candidates and most of its leaders are in prison. Article 33 says that all citizens over the age of 18 have the right to vote and stand for election except those deprived of political rights according to law.

Counter-revolutionary

A term, now replaced in the Criminal Procedure Law of China, amended 1996 with "endangering state security" and defined as: an enemy of the state or any act, "committed with the goal of overthrowing the political power of the dictatorship of the proletariat and the socialist system": Chinese Criminal Code, 1980, Art, 90.

Strike Hard

Campaign aimed at crushing political corruption and crime which in Tibet focuses on "splittism".

Patriotic re-education

A sub-campaign of "strike hard" under which Chinese "work teams" (political re-education and investigation special units) are sent into Tibetan monasteries and nunneries to enforce Communist ideology. Many monks and nuns have been arrested and imprisoned for refusing to comply with work team orders or for questioning the "re-education" campaign.

IS TIBET PART OF CHINA

"A truth that is told with bad intent
Beats all the lies you can invent" - William Blake (1757-1827)

China's position is very simple. It is this. Since the 13th century, during the Chinese Empire, under the Chinese Nationalist Government and under Communism, Tibet was and is a region of China which has been allowed considerable autonomy but over which, China says, it retained territorial sovereignty. The Chinese say their position was consistently maintained right up to the end of the Q'ing dynasty and then after the 1911 Revolution. They say no government of China waived any sovereign rights in Tibet. China says it never considered herself a "suzerain" over Tibet and that that term was introduced by Great Britain and Russia in 1907 without consulting China when they became interested in Tibet and decided to make a secret treaty. The Chinese say that the wording of the 1906 Convention between Great Britain and China was a compromise which recognized China's exclusive rights in Tibet without giving those rights a specific name be it "suzerain" or "sovereign" and that the Simla Convention of 1914, in which Great Britain, China and Tibet recognized that Tibet was under the suzerainty of China and in which China undertook not to turn Tibet into a Chinese province, is not binding on them and that, although initialled by the Chinese plenipotentiary, the Simla Convention was never signed or ratified by the Chinese Government. It simply never came into force.

China also argues that when China was proclaimed a republic, Tibet, Mongolia and Sinkiang were declared to be integral parts of China on equal footing with the provinces of China. (see MONGOLIA, *post*). China blames its absence from Tibet 1913-1950 on British influence in Tibet, and China says its legal capacity over Tibet should in no way be affected by a situation dictated by physical compulsion so long as no other state possessed any title to claim sovereignty over this portion of her territory. China also disputes that it was entirely shut off from Tibet 1913-1950, citing religious missions and sporadic contacts between the Dalai Lama and Beijing.

China says, that there is no international instrument to prove the acquisition of statehood by Tibet or of anything resembling the exercise of *summa potestas* by Tibet as an independent state. China says that Great Britain never went so far as to declare Tibet an independent state or a dependency of its own during all those years when they enjoyed a unique position of exercising dominant influence in Tibet. The Chinese also point to the assertion of the United Kingdom delegate at the Fifth Session of the UN General Assembly in November 1950 on the steering committee's move to postpone El Salvador's request to intercede on behalf of the Tibet: "No one knew exactly what was happening in Tibet, nor was the legal position very clear".

China says, however strong outside pressure to secure independence for Tibet may be, the fact remains that the Tibetans have never been prepared nor willing to assume and fulfil international obligations as a new state and that the legal position of Tibet within the boundaries of China is now clearly defined in the 17-point Agreement. Moreover China considers any United Nations resolutions on Tibet invalid, arguing that the General Assembly considered matters in violation of Article 2(7) of the United Nations Charter, which without prejudice to enforcement measures under Chapter VII, bars the United Nations from intervening in "matters which are essentially within the domestic jurisdiction of any state". (China in the past has also argued that UN resolutions are invalid if the total population of the states voting against the resolution or abstaining exceeds those voting in favour or if it simply considers the resolution "unjust": see Communist China's attitude towards the United Nations, AJIL Vol.62 p.31, note 33). In an official statement issued on 23 October 1959, the People's Republic of China said: "The discussion of the so-called, "Tibet Question" by the UN has been in complete violation of the UN Charter, and the resolution of the UN General Assembly is illegal and void", (Documents 439 (1959)English translation in 2 *Peking Review*, No.43, at 8 (October 27 1959). (Also see, "Legal Position of Tibet" by Tieh-Tseng Li sometime Chinese Ambassador to Iran and Thailand AJIL Vol.50 394.)

Thus on 30 October 1950 the Central People's Government of the People's Republic of China said in a note to the Indian Government:

> "Tibet is an integral part of Chinese Territory. The problem of Tibet is entirely the domestic problem of China. The Chinese People's Liberation Army must enter Tibet, liberate the Tibetan people and defend the frontiers of China. This is the resolved policy of the Central People's

Government ..."

"But regardless of whether the local authorities of Tibet wish to proceed with peace negotiations and whatever the results may be achieved by negotiations, the problem of Tibet is a domestic problem of the People's Republic of China and no foreign interference shall be tolerated. The particular problem of Tibet and the problem of the participation of the People's Republic of China in the United Nations are two entirely unrelated problems ..."

With regard to its record on human rights China claims that the "reunification" of 1951 has been on the whole beneficial to the Tibetan people, "Old Tibet" it asserts was one of the world's regions witnessing the most serious violations of human rights":see Information Office of the State Council of the People's Republic of China, Tibet - Its Ownership and Human Rights Situation, *Beijing Review* (September 28-October 4, 1992), pp.10-43. On human rights issues China constantly strongly asserts that human rights issues are a matter of national sovereignty and that no one has the right to interfere in the internal affairs of another country. The Chinese Communist Party says it stands for the development of state relations with other countries on the basis of "five principles of mutual respect for sovereignty and territorial integrity, mutual non-aggression, non-interference in each other's internal affairs, equality and mutual benefit, and peaceful coexistence". Thus the Chinese Government reject any principles of international law or any United Nations human rights instrument which it says interferes in the domestic affairs of China. It says that the promotion and protection of human rights in the People's Republic of China are not matters of international concern.

But as we shall see in the chapter INDEPENDENCE AND RECOGNITION IN INTERNATIONAL LAW, there is wide recognition among international lawyers that at the time of the invasion in 1950 Tibet fulfilled the criteria of statehood in international law and that in modern international law the taking of territory by force should never be recognized and is unlawful.

Thus the effective test for China's claim to Tibet is not whether China conquered Tibet in the 13th century but whether China had any control over Tibet between 1911-1950, otherwise no former colony anywhere in the world would have obtained independence. This is a question of international law not the domestic law of China. Examination of China's claim that Tibet has always been part of China does not stop in 1913. That would be to ignore the Tibetan Declaration of Independence, the expulsion of all Chinese troops and officials by 1918, the evidence of self-rule and the 1961 United Nations Resolution 1723 calling for the right of the Tibetan people to their fundamental rights and freedoms, including the right to self-determination. Despite Article 4 of China's Constitution which says that all the national autonomous areas are inalienable parts of China, there is no concept of inalienable territory in international law.

TIBET'S STATUS

"The Chinese more, perhaps, than any other people have a mystic reverence for the past which leads them to cling with tenacity to their historical claims over any territory that has at any time formed part of their dominions and, with the fervour of faith, to believe that any people that have once been united to them must in fact still desire that unity, whatever the appearances may be" - Hugh Richardson - b.1905. Head of Lhasa Mission 1936-50

As we have seen Tibet was invaded by China in 1950 and tricked and/or coerced into giving up its independence by signing the so called 17-point Agreement of 23 May 1951.

Tibet says that before the eighteenth century Tibet and China enjoyed equality and mutual independence. Tibet unwillingly and forcibly came under the influence of China in the eighteenth century but by the end of the nineteenth century China's position in Tibet had become little more than a fiction. As Professor Alexandrowicz-Alexander points out (AJIL Vol.48 p.265ff), not infrequently suzerainty, though still continuing on the basis of an historical relationship, can become a nominal title ripe for elimination or conversion into a higher title more favourable to the subordinate state. Tibet's treaty-making powers were recognized by Britain, treating Tibet as a necessary contracting party to the tripartite treaties of 1905 and 1914, even going to the length of war with Tibet in 1903 to secure the frontier and trade between India and Tibet. Had Tibet been territory of China, Britain would have been at war with China in 1903/04.

Accounts of contemporary eye witnesses confirm the almost total disappearance of the Amban's influence by the beginning of the twentieth century (see Percival Landon, "The Opening of Tibet" (NY, 1905), pp.85, 396, 413, 483; Sven Hedin, "Central Asia and Tibet" (1908) p.456; L.A. Waddell, "Lhasa and Its Mysteries" (1905) pp.413, 418. The Chinese revolution of 1911 not only saw the ending of any token Chinese presence in Tibet but ended any personal allegiance of the Dalai Lama to the Manchu Emperors with no replacement allegiance to the Republic of China. But by 1913, Tibet had declared its independence (see Appendix, document 9) and expelled all Chinese representatives and garrisons throughout Tibet. Free of Chinese influence, independent Tibet concluded the Treaty of Urga between Tibet and Mongolia, 29 December 1912, acknowledging mutual independence, Article 2 stating: "The ruler of the Mongol people, Chjebzun damba Lama approves and recognizes the formation of (an) independent (Tibetan) state and the proclamation of the Dalai Lama as ruler of Tibet". (See MONGOLIA, *post*). Shortly afterwards Sir Henry McMahon (Britain's delegate to the Simla Conference) said in his final report: "At the commencement of the year 1913 Tibet was in arms against her neighbour and suzerain China; the Chinese Resident with his escort and troops had been driven from the country and Tibet declared its independence".

Following his return to Lhasa the Dalai Lama issued a proclamation which is regarded by Tibetans as Tibet's formal declaration of independence urging Tibetans: "To safeguard and maintain the independence of our country ..." It was the clearest possible unequivocal rebuff to China's Imperial Decree of November 1908 alluding to China's sovereignty not suzerainty over Tibet. Tibet's opening brief at the Simla Conference 1914 declared: "... Tibet is an independent state and that the precious Protector, the Dalai Lama, is the Ruler of Tibet, in all Temporal as well as spiritual Affairs": Proceedings of the First Meeting of the Tibet Conference held at Simla on 11, October 1913; "Statement of the Tibetan Claims," Foreign Office File, FO 535/16, Annex iv to Enclosure in No.413, p.393 (1914).

Moreover anyone wishing to enter Tibet between 1911-1950 had to obtain permission from the government of Tibet and not from China. Writing in 1926 Sir Francis Younghusband ("The Epic of Mount Everest" p.15) refers to, "the difficulty at the time (1919) in obtaining permission (to climb) from either the government of Nepal or Tibet between which countries Mount Everest is situated".

After the expulsion of the last Chinese troops from Tibet in 1913 and until 1950 there was no Chinese civil or military presence in Tibet. Tibet declared its independence. It had the organization of a sovereign state, controlling its own affairs, internally and externally. In 1914 Tibet ceded to India the Tawamg tract of land. In World War I Tibet offered to send troops to fight on the side of the British. In August and in October 1918 truce agreements were entered into between the governments of Tibet and China at the end of hostilities: see Appendix, documents 7, 8, 13 and 14. During World War II, Tibet remained neutral resisting direct pressure by the governments of Great Britain, the United States and China to allow the transportation of war materials to China through

Tibet. Tibet had its own Army, sending its soldiers to India for military training. It had its own postage and currency and had direct trade relations with its neighbours. Tibetan representatives participated in the first Asian Conference in New Delhi in 1947, displaying the Tibetan national flag on the table as a symbol of Tibetan independence and Tibetan delegates travelled on Tibetan passports which were accepted as valid travel documents by Tibetan diplomats in the United States, Great Britain and other countries.

Having considered the evidence the Report to the International Committee of Jurists by the distinguished Legal Inquiry Committee on Tibet in 1960 found that:

"... Tibet was at the very least a *de facto* independent state when (the 17-point Agreement) was signed in 1951, and the repudiation of this agreement by the Tibetan Government in 1959 was found to be fully justified. In examining the evidence, the Committee took into account events in Tibet, as related in authoritative accounts by officials and scholars familiar at first-hand with the recent history of Tibet and official documents which have been published. These show that Tibet demonstrated from 1913 to 1950 the conditions of statehood as generally accepted under international law. In 1950 there was a people and a territory, and a government which functioned in that territory, conducting its own domestic affairs free from any outside authority. From 1913-1950 foreign relations of Tibet were conducted exclusively by the government of Tibet and countries with whom Tibet had foreign relations are shown by official documents to have treated

Tibet in practice as an independent state".

The 1993 Conference of International Lawyers on Issues relating to Self-Determination and Independence for Tibet also found little serious disagreement that at the time of the entrance of the People's Liberation Army into Tibet in 1950, "Tibet was for all practical purposes an independent state and had been so for an extended period". It further found that "For most of its history Tibet possessed the essential attributes of statehood; was not an integral part of another state; and remains a separate entity despite, at times, having close political ties with the Mongols, the Gurkhas of Nepal, the Manchus of the Qing Dynasty and with the British Empire".

Dr Hienstorfer's conclusions on the legal status of Tibet in his "Opinion Regarding the Legal Status of Tibet by the German Parliamentary Scientific Research Service for International Law", 12 August 1987 commissioned by the German Bundestag are that: "At the time of Tibet's violent incorporation into the Chinese nation it was an independent state. China has not effectively acquired territorial title, as this would be in contravention with the basic principle of the annexation prohibition which is based on the prohibition against violence. The effectiveness of actual domination of a territory does not result in a acquisition of territory within the framework of international law".

The evidence that Tibet was an independent state in 1950 is overwhelming.

INDEPENDENCE AND RECOGNITION IN INTERNATIONAL LAW

"(The Turks) one and all, bag and baggage, shall I hope, clear out from the province they have desolated and profaned" - William Ewart Gladstone 1809 - 1898

The essential characteristics of a new state to enter into relations with another state are independence and recognition. The birth certificate of a new state is usually a formal statement that it is subject to no other sovereignty. But political considerations play a large role in the decision whether to grant or withhold recognition.

The "Proclamation of Independence, 1913" (see Appendix, document 9) is regarded by Tibet as its declaration of independence. Often a declaration of independence is accompanied by some fundamental change of circumstances, such as a revolution or a former power being driven out at the conclusion of a war of independence. Thus in 1824, Britain recognized the new republics of Buenos Aires, Mexico and Columbia as independent states out of the collapsed former Spanish colonies of South America. The recognition of independent Brazil from Portugal in 1825 prompted Canning's famous statement: "I have called the New World into existence to redress the balance of the old".

Britain in the nineteenth century was very much concerned with propping up and keeping the weak empires in China and Turkey out of Russian hands. Practically, the Ottoman Sultan's authority over much of his domain consisted of a vague suzerainty and in portions of his empire, Algiers and the Danube Principalities, which were occupied by foreign powers, the Sultan's power did not even extend to that. But the nineteenth century witnessed new states escaping from Turkish suzerainty. In 1821 there were uprisings in the Danubian (Romanian) Principalities of Moldavia and Wallachia and Greece. The Sultan had little effective control over his far-flung empire and by the policy of divide and rule, foe against foe, let non-Muslims largely govern themselves. The Romanian Principalities, which were in theory autonomous under Ottoman suzerainty, had their traditional privileges protected after 1812 by the Russo-Turkish treaty of Bucharest. But by the 1820s it was clear that Greece could not be left under Turkish suzerainty and the newly-proclaimed independent Greek state came into being in 1830 after the Battle of Naverino Bay where a combined British, Russian and French naval force under Admiral Codrington sank the entire Turkish-Egyptian fleet. Similarly, Belgium declared independence from the United Netherlands and was recognized by Britain in 1830; and in October 1908 Prince Ferdinand of Bulgaria successfully proclaimed his country's complete independence from Turkey, thirty years after the Treaty of Sterfano created an independent Bulgaria, Bulgaria having been nominally part of the Ottoman Turkish Empire from 1396 to 1878. Tiny Andorra was formerly a "fief" under the joint suzerainty of its two joint princes, the President of France, and the Bishop of Urgel who were responsible for foreign relations. In 1993 it became a state with the consent of its two princes, who remain Heads of State.

Since World War II certain states have come into being

through the intervention of the United Nations. In 1950 a procedure was available which should have been applied to Tibet whereby in 1947, Britain (the Mandatory Power) referred the Palestine problem to the United Nations whose first action was to set up the United Nations Special Committee on Palestine. It recommended partition and on 29 November 1947, the General Assembly by a vote of 33 to 13 declared: "The Mandate for Palestine shall terminate as soon as possible, but in any case not later than 1st August, 1948 ... Independent Arab and Jewish states, and the specific international regime for the city of Jerusalem ... shall come into existence in Palestine two months after the evacuation of the armed forces of the Mandatory Power has been completed, but in any case no later than 1st October 1948." Despite lack of support from Britain when the British Mandate terminated on 15 May 1948, the Jewish state of Israel was declared in Tel Aviv and the Provisional Government was recognized immediately by the United States of America as the *de facto* authority of the new state of Israel. On 15 May 1948 recognition was extended to the state of Israel by the Soviet Union and Poland to be followed by several Eastern European and South America countries. Just as it would do in the case of Tibet in 1950 Britain remained silent as Bevin (British Foreign Secretary) attempted to persuade British Dominions and Western Europe to withhold recognition despite South Africa quickly recognizing the state of Israel.

Conversely, Taiwan now has no seat in the United Nations after losing membership to China in 1971, although 27 states still recognize it.

There are a number of different aspects of recognition. The recognition of states by other states; the recognition of governments by other states; collective recognition by the United Nations; the recognition of credentials; the recognition of representatives of a member state of the United Nations; recognition and the Stimson doctrine (that states should not recognize the taking of territory by war or in breach of the UN Charter); recognition in the context of intervention and self-determination. Moreover recognition may be *de facto* or *de jure*. "A *de jure* government is one which - in the opinion of the person using the phrase - ought to possess the powers of sovereignty, though at the time it may be deprived of them. A *de facto* government is one which is really in possession of them, although the possession may be wrongful or precarious": quoted by Banks L. J. in *Luther v. Sago* [1912] 3 KB 543. It should be noted that the recognition of governments is only relevant to exchange of diplomatic relations and has no connection with the recognition of new states in international law. In 1980 the British Government announced it would no longer accord recognition to governments as opposed to states, shifting the focus from recognition to informal dealing: see 408 HL Deb. , cols.1121-2, 28 April 1980.

In the context of the creation of statehood there are two theories. The first says that it is only through recognition that states come into being in international law (the no recognition - no statehood theory). The latter says that once the factual criteria of statehood has been satisfied, the new state exists as an international person, recognition becoming merely a political act and not a legal act in this context: see Shaw,

International Law 4th ed, 146. The so-called "Right of all peoples to self-determination", (see SELF-DETERMINATION *post*) is a separate concept.

Article 1 of the Montevideo Convention on the Rights and Duties of States 1933 lays down the most generally accepted criteria of statehood in international law namely: "(a) a permanent population; (b) a defined territory; (c) a government; and (d) capacity to enter into relations with other states".

This generally accepted definition of statehood was adopted in the United States "Restatement 3d of the Foreign Relations Law", (1987). Section 201 provides: "Under international law, a state is an entity that has [1] a defined territory and [2] a permanent population, [3] under control of its own government, and [4] that it engages in, or has the capacity to engage in, formal relations with other such entities."

In its report "Tibet and the Chinese Peoples's Republic" 1960, the Legal Inquiry Committee on Tibet concluded that according to the norms of international law, "Tibet demonstrated from 1913 to 1950 the conditions of statehood as generally accepted under international law. The view of the Committee was that Tibet was at the very least a *de facto* independent state when the 17-point Agreement was signed in 1951.

In 1994 the United States Congress recognized the Dalai Lama and his representatives as the Tibetan Government in exile. Congress declaring, "Tibet is an occupied sovereign country under international law and that its true representatives of the Tibetan people are the Dalai Lama and the Tibetan Government in exile": Pub L103-236, Title V, 536,

30 April 1994, 108 Stat. 481 (see Appendix , document 18).

The test of statehood followed by the Arbitration Commission of the European Conference on Yugoslavia in Opinion No.1 is that: "a state is commonly defined as a community which consists of a territory and a population subject to an organized political authority" and that "a state is characterised by sovereignty". Opinion No.1 goes on to note that the form of internal political organization and constitutional provisions constituted "mere facts", although it was necessary to take them into account in order to determine the government's sway over the population and the territory. Oppenheimer "International Law", p.120 states that, "a state proper is in existence when a people is settled in a territory under its own sovereign government".

"The European Community Guidelines on Recognition of New States in Eastern Europe and the Soviet Union", 16 December 1991, specifically refers to self-determination and underlines the need to respect the rule of law, democracy and human rights and specifically mentions the requirement for guarantees of minority rights. It notes in particular that recognition requires:

> "respect for the provisions of the Charter of the United Nations and the commitments subscribed to the Final Acts of Helsinki and in the Charter of Paris, especially with regard to the rule of law, democracy and human rights; guarantees for the rights of ethnic and national groups and minorities in accordance with the commitments subscribed to in the framework of the CSCE;
> respect for the inviolability of all frontiers which can

only be changed by peaceful means and by common agreement;

acceptance of all relevant commitments with regard to disarmament and nuclear non-proliferation as well as to security and regional stability;

commitment to settle by agreement where appropriate by recourse to arbitration, all questions concerning state succession and regional disputes".

In 1950 Tibet had a defined territory. It had a permanent population, It had a ruling government. Heinrich Harrer, whose escape from a British internment camp in India to Tibet in 1943 was depicted in his book "Seven Years in Tibet" (which is now a film) describes effective Tibetan Government for both internal and external affairs. Until overrun by China in 1950, Tibet for at least a century had conducted its own external affairs, making treaties* with Britain, successive Chinese Governments (Manchu, Nationalist and Communist), Mongolia and Nepal. It also maintained independent contacts with foreign governments including the United States, see for example, President Roosevelt's correspondence with the Dalai Lama.

But without international recognition a potential state will only have at most *de facto* status or at worst remain unrecognized. Thus the grant of independence by South Africa to its Bantustans in the Transkei and Bophuthatswana was totally unrecognized in international law although it could be said to comply with the criteria for statehood and both the Organization of African Unity and the United Nations called on states not to recognize them because they said they were the tools of apartheid and declared such "independence"invalid. On 16 December 1991, the European Union adopted a declaration on Yugoslavia in which the Community and its member states agreed to recognize the Yugoslavian Republics and shortly afterwards issued statements declaring that the member states of the Community, accepting assurances that the requirements of the Guidelines would be fulfilled, were prepared to recognize Armenia, Azerbaijan, Belarus, Kazakstan, Moldova, Turkmenistan, Ukraine, Uzbekistan, Kirghizstan and Tadzhikistan after the collapse of the Soviet Union.

Serbia, Croatia, Slovenia and Bosnia-Herzegovina were recognized as independent states by member states of the European Union and admitted to membership of the United Nations (membership of which is limited to "states" by Article 4 of the United Nations Charter) at a time when they were engaged in civil war and a considerable part of their respective territories was in dispute.

But the question of recognition is often a matter of political timing. Lithuania is an example of recognition postponed by political events. When Lithuania unilaterally declared independence on 11 March 1990 its declaration went unrecognized because the situation in the old Soviet Union (which had invaded them in November 1939) was unstable and a new Soviet federal structure was still under discussion, and significantly the Soviet Union still maintained substantial control in Lithuania. However the independence of all the Baltic states (Lithuania, Latvia and Estonia) was finally recognized by a large number of states in 1991, after recognition significantly by the Soviet Union.

Another example of international rejection and non-recognition is Rhodesia. United Nations resolutions in 1965, 1966 denied the legal validity of the Rhodesian declaration of independence and called upon member states not to recognize it. The concepts of recognition and self-determination are explained by Shaw, *International Law*, p.145. He says: "It could be argued on the other hand that, in the absence of recognition, no entity could become a state, but this constitutive theory of recognition is not acceptable. The best approach is to accept the development of self-determination as an additional criteria of statehood, denial of which would obviate statehood. This can only be acknowledged in relation to self-determination situations and would not operate in case, for example , of secessions from existing states. In other words, in the case of an entity seeking to become a state and accepted by the international community as being entitled to exercise the right of self-determination, it may well be necessary to demonstrate that the internal requirements of the principal have not been offended. One cannot define this condition too rigorously in view of state practice to date, but it would appear to be a sound proposition that systematic and institutionalized discrimination may invalidate a claim to statehood." Also see, *post*, **Self-Determination**.

Equally no amount of recognition, can make what is not a state into a state and no amount of non-recognition can make a state into a non-state. But as Sir Hersch Lauterpacht maintained "there is a duty on states to recognize a state if it fulfils the conditions of statehood as required by international law" Lauterpacht, n.2, p.6. W.E. Hall in *A*

Treatise on International Law, 1924, p.127 also says that "no state has a right to withhold recognition when it has been earned".

The 1904 Lhasa Treaty between Tibet and Britain, the 1906 Convention between Britain and China, the 1907 Convention between Britain and Russia, the Tibet Trade Regulations 1908 and the 1914 Simla Convention between Tibet, China and Britain (which China initialled but never ratified) are a muddle. Worried that the 1904 Lhasa Convention negotiated by Younghusband went to the extent of recognizing Tibet the British Government devised a procrustean solution. It was to refer *inter alia* to, "the Tibetan Government"; "the territorial integrity of Tibet"; "Tibetan nationalities"; "Tibetan subjects"; "Tibetan High Authorities at Lhasa", yet say in the subsequent treaties that Tibet was under the "suzerainty" of China. Yet whatever the treaties say, the classical rule of international law suggests that Tibet acquired sovereignty even before China was thrown out of Tibet in 1913.

The solution suggested by Professor Shaw is a concept permitting a people to acquire sovereignty over territory pending the establishment of a particular state (see Shaw, *International Law*, p.337) relying on the provision in the 1970 UN Declaration on Principles of International Law concerning friendly relations and co-operation among states that the territory of a colony or other non-self-governing entity, possess, under the United Nations Charter, a separate status from the occupying power. That appears to be the rationale in the 1991 guidelines for the creation of new states in Eastern Europe and the Soviet Union. It would be international law's answer to the question of Tibet.

Even with passage of time annexation by force, however difficult to unscramble, is unlawful in international law. Thus in 1940 the Baltic states were also swallowed up by a mighty neighbour. But Stalin's annexation was never recognized *de jure* by the free world and the control exercised by the Soviet Union was only accepted on a *de facto* basis. Fifty years later despite the depredations of the Soviets and influx of Russians, the Baltic states broke away and wrestled their independence from the old Soviet Union.

* A treaty can be described in a number of ways; a Convention, agreement, regulations, protocol, act, charter, covenant, pact or concordant: see 1969 Vienna Convention on the Law of Treaties. The Convention partly reflects customary law and defines in Article 2 a treaty for the purposes of the Convention as, "an international agreement concluded between states in written form and governed by international law, whether embodied in a single instrument or in two or more related instruments and whatever its particular designation".

SELF-DETERMINATION

"For Freedom's battle once begun, Bequeath'd by bleeding sire to son. Though baffled oft is ever won" - Lord Byron 1799 - 1824

Tibet's claim to self-determination does not depend on whether Tibet is historically part of China. US President Wilson's policy at the end of World War I was the insistence that the settlement of every question whether of territory, of sovereignty, of economic arrangement or of political relationship should only take place upon the basis of free acceptance of that settlement by the people immediately concerned.

After World War II, the principle of self-determination was developed in various United Nations instruments. Article 1 of the United Nations Charter refers to the need for developing "friendly relations among nations based on respect for the principles of equal rights and self-determination of peoples", and Article 55 on "economic and social co-operation" instructs the United Nations to promote higher standards of living, solutions to health and cultural problems and universal respect for human rights in order to create conditions necessary for peaceful and friendly relations among nations, "based on equal rights and self-determination". But these provisions were to do with the obligations and rights of states and not with unrecognized states, groups, or individuals, and until the speeding up of the decolonisation process in the 1960s' independence movements were often suppressed rather than encouraged. In 1950 (GA Res 421, UN GAOR, 5th Sess, Supp. No.20, art.6,

UN Doc A/1775/Corr1 (1950)) the General Assembly decided that an international covenant on human rights should include a right of self-determination for "peoples".

In 1957 the General Assembly resolved that:

"(a) Member states shall, in their relations with one another, give due respect to the right of self-determination;
(b) Member states having responsibility for the administration of non-self-governing territories shall promote the realisation and facilitate the exercise of this right by the peoples of such territories."

The process of de-colonisation was speeded up in 1960 when the General Assembly passed two further resolutions. The first, the Declaration on the Granting of Independence to Colonial Countries and Peoples, GA Res 1514, UN GAOR, 15th Sess., Supp. No.16, UN Doc A/4684 (1960) stigmatized the trusteeship and colonial administrations as great evils and the policy of a gradual end to colonialism favoured by the UN Charter was abandoned in favour of, "a speedy and unconditional end to colonialism". Moreover the principle of meticulous preparation for independence was discarded by the policy statement that: "inadequacy of political, economic, social, or educational preparedness should never serve as a pretext for delaying independence". Colonialism, it declared, was an "impediment to the protection of world peace" taking it outside of international law's proscription against external interference in state affairs. The declaration applies to all territories which have not yet achieved independence. The second resolution, "Principles which should guide Members in determining whether or not an obligation exists to transmit the information called for in Article 73(e) of the Charter". GA Res 1541, UN GAOR 15th Sess., Supp. No.16 at 29 UN Doc A/4684 (1960) provides a number of alternatives to complete independence.

Article 1 of the International Covenant on Civil And Political Rights and Article 1 of the International Covenant on Economic, Social and Cultural Rights, adopted by the General Assembly in 1966, both declare that: "All peoples have the right of self-determination. By virtue of that right they freely determine their political status and freely pursue their economic, social and cultural development". However, both Covenants are unclear as to which people qualify for this right and whether the right is afforded to people through states or as individuals. Article 3 of both Covenants in identical language says: "The States Parties to the present Covenant, including those having responsibility for the administration of Non-Self-Governing and Trust Territories, shall promote the realization of the right of self-determination, and shall respect that right, in conformity with the provisions of the Charter of the United Nations". (Both Covenants have recently been signed by China as a preliminary to full ratification).

The 1970 UN Declaration on the Principles of International Law Concerning Friendly Relations and Co-Operation Among States (GA Res 2625, UN GAOR 25th Sess., 883d mtg., Supp. No.20 at 122 UN Doc A/8028 (1970)) develops the right of equal rights and self-determination still further and offers alternatives to independent statehood including self-determination through free association with an independent state. But although it declares the right of all peoples to have these rights freely determined, the Declaration on Friendly Relations sheds little light as to how the objectives should be accomplished. The Declaration states:

> "By virtue of the principle of equal rights and self-determination of peoples enshrined in the Charter of the United Nations, all peoples have the right freely to determine, without external interference, their political status and to purse their economic, social and cultural development, and every state has the duty to respect this right in accordance with the provisions of the Charter.
>
> Every state has the duty to promote, through joint and separate action, realization of the principle of equal rights and self-determination of peoples, in accordance with the provisions of the Charter, and to render assistance to the United Nations in carrying out the responsibilities entrusted to it by the Charter regarding the implementation of the principle, in order:
>
> (a) To promote friendly relations and co-operation among states: and
> (b) To bring a speedy end to colonialism, having due regard to the freely expressed will of the peoples concerned;
>
> and bearing in mind that subjection of peoples to alien subjugation, domination and exploitation constitutes a violation of the principle, as well as a denial of

fundamental human rights, and is contrary to the Charter.

Every state has the duty to promote through joint and separate action universal respect for and observance of human rights and fundamental freedoms in accordance with the Charter.

The establishment of a sovereign and independent state, the free association or integration with an independent state or the emergence into any other political status freely determined by a people constitute modes of implementing the right of self-determination by that people.

Every state has the duty to refrain from any forcible action which deprives peoples referred to above in the elaboration of the present principle of their right to self-determination and freedom and independence. In their actions against, and resistance to, such forcible action in pursuit of the exercise of their right to self-determination, such peoples are entitled to seek and to receive support in accordance with the purposes and principles of the Charter.

The territory of a colony or other Non-Self-Governing Territory has, under the Charter, a status separate and distinct from the territory of the state administering it; and such separate and distinct status under the Charter shall exist until the people of the colony or Non-Self-Governing Territory have exercised their right of self-determination in accordance with the Charter, and particularly its purposes and principles.

Nothing in the foregoing paragraphs shall be construed as authorising or encouraging any action which would dismember or impair, totally or in part, the territorial integrity or political unity of sovereign and independent states conducting themselves in compliance with the principle of equal rights and self-determination of peoples as described above and thus possessed of a government representing the whole people belonging to the territory without distinction as to race, creed or colour.

Every state shall refrain from any action aimed at the partial or total disruption of the national unity and territorial integrity of any other state or country."

But in distinction to the concept of recognition there is no internationally recognized definition or agreement as to the qualifying circumstances in international law when the right of self-determination is legitimately exercisable. The best available definition of "a people" appears in the report published in November 1989 under the auspices of UNESCO, "Experts on Further Study of the Rights of Peoples":

"A people for the rights of people in international law, including the rights to self-determination, has the following characteristics:

a. A group of individual human beings who enjoy some or all of the following common features:

    (i)   a common history or tradition;
    (ii) racial or ethnic identity;
    (iii) cultural homogeneity;
    (iv) linguistic unity;
    (v) religious or ideological affinity;

(vi) territorial connection;
(vii) common economic life.

b. The group must be of a certain number who need not be large (eg the people of micro-states) but must be more than a mere association of individuals within a state.

c. The group as a whole must have the will to be identified as a people or the consciousness of being a people, allowing that groups or some members of such groups, though sharing the foregoing characteristics, may not have the will or consciousness.

d. Possibly the group must have institutions or other means of expressing its common characteristics and will for identity."

Under this definition, Tibet satisfies each of the criteria giving the Tibetans the right to recognition as a distinct people for the right of self-determination under international law. It should be noted that the United Nations principles of self-determination were particularly geared to the ending of European colonialism or "oceanic colonialism" (the colonisation of land overseas) and whilst it has been largely successful to this end with the exception of the Western Sahara and East Timor it has proved a confused and uncertain doctrine in cases of indigenous, nationalist, secessionalist, democratic and devolutionary self-determination. Writing in 1970, Vernon Van Dyke cynically remarked: "self-determination has become an emotion-laded term in the field of human rights, a shibboleth that all must pronounce to identify themselves with the virtuous.

But in reality the general consensus of nations suggests the preservation of territorial integrity; Biafra and the Confederate States of America are classic examples of the denial of secession and the general proposition is that a segment of the population has no right in international law to break away and form a separate state. But the concept of territorial integrity has no application if a colony or trust territory is entitled to sovereignty or independence. For example, in recent times we have seen the creation of Croatia, Bosnia-Herzegovina and Macedonia and Slovenia out of the former Federal Republic of Yugoslavia leaving behind only Serbia and Montenegro, the break-up of the Soviet Union and the division of Czechoslovakia into the Czech Republic and Slovakia, for little more than a desire for cultural separatism. New states which have arisen out of the old Soviet Union, such as Kazakhstan, Uzbekistan and Turkmenistan have no previous history as independent nations.

In most of these cases the factors and events surrounding the creation of the original unified state were artificial and current-day politics and circumstances have *ex post facto* justified a claim for self-determination and recognition as a separate state. Hence, the right to self-determination is strongest where there is a substantial identifiable minority population within a state which that minority never chose to be part of. In the case of forceable occupation, the voice of the occupied group by its representatives has an unanswerable aspiration to self-determination by independence. That surely is Tibet's position in international law.

Lesser forms of self-determination such as regional government or autonomy within the framework of another state are more appropriate in cases of strong cultural identity within a national framework. Internal self-government exists outside international law; for example devolution in the United Kingdom, Spanish regionalism, and the system of tribal self-government in the United States.

The diversity of situations creating the claim to self-determination is illustrated by the list of non-state groups and peoples claiming some form of self-determination including, the Kurds, the Québecois, the Basques, the Scots, the Welsh, the Palestinians, the Tamils in Sri Lanka, the Karen people in Burma, the Ambonese and Aceh Merdeka in Indonesia, the Chittagong Hill Tribes in Bangladesh, the South Ossetians in Georgia, the Naga people in India and the Western Saharans under *de facto* Moroccan control. (The Unrepresented Nations and People's Organization ("UNPO") founded in 1993 published a list of 26 members representing over fifty million people: see "Unrepresented Nations and People's Organization, Self-Determination in Relation to Individual Human Rights, Democracy and the Protection of the Environment", UNPO GA/1993/CR/1 Conference Report 1993). The catalyst for the winners seems to be strong international pressure and a struggle occasionally pacifist but more frequently violent.

Some commentators argue that the suppression of the Tibetan people is the factor that creates the right to self-determination. Thus, in his book, *Self-Determination of Peoples*, (Cambridge UP (1995) p.95, n.86) Antonio Cassese opines that prior to 1950 Tibet had never been a state entity independent of China and that the issue of Tibet is more a case of the violation of human rights than a case of self-determination.

The case for self-determination in terms of denial of human rights, United Nations 1961 Resolution 1723 and the 1979 UN Declaration on Friendly Relations is cogent because it concentrates on China's occupation of Tibet by force, China's activities in Tibet and conduct towards the Tibetan people. What is needed is a historical debate or arbitration to settle basic facts and to settle once and for all China's claim that before 1950 Tibet was part of China.

CHINA AND HUMAN RIGHTS

"If you want a picture of the future, imagine a boot stamping on a human face - forever" - "1984" by George Orwell, 1903-1950

China's trick is to introduce detailed domestic laws fulfilling on paper its obligations under the international human rights agreements it signs up to, but to carry on with its policies regardless in blatant disregard of human rights.

China's human rights record is appalling. But the human rights situation in Tibet and in Muslim Xinjiang (East Turkestan) is worse because minorities are singled out for particularly harsh treatment. Although prison sentences are handed down to dissidents generally, the Chinese authorities use "splittism" (advocating break away from China) however trivial the expression to persecute minorities. At the end of 1997 there were 1,216 known political prisoners in Tibet accused of splittist crimes but with countless unnamed ones the figure is considerably more. These are just a few examples:

Ngawang Sangdrol is a Buddhist nun from the Garu nunnery just outside Lhasa. She was born in 1977. She was already serving two sentences of imprisonment totalling nine years (three years' imprisonment imposed at the age of sixteen for taking part in pro-independence demonstrations in 1992 and six years for singing nationalist songs in prison in 1993), when along with other nuns, she refused to clean her cell during a re-education programme designed to persuade the women to accept the Chinese appointed

Panchen Lama. As a punishment the nuns were made to stand in the rain by the female brigade commander and Ngawang Sangdrol shouted "Free Tibet". She was badly beaten and her sentence doubled for refusing to stand in the presence of a Chinese official, and for shouting "Free Tibet". Her original sentence was declared unlawful in 1995 by the Working Group on Arbitrary Decisions, a UN Committee which assesses reports of illegal imprisonment; this ruled that her continuing detention was arbitrary because she had been punished for exercising her rights to freedom of opinion and called on China to release her. If she is released in 2010 she will be 33.

In 1989 ten monks from Drepung monastery and one lay Tibetan received sentences ranging from five to nineteen years imprisonment for printing and circulating human rights and political pamphlets including a Tibetan translation of the Universal Declaration of Human Rights. One of the monks, thirty-four year old Ngawang Phulchung, received nineteen years' imprisonment as "leader" of the group. After being jailed in Drapchi prison in Lhasa he was among a group of prisoners who were severely beaten by prison guards in April 1991 for protesting at the treatment of other prisoners.

Jigme Sangpo is a former teacher in a Tibetan primary school now in his sixties. By the time he is released in 2011 Jigme Sangpo will have spent twenty-eight years in prison. He was sentenced in 1983 to fifteen years' imprisonment for "counter-revolutionary propaganda and incitement". He received an additional five- year prison sentence in 1988 for shouting pro-independence slogans in prison. In December

1991 he was beaten for shouting pro-Tibet slogans during a visit to Drapchi prison by the Swiss Ambassador to China, was held in solitary confinement, and his sentence was again increased by eight years.

Chadrel Rinpoche was Abbot of Tashilhunpo monastery and, before his imprisonment, Vice-Chairman of the Sixth Tibet Autonomous Regional Chinese People's Political Consultative Conference of the Tibet Autonomous Region. For the offence of searching for the reincarnation of the Panchen Lama he was sentenced in 1996 to six years' imprisonment on charges of "plotting to split the country", of "leaking state secrets" and "colluding with separatist forces abroad". Two other Tibetans, Jampa Chung, a monk and a businessman called Samdrup, were sentenced to four and two years' imprisonment respectively. (The fate of Gedhun Choekyi Nyima, the little boy recognized as the true 11th Panchen Lama by His Holiness the Dalai Lama on 14 May 1995 is unknown. Gedhun and his family were taken into custody and China refuses to disclose where they are or to confirm whether they are still alive). A puppet Chinese-chosen Panchen Lama of similar age to Gedhun, called Gyaltsen Norbu was enthroned in Shigatse in 1996.

The protection of human rights was considered to be a major role of the United Nations when it was set up in 1945 and the UN Charter and the Universal Declaration of Human Rights form the basis of internationally recognized human rights. All states are under a duty in international law to respect the human rights of its citizens. Article 1(3) of the United Nations Charter declares that its purposes include: "promoting and encouraging respect for human rights and for fundamental freedoms for all without distinction as to race, sex, language, or religion ..." Articles 56, 57 obliges all United Nations members to, "take joint and separate action in co-operation with the Organization for the achievement of ... higher standards of living, full employment and conditions of economic and social progress and development; solutions of international economic, social, health and related problems; and international cultural and educational co-operation; universal respect for, and observance of, human rights and fundamental freedoms for all without distinction as to race, sex, language or religion."

In 1946 the United Nations established a Commission on Human Rights, its first priority was to draft an international Bill of Rights. Despite Conventions on specific areas, for example the General Assembly approval, 9 December 1948 of the Convention on the Prevention and Punishment of the Crime of Genocide and in 1951 the Convention Relating to the Status of Refugees (as amended by a Protocol in 1966) on the treatment of refugees and the setting up of the United Nations High Commission for Refugees, no international bill of rights was agreed until 1966.

Initially the UN General Assembly adopted by a vote of forty-eight to none with eight abstentions the morally binding Universal Declaration of Human Rights on 10 December 1948, GA Res 217A [III], protecting a variety of civil, political and economic rights, and declaring that all individuals are entitled to the rights and freedoms of the Declaration on a non-discriminatory basis. In the absence of an international bill of rights the United Nations Economic and Social Council and the Commission on Human Rights set up by it established working groups and in particular a Sub-Commission on the Prevention of Discrimination and the Protection of Minorities. From the late 1960s a procedure was set up to receive complaints from individuals alleging gross violations of human rights under Economic and Social Council Resolutions 1235 of 1967 and 1503 of 1970. But these measures were not particularly effective and the Economic and Social Council became what has been described as little more than a, "quintessential political body".

In 1966 there was a major development. Two covenants were agreed coming into force in 1976 codifying the principles in the UN Charter and Declaration of Human Rights covering a wide range of human rights, leaving it to states to ratify one or both. They are the International Covenant on Civil and Political Rights and the International Covenant on Economic, Social and Cultural Rights, the former concerned with civil and political rights, the latter concentrating on economic, social and cultural rights. The United Kingdom has ratified both Conventions. But although binding on ratifying states, in international law, adherence to the Covenants involves nothing more onerous than providing periodic reports on national compliance. Although ratifying states can also recognize the jurisdiction of the Covenant's Human Rights Committee to hear complaints from other states that have also agreed this procedure (and if appropriate hold hearings) and to promote a friendly settlement, the inter-state procedure has yet to be put in operation. There are also two optional Protocols to the International Covenant on Civil and Political Rights; under the First Optional Protocol a state may recognize the

Committee's authority to hear petitions from individuals. (The United Kingdom has accepted the inter-state procedure but rejects the individual petition protocol on the ground that the United Kingdom has acceded to the superior European Convention on Human Rights). The Second Optional Protocol adopted by the UN General Assembly 15 December 1989, aims at the abolition of the death penalty.

The rights set out in the UN Charter, the Universal Declaration of Human Rights, the International Covenant on Economic, Social and Cultural Rights and the International Covenant on Civil and Political Rights, include the right to freedom from torture and other cruel, unusual or degrading treatment or punishment, freedom from arbitrary arrest and detention, freedom of opinion and expression and freedom of religion, the rights of peaceful assembly and association and due process of law, and are an authoritative expression of the concept of fundamental human rights in international law. Despite howls of protest from China of interference in its domestic jurisdiction it is a clearly accepted principle of international law that human rights abuse everywhere is the concern of all states and not a matter of domestic jurisdiction.

Reports under the International Covenants on Civil and Political Rights are submitted to the Secretary-General to the Human Rights Committee (which has been in operation since 1977) for consideration. The Committee transmits reports to the state parties and to the Economic and Social Council along with "such general comments as it may consider appropriate". In contrast, the procedure under the International Covenant on Economic, Social and Cultural Rights is that reports under the Covenant are submitted to the Economic and Social Council for consideration in accordance with the Covenant. It then sends reports to the Human Rights Commission for "study and general recommendation": Article 19. In May 1986 a new committee of independent experts, called *rapporteurs,* was established to assist the Economic and Social Council in monitoring states' compliance with their legal obligations under the Covenant.

Reports submitted to the Human Rights Committee in 1977, 1984 and 1989 by the United Kingdom illustrate the reporting procedure and shows how states which genuinely attempt to fulfil their international commitment to human rights do not object to investigations within their domestic jurisdiction. The United Kingdom 1977 report was criticized for being too long on general principles and statements of intent but falling short on detail. The 1977 report provoked questioning on discrimination and equality of opportunity, one member requesting more information on the participation of women in public life and in the judiciary and queried whether higher unemployment rates among Catholics in Northern Ireland was evidence of discrimination against them. There was also questioning on whether the United Kingdom's immigration policy was racially discriminatory, on the burden of proof in race discrimination cases, on prison conditions affecting prisoner's protests and the conditions of remand prisoners. In response to criticism of lack of detail in the 1977 and 1984 reports the 1989 report placed considerable reliance on statistical and research material (mostly governmental).

When considering a government's periodic report the

Human Rights Committee may receive information from non-governmental organizations and pressure groups with an interest in human rights (NGOs): see ESC Resolution 1296[XLIV] of 23 May 1968 concerning arrangements for consulting non-governmental organizations. For example, information was supplied to the Committee concerning the 1989 United Kingdom report by Liberty, Amnesty International, Article 19, Charter 88, the Howard League for Penal Reform, JUSTICE, the Joint Council for the Welfare of Immigrants and the Campaign for the Administration of Justice. Consultations statements may be oral or written. According to statistics supplied by the Non-governmental Organization Officer at Geneva, 33 NGOs participated in the work of the Commission on Human Rights in 1970, 62 in 1980 and 119 in 1982.

The following major human rights agreements have been concluded under United Nations auspices:

Convention on the Prevention and Punishment of the Crime of Genocide, 9 December 1948, 78 UNTS 277 (in force 12 January 1951) **ratified by People's Republic of China in 1983.**

Convention relating to the Status of Refugees, 28 July 1951, 189 UNTS 137 (in force 22 April 1954) **ratified by Nationalist China.**
Protocol to the Convention Relating to the Status of Refugees, 31 January 1966, 606 UNTS 267 (in force 4 October 1967), **Convention and Protocol acceded to by People's**

Republic of China in 1982.

Convention on the Political Rights of Women, 20 December 1952, 193 UNTS 135 (in force 7 July 1954) **ratified by Nationalist China.**

International Convention on the Elimination of All Forms of Racial Discrimination*, 21 December 1965, 660 UNTS 195(in force 4 January 1969) signed 31 March 1966 and **acceded to by People's Republic of China 29 December 1981.**
   Declaration regarding Article 14 (competence of the CERD to receive communications from individuals) (in force 3 December 1982).

International Covenant on Economic, Social and Cultural Rights*, 16 December 1966, 993 UNTS 3, (in force 3 January 1976). **Signed by People's Republic of China on 27 October 1997 as a preliminary to full ratification. N.B. this Covenant has no Optional Protocol enabling the Human Rights Committee to receive communications from individuals.**

International Covenant on Civil and Political Rights, 16 December 1966, 999 UNTS 171 (in force 23 March 1976) **signed by China 4 October 1998.**
   First Optional Protocol to the International Covenant on Civil and Political Rights, 16 December 1966, UN General Assembly Resolution 2200 A [xxI], (in force 23 March 1976) which enables the Human Rights Committee to receive communications from individuals of states party to the Protocol claiming to be victims of violations of any of the

rights set out in the Covenant.

Second Optional Protocol to the International Covenant on Civil and Political Rights, 15 December 1989, UN General Assembly Resolution 44/128 aiming at the abolition of the death penalty.

International Convention on the Suppression and Punishment of the Crime of Apartheid* **acceded to by People's Republic of China in 1983.**

International Convention on the Elimination of all Forms of Discrimination Against Women*, 18 December 1979, GA Res 34/180, UN Doc A/34/46 (in force 3 September 1981) Signed 17 July 1980 and **ratified by People's Republic of China 4 November 1980.**

Convention Against Torture and other Cruel, Inhuman or Degrading Treatment or Punishment*, 10 December 1984, GA Res 39/46, Doc. A/39/51 (in force 26 June 1987) Signed 12 December 1986 and **ratified by People's Republic of China 4 October 1988.**
Declaration regarding Article 21 of the Convention (competence of the Committee against Torture to receive communications by a state party against another state Party) (in force 26 June 1987).
Declaration regarding Article 22 of the Convention (competence of the Committee Against Torture to receive communications from individuals) (in force 26 June 1987).

Convention on the Rights of the Child, 20 November 1989, GA Res 44/25 (in force 2 September 1990) Signed 29 August 1990 and **ratified by People's Republic of China 2 March 1992.**

Accession is a procedure whereby a state becomes party to a treaty of which it is not an original party. The agreements marked with an asterisk contains similar reporting provisions to those of the International Covenant on Civil and Political Rights.

The Vienna Declaration and Program of Action adopted by the World Conference on Human Rights, 25 June 1993, (A/CONF 157/24 (Part I) Chap III) confirmed *inter alia* the indivisibility and interdependence of human rights.

It should also be noted that unless a state agrees to be bound by a treaty by the act of signing, signature is only a preliminary to ratification in the internal government of that state. Thus although China has signed both Covenants, ratification is dependent upon the decision of the Standing Committee of the National People's Congress under Article 67(14) of China's Constitution and by the President under Article 81 (see Appendix, document 15). However Article 18 of the Vienna Convention on the Law of Treaties lays down that between signature and ratification a state must refrain from acts which would defeat the object and purpose of a treaty.

There is also a procedure for direct complaints on human rights issues to the United Nations known as the "1503" procedure, and between 1972 and 1987 about 350,000 complaints were received by the Secretary-General. Generally an admissible complaint to the Commission is more effective because a "1503" is confidential whereas a complaint to the Commission is not.

In 1956 the People's Republic of China embarked on a period of savage persecution in Tibet including the torture and execution of lamas, monks and nuns, rape of nuns, looting and destruction of temples and monasteries. Between 1966 and 1980, particularly during the worst excesses of the Cultural Revolution, the basic human rights of the Tibetan people were systematically violated by the occupying Chinese. Tibetans were the target of the "Destroy the Four Old's Campaign" involving the destruction of Tibetan ideas, culture, customs and habits because China sees the Tibetan language and religion as contributing to "splittism" or secession. Since 1950 some six thousand Buddhist temples and monasteries have been demolished. Some Buddhist universities have also been destroyed and the use of the Tibetan language discouraged. A system of communes was introduced with state control of all food supplies involving rationing according to a system of "work points" earned. China's food policy included forced production of wheat instead of barley (the traditional Tibetan crop) leading to crop failure and widespread famine. In 1960 the International Commission of Jurists in a detailed deliberation and after hearing evidence found that the Chinese People's Republic had violated sixteen articles of the UN Declaration of Human Rights, and that the actions of the People's Republic of China in Tibet clearly fell within the accepted definition of genocide in international law as defined in Article 11 of the United Nations Genocide Convention, which includes:

"... any of the following acts committed with intent to destroy, in whole or in part, a national, ethical, racial or religious group as such:

(a) killing a member of the group;
(b) causing serious bodily or mental harm to members of the group;
(c) deliberately inflicting on the group conditions of life calculated to bring about its physical destruction in whole or in part;
(d) imposing measures intended to prevent births within the group;
(e) forcibly transferring children of the group to another group."

The Commission found that "acts of genocide had been committed in Tibet in an attempt to destroy the Tibetans as a religious group, and that such acts are acts of genocide independently of any conventional obligation". The Commission found four facts relating to the charge of genocide: not permitting adherence to the practice of Buddhism in Tibet; systematically setting out to eradicate Buddhism in Tibet; killing religious figures in pursuit of that purpose; and forcibly transferring large numbers of Tibetan children to a Chinese materialist environment to prevent them having a Buddhist upbringing. (Recently the Dalai Lama and others have suggested that the massive influx of Han Chinese settlers in Tibet with the intention of pushing the indigenous Tibetans into an insignificant majority is a form of genocide. These "settlers" include military, administrative and professional workers, technicians, skilled and unskilled workers, farmers, traders, entrepreneurs and prisoners, many of whom are required to remain in Tibet after release).

China's Government, however, does not accept that human rights are of universal concern. It believes that what it does to its people is its own business. In 1989, the Sub-Commission on the Prevention of Discrimination and Protection of Minorities requested the UN Secretary-General to transmit to the Commission on Human Rights information provided by the Chinese Government and other reliable sources on the Tiananmen Square massacre. This was the brazen official response of the Chinese Government:

> "Last June there occurred in Beijing a rebellion which was supported by hostile forces abroad and constituted an attempt to overthrow the legitimate government of the People's Republic of China and subvert the socialist system set forth in the Constitution through violent means. The Chinese Government took resolute measures to quell the rebellion in the interests of the overwhelming majority of the Chinese people. This is entirely China's internal affair and is a matter different in nature from the question of human rights. However, with the plotting and encouragement of some Western members, the Sub-Commission on the Prevention of Discrimination and Protection of Minorities adopted resolution 1989/5 at its forty-first session. This is a brutal interference in China's internal affairs while hurting the feeling of the Chinese people. The Spokesman of the Foreign Ministry of the

People's Republic of China issued a statement of 2 September 1989, solemnly declaring the firm objection of the Chinese Government to the resolution and deeming it to be illegal and null and void."

Looking at Chapter II of China's Constitution, which is China's Bill of Rights, and the Criminal Procedure Law of China (as amended March 1996) one might think that China shows model respect for human rights. The grisly truth is that in China within the framework of "the people's democratic dictatorship" human rights are virtually non-existent.

Protection from torture, inhuman and degrading treatment

Although China ratified the United Nations Convention Against Torture and Other Cruel, Inhuman or Degrading Treatment or Punishment in 1988, allegations of torture in Chinese and Tibetan prisons continue to be made. Article 1 of the Convention defines torture as "... any act by which severe pain or suffering whether physical or mental, is intentionally inflicted on a person for such purposes as obtaining from him or a third person information or a confession, punishing ... intimidating or coercing ... or for any reason based on discrimination of any kind, when such pain or suffering is inflicted by or at the instigation of or with the consent or acquiescence of a public official or other person acting in an official capacity". Article 2 of the Convention stipulations that state parties must, "... take effective legislative administrative, judicial or other measures to prevent acts of torture in any territory under its jurisdiction". Article 10(1) states: "All persons deprived of their liberty shall be treated with humanity and with respect for the inherent dignity of the human person". But although China has complied in part by introducing Article 43 of its revised Criminal Procedure Law which states that "The use of torture to coerce statements and the gathering of evidence by threats, enticement, deceit or other unlawful methods are strictly prohibited", and Article 18 which states that, "Cases involving ... (the) violation of the personal and democratic rights of citizens committed by power-abusing state-organ functionaries, such as illegal detention, the acts of extorting a confession by torture, retaliation and framing and illegal searches, are to be filed for investigation by the people's procuratorates", first-hand accounts of prisoners and the number of deaths of prisoners in custody tortured indicates that despite Articles 18 and 43 torture continues to be routine in questioning prisoners. The Lawyers Committee for Human Rights ("Opening to Reform?" An Analysis of China's Revised Criminal Procedure Law, October 1996, p.69) also found China in breach of the Torture Convention by not making the exclusion of illegally-gathered evidence a basic principle of the China's criminal process.

The United Nations Special Rapporteur on Torture, P. Kooijmans, in his report to the 1990 session of the United Nations Commission on Human Rights (UN Document E/CN4/1990/17) stated that he had addressed letters to the Chinese Government regarding alleged torture of Tibetans who had been convicted of involvement in demonstrations, including beatings with electric batons, cattle prods and rifle butts during questioning, hanging of detainees by their thumbs, ankles or wrists and suspension from ceilings or prison bars. Prisoners testified that they were doused with ice water or held down in tubs of cold water in winter. Buddhist monks and nuns appear to have been singled out for particularly harsh prison treatment. (For a first-hand account of torture and prison conditions in Tibet see "Fire Under the Snow" by Palden Gyatso, Harvill Press, 1997.) He also alleged that prison authorities sometimes charge relatives a collection fee for the corpses of those killed in police custody or demonstrations. The United Nations Committee Against Torture at its fourth session in Geneva held in spring 1990, requested China to provide more details on measures to stamp out torture and submit an additional report by the end of the year. The Chinese Deputy Chief Procurator, Liang Guoqing, admitted that in the first quarter of 1990 his department investigated 2,900 cases of "perverting justice for bribes, extorting confessions by torture, illegal detention and neglect of duty". Of these more than 490 were "major cases, involving deaths and injuries, as well as serious economic losses".

Tibetan nuns seem to suffer particularly in prison. Reports of at least twelve deaths of prisoners after a protest in Drapchi prison in May 1998 include six nuns. The Chinese prison authorities say they committed suicide. The names of the nuns are Ngawang Choekyi (26), Tashi Lhamo (24), Choekyi Wangmo, Lobsang Wangmo, Dekyi Yangzom (21) and Khedron Yonten. The Prison Law was adapted by the Standing Committee in December 1994. It outlines the appropriate treatment of prisoners, forbidding torture and forced confessions.

Freedom of religion, thought, conscience and association

In 1998, 7,156 monks and nuns were expelled from monasteries and nunneries as China intensified persecution of Tibetan Buddhism under the "strike hard" and the accompanying "patriotic re-education" campaign introduced in 1996, designed to wipe out Tibetan nationalism. The strike hard campaign has now been extended to secular Tibetan society. In 1998 the arrest of 327 monks, nuns and lay people was recorded in connection with the strike hard campaign. Some were arrested for possessing a picture of the Dalai Lama, opposing the Chinese appointed Panchem Lama or failing to obey work team orders. Tibetans are routinely forced to denounce the Dalai Lama and new measures have been introduced to force monks and nuns into retirement at the age of sixty and to subject admission into monasteries and nunneries to strict state control Recently fourteen monasteries and nunneries have been shut down and a number demolished on the pretext that they were built with foreign money.

Article 18,1 of the Covenant on Civil and Political Rights specified that, "Everyone has the right to freedom of thought, conscience and religion. This right shall include freedom to have or adopt a religion or belief of his choice, and freedom, either individually or in community with others and in public or private, to manifest his religion or belief in worship, observance, practice and teaching". Under Article 18,2 "No one shall be subject to coercion which would impair his freedom to have or to adopt a religion or belief of his choice." And Article 27 stipulates that, "In those states in which ethnic, religious or linguistic minorities exist, persons belonging to such minorities shall not be denied the right, in community with other members of their group to enjoy their own culture, to profess and practice their own religion, to use their own language." China says that its Constitution stipulates that freedom of religious belief is one of the fundamental rights of citizens and that the Chinese Government respect and protects its citizens' right to freedom of religious belief. Article 35 of China's Constitution says that, "Citizens of the People's Republic of China enjoy freedom of speech, of the press, of assembly, of association, of procession and of demonstration." Article 36 guarantees freedom of religious belief and state protection of "normal religious activities" and similarly Article 11 of the Law on Regional Autonomy specifies that, "The organs of self-government of national autonomous areas shall guarantee the freedom of religious belief to citizens of the various nationalities." But although section 127 of China's Criminal Law provides that officials who deprive citizens of religious freedom are subject to a penalty, up to two years' imprisonment, no one has been prosecuted.

Protection from slavery and forced labour

Article 8 of the International Covenant on Civil and Political Rights prohibits slavery in all forms and stipulates, "No one

shall be required to perform forced or compulsory labour."
In 1998 various compulsory unpaid labour programs were set up in Tibet in connection with road construction by the Chinese Government in Chamdo and Shigatse and in mining and the construction of a hydro-electric plant. Harry Wu records that there are 1155 prison factories and farms in China (loagai) housing 8/10 million prisoners of whom a tenth are political prisoners. He also revealed China's brisk trade to order in organs taken from executed prisoners, sometimes he says, removed before execution: Harry Wu, *Troublemaker*, Chatto and Windus 1996.

Violation of subsistence rights

In 1997 the average income of Tibetans living in rural areas was 1,040 yuan p.a. ($130), a fifth of urban dwellers' earnings. Just under 87% of Tibetans live in rural areas. Evidence suggests that improvements and investment in the TAR economy benefit Chinese settlers and not Tibetans. Not only are Tibetans extensively taxed but the enforced sale of grain, butter and other products at minimum rates to the state and the policy of forcing Tibetans to make unwanted purchases of commodities such as fertilisers and barbed wire from the state further depletes subsistence levels. In the towns Tibetan girls are increasingly forced into prostitution as the only means of subsistence.

But Article 13 of China's Constitution says, "The state protects the right of the citizens to own lawfully earned, income, saving, houses and other means of livelihood." The violation of subsistence rights is also contrary to points 13 and 14 of the 17-point Agreement. Article 11 of the Covenant on Economic Social and Cultural Rights, "recognizes the right of everyone to an adequate standard of living for himself and his family, including adequate food, clothing and housing, and to the continuous improvement of livelihood". Article 1,2, of the International Covenant on Civil and Political Rights includes the right of all peoples to "freely determine their political status and freely pursue their economic and cultural development". Article 1,3 states, "In no case may a people be deprived of its own means of subsistence".

Freedom of expression and opinion

Article 19,1 of the Covenant on Civil and Political Rights states, "Everyone shall have the right to hold opinions without interference" and under Article 19,2, "the right to freedom of expression: This right shall include freedom to seek, receive and impart information and ideas of all kinds, regardless of frontiers, either orally, in writing or in print, in the form of art, or through the media of his choice." Equally Article 35 of China's Constitution says that everyone in China enjoys freedom of speech, of the press, of assembly, of procession and of demonstration.

The following cases are typical. Ngawang Kyonmey was arrested on 18 September 1998 for conspiring to hand a letter to Mary Robinson, the UN High Commissioner for Human Rights during her visit to Tibet. Two to five year prison sentences have been handed down for pasting up posters, flying the Tibetan national flag, distributing leaflets concerning the reincarnation of the Panchem Lama or shouting: "Free Tibet". The use of the internet is also monitored as Lin Hai found to his cost when he was arrested in March 1998 and sentenced in Shanghai to two years imprisonment for sending 30,000 e-mail addresses to a dissident publication. There is also strict control of radio and television.

Right to education

Educational levels in the Tibet Autonomous Region are considerably lower than in China and any other Autonomous Region. The Specialized Plan for the TAR Territory, 1993, shows that in 1990 21.92% of the non-Han population received primary education compared to 43.47% in China as a whole. 73.27% of the non-Han population was illiterate or semi-literate (84.22% among women) compared to 29.86 in China. 2.96% of Tibetans received junior secondary education as opposed to 18.80% of the population in China and with regard to university education 0.09% graduated in the Tibet Autonomous Region as opposed to 0.42% in China.

Article 28(1) of the Convention on the Right of the Child guarantees, "the right of the child to education, and with a view to achieving this right progressively and on the basis of equal opportunity (a) make primary education compulsory and available free to all; (b) encourage the development of different forms of secondary education, including general and vocational education, make them available and accessible to every child, take appropriate measures such as the introduction of free education and offering financial assistance in case of need"; (c) make higher education accessible to all on the basis of capacity by every appropriate means; (d) make educational and vocational information and guidance available and accessible to all children; (e) take measures to encourage regular attendance at schools and the reduction of drop-out rates". Article 30 stipulates: "In those states in which ethnic, religious or linguistic minorities or persons of indigenous origin exist, a child belonging to such a minority or who is indigenous shall not be denied the right, in community with other members of his or her group, to enjoy his or her own culture, to profess and practice his or her own religion, or to use his or her own language".

Article 46 of China's Constitution states that citizens have "the duty as well as the right to receive education" and China's Education Law enshrines the principle of "equal educational opportunities regardless of race, nationality, sex, occupation, financial status and religion". Article 37 of the Law on Regional National Autonomy requires the government of national autonomous areas to "develop education for the nationalities by eliminating illiteracy, setting up various kinds of schools, spreading compulsory primary education, developing secondary education and establishing specialized schools for the nationalities, such as teachers' schools, secondary technical, national schools and institutes of nationalities to train specialized personnel from among the minority nationalities."

The simple truth is that education is deliberately withheld from most Tibetan children. In 1993 TAR Chairman, Gyaltsen Norbu, conceded that by the end of 1993, approximately one third of Tibetan children were unable to go to school due to financial restraints. Even where schools exist standards are often poor. The charging of fees and selective enrolment procedures further limits education opportunity for Tibetans. The principal use of Chinese in schools is another denial. Traditionally monasteries and nunneries provided education in Tibetan culture and philosophy but by prohibiting and expelling young monks and nuns China also violates the rights of Tibetan children to education.

Enforced birth control and Women's rights

Article 49 of China's Constitution, stipulates "Marriage, the family and child are protected by the state. Both husband and wife have the duty to practice family planning". But China's surging population problem is not Tibet's problem. China's solution in Tibet is to flood Tibet with Han Chinese settlers.

Article 44 of the Law on Regional National Autonomy provides: "In accordance with legal stipulation, the organs of self-government of national autonomous areas, shall, in the light of local conditions, work out measures for family planning" (see Appendix, documents 16). The size of families is restricted by a quota system. In urban areas particularly by a harshly applied 'One Child Programme'. Those working in official positions are allowed two children, farmers are permitted three. Violence used to implement this policy in the name of family planning routinely includes forced sterilisation, abortion, and beating of pregnant women: see Amnesty International publication, 'China No One is Safe', 1996. By these means China aims to start to achieve a reduction in population after the year 2,000. The definition of genocide in the UN Convention on the Prevention and

Punishment of the Crime of Genocide means any acts committed with the intent to destroy, in whole or in part, a national, ethnic, racial or religious group, and includes in Article IId the imposition of ... 'measures intended to prevent births within the group'. In 1998 the Tibet Centre for Human Rights and Democracy received 432 reports of Tibetan women being sterilised against their will.

Fines are imposed for exceeding quotas and children born in excess of quota cannot be registered which means they are denied a ration card that entitles them to food, education and land rights.

Arbitrary arrest

Arbitrary arrest is defined by the UN Working Group on Arbitrary Detention as: "deprivation of freedom when the facts giving rise to the prosecution or conviction concern the exercise of the rights and freedoms protected by certain articles of the Universal Declaration of Human Rights and the International Covenant on Civil and Political Rights." Article 9 of the Covenant on Civil and Political Rights states: "Everyone has the right to liberty and security of person. No one shall be subjected to arbitrary arrest or detention. No one shall be deprived of his liberty except on such grounds and in accordance with such procedure as are established by law." Amnesty International's latest report on China says: "The past year saw the arbitrary detention of possibly thousands of protesters and suspected government opponents, the continued imprisonment of thousands of political prisoners, grossly unfair trials, widespread torture and ill-treatment in police cells, prisons and labour camps and the extensive use of the death penalty ..." Despite some changes Chinese legislation still allowed more than 200,000 people to be detained in 1997 without charges or trial for re-education through labour.

Denial of right for fair trial

Article 14 of the Covenant on Civil and Political Rights says that: "All persons shall be equal before the courts and tribunals. In the determination of any criminal charge against him, or of his rights and obligations in a suit at law, everyone shall be entitled to a fair and public hearing by a competent, independent and impartial tribunal established by law ..." "Everyone charged with a criminal offence shall have the right to be presumed innocent until proved guilty according to law".

In its 1998 Report, Amnesty International stated that political trials continue to fall far short of international standards, with verdicts and sentences decided by the authorities before the trial, and appeal hearings usually a formality.

Rights of the Child

The right of the child to education has already been noted. There is evidence that Tibetan children are imprisoned for political offences; for example, 11 years' old Tenzin Tsedup was arrested and badly beaten after taking part in a demonstration in Lhasa. He was sentenced to one year in prison and, on release, fled to India. The abduction of the boy 11th Panchem Lama by the Chinese Government is a grave violation of his human rights.

Article 37(b) of the Convention on the Rights of the Child states: "No child shall be deprived of his or her liberty or arbitrarily. The arrest, detention or imprisonment of a child shall be in conformity with the law and shall be used only as a measure of last resort and for the shortest appropriate period of time."

Other ethnic minorities are also victims of China's abuse of human rights in retaliation for demands for self-determination, respect for cultural identity or religious freedom. A similar pattern of abuses against Muslim ethnic groups in Xinjiang Autonomous Region and the Ili Kazak Autonomous Prefecture is known to occur, and also against Han Chinese trying to exercise fundamental human rights, for example those who suffered from the brutal putting down of the Tiananmen demonstration in 1989 and the subsequent imprisonment and execution of participants. Charges against ethnic detainees have included "seeking to split the motherland", "hooliganism" and "endangering public order", which crimes carry the death penalty. Evidence suggests that Tibetans are singled out for particularly harsh treatment by the Chinese courts, which is routinely unfair and inhuman, and without regard to international standards. The Tibetan people, moreover, have been marginalized by a vast influx of Han Chinese immigrants. Tibet under Chinese occupation has been stigmatized as showing the worst characteristics of an oppressive colonial administration: see the UNPO Report, "China's Tibet - The World's Largest Colony (Report of a Fact-Finding Mission and Analysis of Colonialism and Chinese Rule in Tibet", January 1998).

Through the veneer of talk about China signing up to international human rights covenants, the contempt of the Chinese authorities for human rights is only too transparent. On 9 September 1998, outside the Hilton Hotel, Beijing, Chu Hailan the wife of jailed labour activist Liu Nianchun was seized and kicked by six policemen and hotel security staff when attempting to do no more than meet Mary Robinson, the United Nations High Commissioner for Human Rights. Other individuals were arrested for trying to hand her letters. So much for human rights in lawless China.

MONGOLIA

"The day may dawn when fair play, love for one's fellow men, respect for justice and freedom, will enable tormented generations to march forth triumphant from the hideous epoch in which we have to dwell. Meanwhile never flinch, never weary, never despair" - Winston Churchill, April 1955, 1878-1965

Tibet and Mongolia have distinct historical parallels. They are regarded as sister states. Both lost their independent status but, whereas Outer Mongolia emerged from a terrible past and is a fully independent state today, Tibet is still an occupied country. Mongolia has a population of just over two million. It is basically a nomadic herding society about the size of Tibet and its Buddhist population once suffered terrible religious persecution in the 1930s. All but six of Mongolia's 800 monasteries and nunneries were destroyed by the Communists. It too was a theocracy under the spiritual leadership of a living Buddha, Jebtsundamba Hutuktu but when the eighth reincarnated descendant died on 20 May 1924 the communist government in power at the time prohibited a search for his reincarnate successor, the line died out and Mongolia lost its spiritual ruler. A ninth Hutuktu Bogd Haan was found in Tibet. He lives in exile in India.

By 1732 Mongolia was also under the influence of Manchu China. Inner Mongolia has been absorbed by China but, with the ending of Manchu rule in 1911, both Outer Mongolia and Tibet seized the opportunity to assert their independence and on 1 December 1911, Mongolia declared independence from China proclaiming the Jebtsundamba Hutuktu its Bogd Haan

(Holy King). Tibet followed with its Proclamation of Independence in 1913 (see Appendix, document 9). On 29 December 1912 Article 2 of the Treaty of Urga between Tibet and Mongolia declared: "The ruler of the Mongol people, Chjebzun damba Lama approves and recognizes the formation of (an) independent (Tibetan) state and the proclamation of the Dalai Lama as ruler of Tibet". On 25 May 1915 the Treaty of Kyakhta between Mongolia, China and Czarist Russia was signed granting Outer Mongolia limited autonomy. In 1919 Chinese troops occupied the capital Ulan Bator, to be driven out in February 1921 by retreating anti-communist White Russians. In July 1921 joint Mongolian and Bolshevik forces captured Ulan Bator and the People's Government of Mongolia was declared on 26 November 1926 under the 28 year-old Mongolian "red hero" Damdiny Sukh and, with the backing of Lenin, all White Russians and Chinese were driven out of Outer Mongolia. Later, under the protection of Stalin, Mongolia secured in the Yalta Agreement between the Allies in February 1945 (with Chang Kai-shek's consent) a plebiscite in Mongolia after World War II and in due course Mongolia voted in favour of total independence. But it was not until 1961 that Mongolia gained full admission to the United Nations and was eventually fully recognized as an independent sovereign state. Inner Mongolia remains under Chinese control.

With the break-up of the Soviet Union the Russians simply pulled out and, Mongolia became a democracy; there has been a Buddhist religious revival and some of Mongolia's former communist leaders have entered monasteries. In 1996 the Democratic Party won a landslide victory.

At the 1992 UN Earth Summit in Rio, Mongolia proposed that the whole country be declared a special biosphere reserve. With $750 million from the UN Development Fund Mongolia doubled the area of the Great Gobi National Park (the size of England) by adding seven million hectares. As we shall see, a similar concept that Tibet should become a biosphere was part of the Dalai Lama's "Five Point Peace Plan".

In August 1995 The Dalai Lama presided over the first Kalachakra initiation in Mongolia for 60 years.

In Inner Mongolia, an indication of Tibet's possible fate, Han Chinese settlers now outnumber the remnant Mongolian population by 20:1.

CONSTITUTION OF THE PEOPLE'S REPUBLIC OF CHINA AND LAW ON REGIONAL NATIONAL AUTONOMY

"Every Communist must grasp the truth, "Political power grows out of the barrel of a gun" - Mao Zedong 1893-1976

Within China's existing constitutional set-up true Tibetan autonomy is impossible. China's brand of communism is ring-fenced by the concept of one nation which actually curtails minority identity. The current Constitution of the People's Republic of China (see Appendix, document 15) was adopted by the 5th National People's Congress on 4 December 1982. It sets out the structure of state government. Local government is dealt with in the Law on Regional Autonomy (see Appendix, document 16). But the all important Chinese Communist Party has its own Constitution (see Appendix, document 17) adopted 22 September 1982. The three estates in China are the state executive, the armed forces and the Communist Party. Although their powers overlap the CCP rules in China.

In a move to a more collective form of leadership in 1982 the posts of party Chairman and Vice-Chairman were replaced by the post of General Secretary of the Central Committee shifting power back to the Standing Politburo Committee which is the highest Party authority. Under the Constitution the posts of PRC President and Vice-President are restored and the State Council comprising the Premier, Vice-Premiers, State Councillors, Ministers in charge of Commissions, Auditor General and Secretary General is the highest organ of state administration.

Table showing PRC system of government

Organs of state power

National People's Congress
(highest state legislature)
↓
Standing Committee
(consisting of Chairman, Vice Chairman, Secretary General & members)
↓
President & Vice-President
(elected by National People's Congress)
↓
State Council
(highest organ of state power appointed by the President - consisting of Premier, State Councillors, Ministers in charge of Ministries, Ministers in charge of Commissions, the Audit or General and the Secretary General:
Note: all Ministries report to State Council except PLA which reports to Communist Party Military Affairs Commission)
↓
People's Congresses and their Standing Committees at local level
(Responsible to State Council)

Chinese Communist Party organs of government

National Party Congress
(highest Communist Congress - 1,500 members)
↓
Party Congress Central Committee
(Headed by its Secretary General and consists of 300 members. It elects the Party Central Committee and the Standing Politburo Committee)
↓
Party Congress Central Committee Politburo
(15/25 members - issues instructions to CCP members)
↓
Standing Politburo Committee
(highest CCP authority headed by Secretary General of Central Committee)
↓
Local Party Organizations

Military Commission of Central Committee
(Note: Armed forces are supervised by the Chinese Communist Party)

Central Military Commission
(Comprising Chairman, Vice Chairman and members whose Chairman is responsible to the National People's Congress and its Standing Committee.
Note has very little power)

The pivotal principle of the Constitution is the maintenance of, "a socialist state under the people's democratic dictatorship led by the working class and based on the alliance of workers and peasants": Article 1. Political objectives are set out in the Preamble. Citizens rights and obligations are dealt with in outline and specific laws have been enacted defining civil rights, for example the Prison Law 1994 which mandates humane treatment of prisoners and forbids torture and forced confessions. But as the Constitution frankly admits, China is a socialist dictatorship. Accordingly four tenets, generally known in China as "the principles of the four upholds", have been written into the Preamble, namely (1) Adherence to the socialist road, (2) loyalty to the Communist Party leadership, (3) following through with the dictatorship of the proletariat and (4) adherence to Marxism-Leninism-Mao Zedong thought and Deng Xiaoping theory as its guide to action.

In China the will of the state is absolute. That is the meaning of " peoples democracy" under the Constitution. Individual rights are set out in Chapter II (Articles 33-56) but those rights are conditional on acceptance of the state's dictats. Those who the Chinese authorities perceive to oppose the system are deemed to have endangered state security and are dealt with harshly under China's criminal law. Thus

Article 3 says: "All citizens enjoy the rights and at the same time must perform duties prescribed by the Constitution and the law".

Since 1982 China has signed international human rights covenants and the Constitution has been amended. But the constitutional amendments are all concerned with economic liberalisation and, as we have seen, China falls far short of the standards laid down in the human rights covenants. The strangle hold on dissent is tighter than ever. Despite Article 35, there is no freedom to express opposition to the Party-led single party political system or to challenge China's leaders or form of government and those who do so end up in prison. Although China's revised Criminal Procedure Law (which came into force on 1 January 1997) provides the right to a defence lawyer and public trial, every year countless victims are detained without charges or sentenced without trial to years of imprisonment called "re-education, through labour" for political crimes, at the discretion of the police or local officials, and some prisoners are even sentenced to death. Those who are charged do not have fair trials. Legal representation is non-existent or very poor. Verdict decided before the evidence is heard is common. Torture of prisoners, political interference in the judicial process, repressive criminal legislation, harsh punishment including lengthy extended terms of imprisonment and the death penalty are frequently imposed. Yet addressing the UN General Assembly in 1986, the Chinese Foreign Minister, Wu Xueqian said: "The Covenants have played a positive role in realising the purposes and principles of the UN Charter concerning respect for human rights" and that, "the Chinese Government has consistently supported those purposes and principles".

The Constitution was amended on 15 March 1999 to provide that in the non-public sector of the economy comprising the individual and private sectors, operating within the limits prescribed by law is an important component of the socialist market economy. The previous wording said private business was a supplement to the socialist public-owned economy. Another amendment says that the People's Republic of China shall be governed according to law and shall be built into a socialist country based on the rule of law.

On paper the National People's Congress is the highest state legislative body. Between annual planning sessions of its 3,000 members its permanent body is the important Standing Committee of the People's Congress. Below the National People's Congress are Local People's Congresses at various levels. All administrative, judicial and procuratorial organs of the state are responsible to the State Council except the PLA which reports to the Military Affairs Commission of the Communist Party. Article 3 declares that state organs of the People's Republic of China apply "the principles of democratic centralism". Representatives of the National People's Congress and local assemblies are "elected" from lists of candidates drawn up exclusively by the CCP.

Chapter III (Articles 57 to 135) sets out the structure of government. The Head of State is the President. The Vice-President shares some presidential duties and can take over if the President is incapacitated. Citizens of the People's Republic of China have the right to vote and stand for election to the National People's Congress, which elects the

President and Vice-President, Chairman of the Central Military Commission, President of the Supreme People's Court and Procurator General. It chooses the premier of the State Council and the Vice Premier and others upon nomination: see Article 60. The President's designated powers include the power to promulgate statutes pursuant to National People's Congress decisions, to appoint and receive the Premier, Vice Premiers, State Councillors, Ministers in charge of Ministries or Commissions, the Auditor General and Secretary General of the State Council. The President can confer state honours, pardon criminals, proclaim martial law, declare a state of war and issue mobilisation orders: Article 80. The President also receives foreign diplomatic representatives. He can appoint and recall ambassadors, ratify treaties and important agreements concluded with foreign states: Article 81.

The highest executive body is the State Council; its membership appointed by the President, comprises the Premier and his deputies, State Councillors, Ministers in charge of Ministries or Commissions, the Auditor General and the Secretary General. The Premier has overall responsibility for the State Council and Ministers have overall responsibility for the Ministries or Commissions under their charge: Article 86. The President, Vice-President, the Premier and his deputies cannot serve for more than two consecutive sessions of the National People's Congress which amounts to ten years but when their time in any particular office has expired, State Council members often switch jobs and stay on.

The functions and powers of the State Council (which

includes all the main powers of government) are set out in Article 89. The State Council is responsible to the National People's Congress and when not in session to its Standing Committee: Article 92.

Articles 93 and 94 establish a Central Military Commission which is responsible to the Party Congress Central State Politburo. Its chairman wields considerable power and in June 1983 the National People's Congress elected the powerful Deng Xiaoping as Chairman of the new Central Committee Military Commission and the veteran politician Li Xiannian as State President.

Section VII, Articles 123 to 128, provide for the establishment of the People's Courts. The Supreme People's Court is the Highest Court, and there are local people's courts at different levels, military courts and other special people's courts: Article 124. Articles 126 to 133 deal with the people's procuratorates (the state prosecution service). Articles 134 and 135 deal with procedure in the people's courts and procuratorates. The Constitution provides for an independent judiciary but in practice the judicial system is subject to political guidance from the government and Politburo, particularly in sensitive cases. The highest CCP organ of state is the National Party Congress. Its 1,500 members elect the smaller 300 member Party Congress Central State who elect the Party Congress Central State Politburo. Their 15/25 members issue instructions to party organizations including the PLA. The highest CCP authority is the Standing Politburo Committee headed by the General Secretary. Li Peng, premier 1988-1998, is Chairman of the National People's Congress and also a member of the Standing Politburo State.

Articles 95-111 deal with Local People's Congresses and local government at various levels. The provisions for the establishment of the organs of self-government of National Autonomous Areas are contained in Section IV, Articles 112 to 122. Section IV applies to Tibet but in reality "autonomy" is a bogus delegation of powers as local government slavishly follows instructions from Beijing, mostly inimical to the interests of the Tibetan people. The organs of self-government are described as the "the People's Congresses and the people's governments of autonomous regions, autonomous prefectures and autonomous counties": Article 112. In the People's Congress of an autonomous region, prefecture or county, in addition to the deputies of the nationality or nationalities exercising regional autonomy in the administrative area, the other nationalities inhabiting the area are also entitled to appropriate representation in the People's Congresses and chairmanship and vice-chairmanship of the Standing Committees: Article 113. Article 114 says that the administrative head of an autonomous region, prefecture or county shall be a citizen of the nationality or of one of the nationalities exercising regional autonomy in the area concerned. Article 115 says that the organs of self-government of autonomous regions, prefectures and counties exercise the functions and powers of local organs of state as specified in section V. At the same time, Article 115 goes on to say, "they exercise the power of autonomy within the limits of their authority as prescribed by the Constitution, the law of regional national autonomy and other laws and implement the laws and policies of the state **in the light of the existing local situation**" (author's emphasis). Article 116 curtails the power of the organs of government in national autonomous areas by specifying that People's Congresses of national autonomous areas have the power to enact autonomy regulations and specific regulations in the light of the political, economic and cultural characteristics of the nationality or nationalities in the areas concerned, and that the autonomy regulations and specific regulations of the autonomous regions shall be submitted to the Standing Committee of the National People's Congress for approval before they go into effect. Article 117 deals with finance and Article 118 is concerned with local development plans.

Article 119 lays down the blueprint for cultural suppression. It says: "The organs of self-government of the national autonomous areas independently administer, educational, scientific, cultural, public health and physical culture affairs in their respective areas, **protect and cull** through the cultural heritage of the nationalities and work for the development and flourishing of their cultures." The strange use of the word "cull", usually used in the context of controlling animal populations, ominously suggesting suppression or at worst destruction of what is seen as a threat by China. Article 120 authorizes the raising of local public security forces for maintenance of public order. Article 121 specifies use of the local languages in the organs of self-government. Article 122 provides for state financial, material and technical assistance to accelerate economic and cultural development. Article 122 also provides for state help in occupational training.

General rights set out in Chapter I, Articles 1 to 3, define the state's role. The Constitution specifies certain individual liberties but also says that those rights can be curtailed and modified by overriding considerations of "the socialist system". Freedom within the constitutional framework is made subject to the interests of "the state, of society and of the collective, or upon the lawful freedom and rights of other citizens": Article 51. The duty of citizens in Article 52 is to "safeguard the unity of the country and the unity of its nationalities"and the duty in Article 53 is to, "abide by the Constitution and the law, keep state secrets, protect public property and observe labour discipline and public order and respect social ethics". Similarly Article 54 says: "It is the duty of citizens to safeguard the security, honour and interests of the Motherland; and not commit acts detrimental to her security, honour and interests." And in Article 55: "It is the sacred obligation of every citizen ... to defend the Motherland and resist aggression." Article 4 proclaims that all nationalities are equal. Discrimination against minorities is prohibited but co-joined with that is a statement that "any acts that undermine the unity of the nationalities or instigate their secession are prohibited". Article 4 goes on to declare that: "All the national autonomous areas are inalienable parts of the People's Republic of China". Article 4 also says that the people of all nationalities have the freedom to use and develop their own languages and to preserve or reform their own way of life. Article 4 of the 1999 amendment contains an additional statement that China shall be governed according to the rule of law of a socialist country. Article 5 proscribes all acts in violation of the Constitution. Articles 6 to 15 explain the basis of the socialist economic system. Article 15 ends with a warning: "Disturbance of the orderly functioning of the social economy or disruption of the state economic plan by any organization or individual is prohibited". Articles 13 to 29 sets out state responsibilities for its citizens. Article 32 deals with the protection of foreigners.

As we shall see below Article 30 provides for division of China into provinces, autonomous regions and municipalities; Tibet being an Autonomous Region. Article 30 also implements in "the Law on Regional Autonomy for Minorities in the People's Republic of China, 1984", the preamble of the latter stating that "the (PRC) is a multinational state jointly founded by the people of various nationalities. Regional national autonomy means that the minority nationalities, under state leadership, practice regional autonomy in areas where they live in concentrated communities and set up organs of self-government for the exercise power of autonomy." Article 31 allows for the setting up of Special Administrative Regions, which is the status of Hong Kong.

Chapter II headed "The Fundamental Rights and Duties of Citizens", is China's Bill of Rights. But they are hollow rights shackled with duties to the state, so that Article 33 which promises PRC citizens equality before the law says: "Every citizen enjoys the rights and at the same time must perform the duties prescribed by the Constitution and the law." Article 34 contains the right of all citizens over 18 to vote. Article 35 contains fundamental rights which are not in fact allowed. It says: "**Citizens of the People's Republic of China enjoy freedom of speech, of the press, of assembly, of association, of procession and of demonstration**" (author's emphasis). Article 36 purports to guarantee freedom of religious belief. But the rider makes it clear that the state will not tolerate any religious activities which in its opinion disrupts public order, impairs the health of citizens or interferes with the educational system of the state. The rider is used by the central authorities to persecute *inter alia* Buddhists, Catholics and the Falun Gong. The rider to Article 36 ominously adds: **"Religious bodies and religious affairs are not subject to any foreign domination"**. **Article 37 states that freedom of the person is inviolable and provides that no one can be arrested except with the approval or by a decision of a people's procuratorate or by a decision of a people's court**. Article 38 makes the personal dignity of citizens inviolable. **"Insult, libel, false charge or frame-up directed against citizens by any means is prohibited"**. Article 39 says that the home is inviolable and prohibits unlawful search or intrusion. Article 40 protects freedom and privacy of correspondence but goes on to except the needs of state security or investigation into criminal offences and says that **"public security or procuratorial organs are permitted to censor correspondence in accordance with the procedures prescribed by Law**. In fact censorship is routine. Article 41 gives citizens the right to criticise and make suggestions to any state organ or functionary but **"fabrication or distortion of facts for the purposes of libel or frame-up is prohibited."** Article 42 says that citizens have the right and duty to work, and contained in Article 43 is the right to rest. Article 45 deals with retirement entitlements and Article 45 with social security arrangements. Articles 46 declares the right of citizens to receive education. Article 47 contains the right to indulge in scientific and cultural pursuits. Article 48 gives women equal rights. Article 49 recognizes that the state protects marriage, the family and mother and child. It goes on to declare that both husband and wife have a duty to practice family planning, and imposes a duty on parents to rear and educate their children and on adult children to support and assist their parents. Violation of freedom of marriage and maltreatment of the old, woman and children is prohibited. Article 50 says that the PRC will protect the rights and interests of overseas PRC nationals. Articles 55 and 56 concern military service and the duty on PRC citizens to pay their taxes.

The Law of the People's Republic of China on Regional National Autonomy

In 1965 China designated Tibet an Autonomous Region of China. The Autonomous Regions of China are, Tibet, Xinjiang, Inner Mongolia, Ningxia, and Guangxi. Genuine autonomy involves independent devolved government. True autonomy also recognizes and implements the principles of international human rights. Although the 17-point Agreement was thought by Tibet to grant real autonomy, the ethos of the Regional Autonomy Law is strict adherence to centralist basic policy adopted by the Chinese Communist Party. In reality, the Autonomous Region of Tibet is subservient to the totalitarian regime in Beijing and although lip service is given to certain fundamental rights the Tibetans have been the victims of gross human rights violations to the extreme of genocide. Whilst it is true that there are many

Tibetan ethnic representatives in the organs of the Tibet Autonomous Region they are not democratic representatives of the Tibetan people and for the main part communist hardliners. Thus for example the Martial Law Decrees of 7 March 1989 were issued by Dorjie Ceiring, Chairman of the People's Government of the Tibet Autonomous Region. In 1993 he was appointed Minister of Civil Affairs thus becoming the first Minister of Tibetan nationality. The Tibet People's Congress itself regularly introduces repressive legislation, for example since 1994 regulations have been promulgated on religious activities entitled, "Regulations on the Democratic Management of Lamaseries", "The Management of Religious Affairs in Tibet" and "The Detailed Rules on the Reincarnation of the Living Buddha". Economic decentralisation has also increased the harsh authority of regional officials many of whom are Tibetans.

To see how the Tibet Autonomous Region is governed it is necessary to examine three Constitutions: the Constitution of the People's Republic of China ("the Constitution"), the Law of the People's Republic of China on Regional National Autonomy 1984 ("the Autonomy Law") and the Chinese Communist Party Constitution ("the CCP Constitution", partly amended 18 September 1997 to take Marxism-Leninism-Mao Zedong Thought and Deng Xiapong Theory as its guide to action): see Appendix, documents 15, 16, 17. Imposed on Tibet's unique culture is a system based on the cardinal principles of the four upholds set out in the CCP Constitution.

All the freedoms promised in the Autonomy Law have been grossly violated by China. The freedom of religious belief contained in Articles 10 and 11 mirroring Article 36 of the Constitution are mythical. Significantly, Article 35 of the Constitution guaranteeing freedom of speech, of the press, of assembly, of association, of procession and of demonstration is not repeated in the Autonomy Law. The "cadres", referred to in Article 22 of the Autonomy Law and Articles 6, 33, 34 of the CCP Constitution are Chinese-led work teams who descend on Tibetan monasteries and nunneries and attempt to indoctrinate the monks and enforce Communist ideology through patriotic re-education", as a sub-campaign of "Strike Hard". Manifestations of support for the Dalai Lama or for an independent Tibet are crimes under Chinese law carrying severe penalties.

The CCP Constitution sets out Chinese Communist hard-line Marxism-Leninism thought. Although the Chinese Communist Party revised its Constitution in 1997 and adopted Deng Xiaoping ideas of economic reform and opening China to the outside world, the party's ultimate goal remains "to materialize a communistic social system" in a "people's democratic republic". Socialism it claims will triumph over capitalism. The revolutionary struggle it proclaims is against "imperialism, feudalism and bureaucratic capitalism" ... "developing socialist economy politics and culture". Although religion and democracy are anathema to the communist creed paradoxically the Chinese have enthusiastically embraced capitalism.

Under the Chinese electoral system all candidates are chosen by the Communist Party. Alternative political parties are banned. In November 1998 over 30 members of the Chinese Democracy Party were detained. Three of its leaders,

Wenli, Wang Youcai and Qin Yongmin were tried for attempting to organise and register The Chinese Democracy Party as an opposition party and for allegedly colluding with foreign forces to "subvert state power" and sentenced to 13, 11 and 12 years respectively in closed trials.

Under the Constitution, the Autonomy Law and CCP Constitution Tibet can never be truly autonomous. If China's leaders cannot even tolerate the harmless Falun Gong movement what chance has the survival of Tibetan Buddhism and culture.

THE STATUS OF HONG KONG

"In the Far East, the dominant long term questions concerned the future role and development of a political and military super power, the People's Republic of China, and an economic super power Japan although for Britain it was the future of Hong Kong which had to take precedence over everything else" - Margaret Thatcher, "The Downing Street Years", 1993

The Treaty of Nanking 1842, granted foreigner the right to reside and trade at several "treaty ports" and ceded Hong Kong Island to Great Britain at the end of the first Opium War which had been fought as a result of China's opposition to the importation of opium. War from 1858 to 1860 extended foreign privileges and opened the interior of China to Christian missionaries and the rivers to foreign shipping. Between 1841 and 1997 Great Britain occupied Hong Kong Island and leased the New Territories from China making up 90% of land in the colony as a Crown Colony. After 1950 the People's Republic of China declared the treaties ceding Hong Kong to Great Britain were invalid because Great Britain obtained them by force. Accepting the inevitable return of the New Territories to China in 1997, the British Government submitted to the Chinese proposal for the return of all Hong Kong under the "one country", "two systems" originally proposed by China for Taiwan in 1980.

The Sino-British Joint Declaration on the Question of Hong Kong came into effect on 27 May 1985. It has been registered by both sides as a treaty with the United Nations. (Article 80 of the Vienna Convention on the Law of Treaties 1969 allows registration at the United Nations to give publicity without guaranteeing enforcement and avoid secret treaties). According to the Joint Declaration, China has promised that:

(1) Hong Kong will become a Special Administrative Region of China and through the enactment of the Basic Law the socialist system and socialist policies will not be practised in Hong Kong and Hong Kong's previous capitalist system and life-style shall remain unchanged for fifty years;

(2) Hong Kong shall enjoy a high degree of autonomy;

(3) except for foreign and defence matters, Hong Kong will have executive, legislative and independent judicial power including that of final adjudication;

(4) the laws previously in force in Hong Kong shall be maintained;

(5) the courts of Hong Kong shall exercise judicial power independently and free from any interference;

(6) Hong Kong shall use its financial revenues exclusively for its own purposes and they shall not be handed over to China;

(7) Hong Kong shall maintain the capitalist economic and trade systems previously in place and shall decide economic and trade policies on its own;

(9) the monetary and financial systems previously practised in Hong Kong, including the systems of regulation and supervision of deposit-taking institutions and financial markets, shall be maintained;

(10) Hong Kong may maintain and develop relations and conclude and implement agreements with states, regions and relevant international organizations;

(11) international agreements to which China is not a party but which are implemented in Hong Kong may remain in effect;

(12) the maintenance of public order shall be the responsibility of the Hong Kong Special Administrative Government, and Chinese military forces stationed in Hong Kong will be for the purpose of defence and will not interfere in the internal affairs of Hong Kong;

(13) Hong Kong shall maintain the rights and freedoms as provided for by the laws previously in force in Hong Kong, including freedom of speech, of the press, of assembly, and of association; and

(14) holders of valid travel documents shall be free to leave Hong Kong without special authorization.

Critics of the Joint Declaration compare it to the 17-point Agreement with Tibet and point to China's poor record of treaty observance. They say that autonomy means genuine self-government and that the "autonomy" in the Joint Declaration is qualified. Article 11 of the Basic Law says: "The Hong Kong Special Administrative Region is a local administrative region of the People's Republic of China enjoying a high degree of autonomy under the Central People's Government". They say that China's promise to keep the law previously in force ("the common law, rules of equity, ordinances, subordinate legislation and customary law") is qualified by the rider, "save for any that contravene the Basic Law". Critics add that the Basic Law which was adopted by the National People's Congress of the People's Republic of China in April 1990 conflicts with the Joint Declaration, for example, the Standing State of China's National People's Congress they say has the power to invalidate Hong Kong's laws which, in its opinion, do not comply with the Basic Law and that whenever a Basic Law provision affecting central government is before the Hong Kong courts, the court must consult the Standing Committee. There is concern whether Hong Kong's new Court of Final Appeal (which replaces appeals to the Privy Council in London) will be excluded from questions as to the scope of Basic Law exemptions from its own jurisdiction and whether the panel of six external judges - two each from England, Australia and New Zealand, might be excluded from politically sensitive cases.

The area of Tibet that was formerly known as Outer Tibet is a "National Autonomous Region of the People's Republic of China" under Article 30(1) of China's Constitution. In May 1992 China designated the Tibet Autonomous Region as a "Special Economic Zone", not to be confused with Hong

Kong's status as a "Special Administrative Region of the People's Republic of China defined under Article 31 (see Appendix, document 15). Chapter III, Section IV, Articles 112-122 of China's Constitution sets out the mechanism of national autonomous government. Unlike a special administrative region, an autonomous region selects and sends deputies to the National People's Congress : see Article 59.

But the autonomy of an autonomous region under Section IV actually amounts to very little and, despite the high flown language promising respect for certain fundamental rights, China's criminal law punishes harshly any acts or expression of opinion which in the opinion of the authorities might undermine the unity of greater China or instigate secession of any minority nationality: see Article 4, which goes on to declare:" All the national autonomous areas are inalienable parts of the People's Republic of China".

Hong Kong should heed the broken solemn pledges made to Tibet in the 1951 17-point Agreement. The guarantees in the Joint Declaration depend on China's dependence on Hong Kong's economy and China's goodwill but it has already been suggested that China has broken the Joint Declaration. Of concern is the independence of the prosecution service in dealing with corruption and the placing of all Chinese state agencies beyond the reach of Hong Kong law. Moreover only one third of the new 60-seat Legislative Council is elected by the general public under a complex system of proportional representation which hampers Hong Kong's democratic parties. The other 40 are chosen by a narrow élite. Significantly, the Basic Law guarantees that the International Covenant on Civil and Political Rights will continue to apply in Hong Kong with reporting requirements. How Hong Kong fares in the long term remains to be seen. Recently the Hong Kong Government has moved to quash a court ruling giving 1.5 million children of Hong Kong residents the right of abode in Hong Kong.

In an agreement on similar lines to the Joint Declaration on Hong Kong, Portugal on 19 December 1999 ceded back to China, Macau, which had been a Portuguese colony since 1557, leaving Taiwan now as the main target for Chinese reunification. The unity of China, Taiwan, Hong Kong, Macao and overseas Chinese according to the policy of one country is China's objective. One country, two systems is the aim of the Chinese Communist Party in those territories. It has been proposed by some commentators that Tibet might also become a Special Administrative Region, but cosmetic change is not enough. As in Hong Kong basic freedoms must be guaranteed. A meaningless exercise of simply changing names on the door will do nothing.

BRITISH QUIET DIPLOMACY

"My [foreign] policy is to be able to take a ticket at Victoria Station and go anywhere I damn well please" - Ernest Bevin 1881-1951, British Foreign Secretary 1945-1951

British interest in China extends back to Elizabethan times. In 1566 Sir Humphrey Gilbert published "A Discourse to Prove a Passage by the Northwest to Cathaia"(China), which eleven years later Drake tried to find. The European powers quickly realised that mainland China could not be colonized and exploited China by developing its' harbours.

In 1852 Disraeli, writing about the British Empire, said: "these wretched colonies will all be independent in a few years, and are a millstone around our own necks". But within thirty years a new jingoist spirit had taken over British foreign policy. Dicey the famous jurist, expressed it in his book "Law and Public Opinion in England" shortly before the outbreak of World War I in a way which modern Chinese would understand: "Imperialism to all who share it is a form of passionate feeling, it is a political religion for it is public spirit touched with emotion."

Nineteenth century Britain saw Tibet as a frontier of empire, a buffer state against any Russian threat to its supremacy in British India. In 1903, Britain embarked on its last imperial adventure and invaded Tibet. But Britain's Tibet policy was muddled, creating problems that were never resolved and when Britain finally left India in 1947 it committed the final act of betrayal by cravenly failing to support Tibet at the critical moment in 1950.

The personality and opinions of British foreign secretaries (and in the past colonial secretaries) dominates foreign policy. Foreign secretaries range from the good to the naive, from the active to the lazy and incompetent. In his published memoirs ("In My Way", Gollancz 1972) George Brown, Labour's Foreign Secretary 1966-1968, wrote: "But obviously there were vast areas of the world of tremendous importance to us and to our allies which I hardly knew at all and on which I had to be fully briefed. The Foreign Office is equipped to give the best information, the best briefing on any international issue one cares to mention. But what bothers me, made as I am, was the thought that it was they who were deciding the areas I should be briefed about, and I quickly became aware that, unless I was very determined, I would inevitably become the purveyor of views already formed in the Office."

The political spectrum is also reflected in British foreign policy. Thus in 1950 Ernest Bevin (Labour's anti-Zionist and pro-China Foreign Secretary 1945-1951) said that the position of Tibet was uncertain and the invasion of Tibet was not a threat to world peace. Even if Bevin was unsure about Tibet's status, he knew full well that the Chinese invasion of Tibet was contrary to international law. "Tibet is redundant to Britain's interests", says a Foreign Office document of the Fifties. "We therefore consider any attempt to intervene in Tibet would be impractical and unwise. We have no interest in the area sufficiently strong to justify the certain risks involved in our embroiling ourselves with the Chinese on this question".

Yet seven years earlier, Sir Anthony Eden (Conservative Foreign Secretary 1937-1940;1941-1945;1951-1955) in 1943 formally expressed an opinion of the status of Tibet to the Chinese Foreign Secretary in which he said that Tibet has enjoyed *de facto* independence since 1911 and that the British Government had always been prepared to recognize Chinese suzerainty over Tibet on the condition that Tibet is regarded as autonomous: F0371/93001. Speaking of security in South East Asia, Sir Anthony said in his memoirs, "Full Circle", p.143, Cassell, 1960: "... security is still under menace, as has been shown by the ruthless occupation of Tibet by Chinese military power. Tibet in 1959 is the Albania of Good Friday 1939" (Mussolini's invasion of Albania, April 1939).

The Bevinesque ethic was: "What you have got to do in foreign affairs is not to create a situation". In 1993 the then British Foreign Secretary, Douglas Hurd was roundly condemned by China for meeting the Dalai Lama; more recently Chris Patten, the last British Hong Kong Governor, urged the West to be more robust with China and not react to Beijing's demands with a "pre-emotive cringe".

The Blair government's policy on Tibet was explained in a short debate. On 1 April 1998 the House of Commons found 32 minutes of parliamentary time for a Friday afternoon debate on Tibet (see Appendix, document 19). Mr Harry Cohen, backbench Labour MP for Leyton and Wanstead, opening the debate said:

"I have great respect for the progress that China has made, especially economic and social progress, but it should not expect to flout long-accepted international standards without serious criticism. It has flouted those established standards to a major extent in Tibet. I hope that the government will tell the Foreign Minister that colonisation, imperialism - a word that they will understand - attempts to extinguish a unique cultural heritage and the denial of proper human rights in Tibet are unacceptable ..."

"The legal status of Tibet has a long history, but it was a *de facto* independent state between 1913 and 1950. Central Tibet was ruled from Lhasa. It demonstrated all the conditions of statehood generally accepted under international law. It was a people, a territory, and it had a government who conducted their domestic affairs free from outside authority. Then came the Chinese invasion. In 1951, a 17-point Agreement between Mao Tse-Tung and the Dalai Lama was signed. The Dalai Lama had no choice but to sign it in the wake of the Chinese Takeover. It was a *fait accompli* ..."

"To call what is happening in Tibet repression is the kindest way of putting it; one might call it an inexorable cultural and religious genocide; but whatever one calls it, it is not acceptable in a modern world. It is Maoist fundamentalism - a form of nationalism that incorporates racism, insists that only Chinese standards are acceptable and does not allow diversity or different cultural or religious beliefs."

Speaking for the government in reply, the Minister of State, Foreign and Commonwealth Office (Derek Fatchett) had nothing new to say. He said that, "successive British Governments have regarded Tibet as autonomous, while recognizing the special position of China there. That continues to be the government's view. Tibet has never been internationally recognized as independent and the government do not recognize the Dalai Lama's Government in exile. However we strongly believe that Tibetans should have a greater say in running their own affairs in Tibet, and we have urged the Chinese authorities to respect the distinct cultural, religious and ethnic identity of the Tibetan people."

This has been the policy of successive British Governments from about 1979. Hitherto from about the end of the nineteenth century Britain had said that China's authority was an authority based on nominal suzerainty which afforded a high degree of Tibetan autonomy. Apart from Sir Anthony Eden no British minister has ever recognized that Tibet fulfilled the criteria of *de facto* statehood or explained what it understands autonomy to mean. Thus Lord Brabazon of Tara in the House of Lords on behalf of the Thatcher Government on 3 July 1990 said: "Successive governments have regarded Tibet as autonomous, while recognizing the special position of the Chinese authorities there." What Derek Fatchett was prompted to say on 1 April 1998 was the same foreign office gramophone record.

But the thrust of British foreign policy on Tibet in the late nineteenth century was that China had a weak form of suzerainty over Tibet and that Britain as the sovereign power in India could exercise a certain amount of local predominance in Tibet (the justification for the Younghusband Expedition). On 2 May 1904, Mr Labouchere (MP for Northampton) asked Mr Broderick, the Secretary of State for India at the height of the Younghusband Expedition, a pertinent House of Commons question:

> "... what is our precise position towards China in regard to Tibet; is Tibet an independent kingdom or is it a portion of the Chinese Empire; has the representative of China in Tibet full powers from his government to enter into a treaty with us; and, if so, would this treaty be valid being ratified by the Chinese Government in Pekin; or have we - assuming Tibet to be a dependency of China - obtained any assurance from the Chinese authorities that if we sign a treaty with Tibet such treaties would be binding on China."

But Mr Broderick replied evasively:

> "For information regarding the status of Tibet I must refer the Hon Member to the blue book. (1904 cd 1920 lxvii 779) The negotiations will be conducted jointly with the Chinese Amban and the Tibet representatives. The Chinese Government has been duly apprised of the action of Her Majesty's Government."

A blue book is simply a British Government publication in a blue cover. 1904 cd 1920 lxvii 779 is the first of four blue books containing government papers relating to Tibet for that period. (Also see 1904 cd 2054 lxvii 1103;1905 cd 2370 lviii 433 and 1910 cd 5240 lxviii 615). Of particular interest among the mass of documents (No.66) is a letter [8 January 1903] from the Government of India, Foreign Department to Lord George Hamilton, Secretary of State for India (Broderick's predecessor):

> "... A little while back we spoke of acceptance of the Chinese proposals subject to a qualification. What we meant was this. In our view the attempt to come to terms with Tibet through the agency of China has invariably proved a failure in the past, because of the intervention of this third party between Tibet and ourselves. We regard the so-called suzerainty of China over Tibet as a constitutional fiction - a political affectation which only has been maintained because of its convenience to both parties ... We may remark that there are, in the present circumstances of Tibet, special reasons for insisting that Tibet herself shall be a prominent party to any new agreement. For the first time for nearly half a century that country is under the rule of a Dalai Lama (the 13th) who is neither an infant nor a puppet, but a young man, some 28 years of age, who, having successfully escaped from the vicissitudes of childhood, is believed to exercise a greater personal authority than any of his predecessors, and to be *de facto* as well as the *de jure* sovereign of that country ..."

In 1902 Lord Curzon had complained to Hamilton, "... that there should exist within less than three hundred miles of the boarders of British India a state and a government with whom political relations do not so much as exist, and with whom it is impossible even to exchange a written communication." Almost fifty years later (6 November 1950) Ernest Bevin told the House of Commons. "We have over a long period recognized Chinese suzerainty over Tibet but only on the understanding that Tibet is regarded as autonomous:" *Official Report*; vol. 480, c. 602.

When asked to state the government's position on Tibet on 25 March 1959 the Secretary of State for Foreign Affairs referred to Ernest Bevin's statement and said: "This is still her Majesty's position. Our present information does not suggest that there is any threat to world peace arising out of the unrest in Tibet. Nevertheless we shall continue to study closely any reliable information which may emanate from that area." In 1959 Britain did not support United Nations resolution 1353 and abstained. In a House of Lords Debate on United Nations resolution 1353 (4 May 1960), Lord Lansdowne speaking for the government while expressing profound regret for the events in Tibet said: "We could not however support a resolution which dealt with human rights in a particular territory and which moreover rested on a juridical assumption about the status of Tibet about which there are contrary interpretations." Foreign Office policy on Tibet was further discussed in 1973 when Baroness Tweedsmuir told the House of Lords on behalf of the Heath administration (6 November 1973): "So far as the status of Tibet is concerned, we have , over a long period, recognized Chinese suzerainty over Tibet. This has been on the understanding that Tibet is regarded as autonomous. It was proclaimed an autonomous region in 1965."

Speaking in the United Nations General Assembly on 12 December 1961, the United Kingdom representative had earlier repeated the position of the United Kingdom

Government that it had in the past recognized Chinese suzerainty over Tibet only on condition that Tibet retained its autonomy. He added as his predecessors should have said in 1950 and 1960 that the United Kingdom could not agree that any such suzerainty entitled the Chinese Government to claim immunity from world condemnation for depriving the Tibetan people of their fundamental rights.

Britain is one of China's important trading partners. In 1997 the value of UK exports to China was £1,686,000,000 whereas UK imports from China amounted to £5,540,000,000. But by 1998 exports to China had fallen to £1,475,000,000 whereas total imports into the UK had risen to £6,065,000,000: source China-Britain Trade Review, April 1999. (In 1995 China imported a staggering $132 billion of goods from the United States and exported $150 billion in total.) The priority behind the Blair Government's policy of a "broad co-operative new relationship with China" and "quiet diplomacy" is the promotion of trade without regard to the trading imbalance.

But so long as China continues to receive massive foreign aid and investment and a handsome trade balance in its favour, China's hard liners will never change their policies. With the constraints of protecting Hong Kong gone, why is Britain so afraid to criticise China. China's leaders are sensitive to international criticism; strong criticism of China never prevented the United States building a leading trading relationship with China. Instead of making meaningless and harmful statements about Tibetan autonomy and China's special position in Tibet, the British Government should admit that Tibet is an occupied state and start making genuine and positive statements about human rights and Tibet's right to self-determination. It should begin by saying that trade and human rights go hand in hand.

Ironically, Britain, which took the leading role in the Serbian-Kosovo conflict, shuts up and leaves it to the United States or the European Union when it comes to Tibet. Before Tony Blair met President Jiang Zemin in Beijing in October 1998, Bao Tong, sometime political adviser to disgraced party chief Zhao Ziyang at the time of the Tiananmen massacre, urged Tony Blair to speak out publicly on the subject of human rights to encourage the political reform movement. The meeting was held behind closed doors, after a few quick sentiments on human rights it moved on to more pressing matters affecting trade.

Shortly after the British Government's sycophantic welcome of President Zemin in October 1999, the Chinese Government embarked on a more energetic crackdown on dissent in Tibet.

UNITED STATES POLICY ON TIBET

"The key lies in America" - Winston Churchill, 17 July 1940, 1878-1965

Unlike Great Britain's tight lip policy, America has been a consistent outspoken critic of China in relation to Tibet and China's human rights record. The United States Congress has also recognized the government of the Dalai Lama as the Tibetan Government in exile. The United States is also China's largest trading partner.

Following the European pattern of exploiting China's harbours, the United States was already trading fur and sandlewood to China in the eighteenth century. In 1844 Caleb Cushing negotiated a treaty with China by which US ships obtained access to ports already open to Europeans. In 1899 the United States introduced an "open door" policy promising not to interfere in China in exchange for a Chinese tariff Commission headed by Americans and Europeans to fix and collect excise duties (in 1908 Japan also acceded to the United States "open door" policy).

Although the United States took part in a joint expedition to relieve the legations at Beijing during the Boxer Rebellion in 1900, in a Note, 3 July 1900 Secretary of State John Hay reassured China that it was the policy of the United States to preserve Chinese territories and administrative entity and safeguard for the world the principle of equal and impartial trade with all parts of the Chinese Empire, and later President Theodore Roosevelt relieved China of its Boxer indemnity. After the fall of the Manchu Empire, China fell apart into warring factions and in 1922 the United States participated in the Nine Powers Treaty, by which the powers with interests in the far east promised to "safeguard the rights and interests of China", agreeing to respect her sovereignty, independence and administrative integrity and to refrain from creating spheres of influence or seeking special privileges or concessions.

But in 1931, in violation of the Kellog Pact and Covenant of the League of Nations, Japan's General Hyashi invaded Manchuria and declared the puppet independent kingdom of Manchukuo and began an undeclared war against Kuomintang China under Chiang Kai-shek which was to continue until the defeat of Japan in 1945. It was United States policy to support Chiang Kai-shek. Kuomintang China was part of an alliance of Russia, the United States and Britain that continued throughout World War II. But the end of World War II did not bring peace to South East Asia and saw the beginning of new Communist-inspired turmoil which in turn affected Tibet.

Throughout World War II, Mao Zedong, whose forces controlled part of northern China, refused to fight the Japanese. Once Japan surrendered Mao unleashed his forces against his war weary Kuomintang enemy. The United States did not intervene as its ally Chaing Kai-shek was swept out of mainland China by Mao's forces. In 1949, Stalin and Mao signed a treaty promising mutual assistance against aggression by Japan or any other state. Faced with the weak imperial powers, Britain , France and the Netherlands, new wars soon broke out. In Indo-China, Ho Chi Minh tried to force out the French; there was an attempted communist coup in the former Dutch colony of Indonesia and a guerrilla war in Malaysia. In June 1950 South Korea was invaded by communist forces and the United Nations Security Council (which the Soviet Union was then boycotting), on a United States motion condemning the attack as an act of aggression, opened the way for President Truman, on behalf of the United Nations Security Council, to order United States forces to come to the aid of South Korea's President Syngman Rhee and, in the ensuing conflict, it is estimated that 750,000 Chinese were killed. Simultaneously by the end of 1951 China had annexed the whole of Tibet.

No sooner was a Korean truce signed in July 1953 than further wars broke out in South Vietnam, Laos and Cambodia. From 1949 until President Nixon negotiated the withdrawal of United States forces from Vietnam and began in 1974 the process of reconciliation, China and the United States were implacable foes.

Under the United States Constitution responsibility for international and foreign affairs lies in Congress (the Senate and House of Representatives). But the exercise of executive powers with respect to foreign policy lies with the President who exercises a plenary and primary authority to negotiate treaties and develop foreign policy: see *United States v. Curtiss-Wright Corp*, 299 US 304 (1936) where the Supreme Court held that the general principle which denies the delegability of legislative authority does not preclude broad delegation to the President in the field of foreign policy. Justice Sutherland said: "In this vast external realm, with its important, complicated, delicate, and manifold problems, the

President alone has the power to speak or listen as a representative of the nation", thereby sustaining the validity of a joint resolution of Congress authorising the President in his discretion and on such terms and conditions as he may find to be in the interest of the United States to impose an embargo upon the sales of arms or ammunition to the nations involved in the armed conflict in the South American Chaco War. No part of a treaty has ever been declared unconstitutional by the Supreme Court and in consequence since World War II presidential power over foreign affairs has grown unchecked. The framers of the Constitution required that the President make treaties but only with the advice and consent of the Senate. But in *Goldwater v. Cartery* (1997) the Supreme Court dismissed Senator Barry Goldwater's challenge to President Carter's action, terminating a mutual defence treaty with Taiwan without seeking the Senate's prior approval. In Justice Rehnquist's plurality opinion the role of the Senate in treaty termination was non-justiciable. In consequence of the Goldwater decision the Reagan administration terminated, modified and re-interpreted many treaties without seeking the advice and consent of the Senate. Thus the executive order conditioning China's most favoured nation trade status was a presidential act.

From 1987 to 1997 the following measures concerning Tibet have been put down in Congress:

Foreign Relations Authorization Act for Fiscal Year 1888-89 (1987);
Congressional Resolution S Con Res. 129 (1988);

Congressional Resolution S. Res 82 (1989);
Congressional Resolution H Con Res 63 (1989);
Congressional Resolution 75; Congratulations to Dalai Lama for Nobel Peace Prize (1989);
Congressional Concurrent Resolution (1991);
Foreign Relations Authorization Act for Fiscal Years 1992-93 (1991);
Senate Resolution 271 (March 1992);
Congressional Record 119: Staff Trip Report (August 1992);
Most Favoured Nation Waiver Authority (1993);
Foreign Relations Authorization Act for Fiscal Years 1994-95, (1993)
Congressional Resolution S. Res 169 (1995);
Congressional Resolution SJ Res. 43 (1995);
HR 1561 (1996) State Department Authorization Bill;
Congressional Resolution S. Res 19 (1997).

But the President and Congress do not always agree and despite the robust approach of Congress to relations with China, US presidents since Carter have made their own foreign policy.

The first official diplomatic contact between Tibet and the United States came in 1942 when Captain Ilia Tolstoy and Lieutenant Brooke Dolan, assigned by the Office of Strategic Services in Washington to organize supply routes to China through Tibet, were received by the seven year-old Dalai Lama in Lhasa as head of state. The following letter from President Roosevelt was delivered:

"THE WHITE HOUSE
WASHINGTON, July 3, 1942

Your Holiness:

Two of my countrymen, Ilia Tolstoy and Brooke Dolan, hope to visit your Pontificate and the historic and widely famed city of Lhasa. There are in the United States of America many persons, among them myself, who, long and greatly interested in your land and people, would highly value such an opportunity.

As you know, the people of the United States, in association with those of twenty-seven other countries, are now engaged in a war which has been thrust upon the world by nations bent on conquest, who are intent upon destroying freedom of thought, of religion and of action everywhere. The United States are fighting today in defence of and for the preservation of freedom, confident that we shall be victorious because our cause is just, our capacity is adequate and our determination is unshakable.

I am asking Ilia Tolstoy and Brooke Dolan to convey to you a little gift in token of my friendly sentiment towards you.

With cordial greetings, I am

Very sincerely yours,
(signed) Franklin D. Roosevelt"

Although Tibet refused to compromise its neutrality by allowing supply routes, at the end of World War II the

Regent, Taktra Rimpoche sent a mission to India to congratulate the Allies on their victory, through the Viceroy, Lord Wavell. Complimentary messages and presents were also delivered to the United States Government through its representative in New Delhi. But the failure of the Tibetan Government to create an alliance with the United States was to prove a serious misjudgment.

In October 1947 Tibet sent a trade delegation (travelling on Tibetan passports) to India, Great Britain, the United States and China. In Great Britain the delegation met Prime Minister Attlee and when the delegation reached Washington it was received by Secretary of State, George Marshall, without the presence of the Nationalist Chinese Ambassador who had offered to accompany them.

Whilst Britain has dissembled over Tibet, since 1950 Tibet has received the firm support of the United States in Congress and in the United Nations. In 1954 John Foster Dulles told leading journalists that US policy in the Asia and the Middle East has been badly hampered by a tendency to support Britain and French colonial views.

The US Tibet Act 1987 strongly condemns China's human rights abuses in Tibet and was signed by President Reagan on 22 December 1987. Previously in 1986, Congress amended the 1945 US Export-Import Bank Act giving Tibet the status of a separate state (which the President later retracted). In June, 1987, the House of Representatives passed an amendment to the Foreign Relations Authorisation Act denouncing Chinese human rights violations in Tibet and in September the Dalai Lama testified before a Congressional Human Rights Committee on his "Five Point Peace Plan" which was accepted in the final version of the US Tibet Act.

The US Tibet Act was followed by the State Department Appropriation Act 1987 condemning Chinese human rights violations in Tibet, calling on China to release all political prisoners, tying arms sales to China to a presidential assessment of respect for human rights in Tibet, granting scholarships and aid to Tibetan refugees and endorsing the Dalai Lama's Five Point Plan for Tibet. Another Bill condemning human rights violations in Tibet and supporting Tibetans in Tibet and in exile was proposed in the House of Representatives on 11 May 1988 by Congressmen Charlie Rose, Tom Lantos, Gilman, Conyers, Dornan and Porter. In August 1988, Tom Lantos introduced a resolution calling for the immediate cessation of all visas to Chinese officials until China approved visas without delay for all members of Congress who had requested them to visit Tibet. Soon afterwards, a three member delegation led by Senator Patrick Leahy visited Tibet for three days condemning human rights abuses in Tibet in their subsequent report.

The Foreign Relations Authorization Act 1996-1997 (see Appendix, document 18) authorized a United States Special Envoy for Tibet with the rank of ambassador to promote substantive negotiations between the Dalai Lama or his representatives and senior members of the Chinese Government and to promote good relations between the Dalai Lama or his representatives (including meetings with members of the Tibetan Government in exile) and to travel regularly throughout Tibet and Tibetan refugee settlements. The Act says that his duties include consulting with Congress on policies relevant to Tibet and the future and welfare of the

Tibetan people, co-ordinating United States governmental policies, programs and projects concerning Tibet and reporting to the Secretary of State. The Act also provides for educational and cultural exchanges for Tibetans. In the fiscal years 1996-1997, 30 scholarships were made available to Tibetan students, all of which were taken up. The Act also provides for the setting up of Radio Free Asia to provide a forum of opinion within Asian nations whose people do not fully enjoy freedom of expression.

In 1998 Congress passed and the President signed into law the International Religious Freedom Act which created an Office of International Religious Freedom mandatory annual report on international religious freedom country by country.

Outspoken criticism worries China. President Clinton's public comments on China's rule in Tibet and human rights during his summit visit to China at the end of June 1998 prompted the Chinese leadership to permit the live and uncensored lengthy press conference by President Jiang Zemin and President Clinton whose public debate included the Tiananmen Square massacre and human rights issues. Most surprising of all was President Jiang's monologue on Tibet listing his conditions for opening talks with the Dalai Lama.

But United States condemnation, however strong has not been enough to deter China. There must be international strategy linking trade to human rights and democratic reform in China. After giving China aid and trade concessions without insisting on an improvement in human rights and allowing China access to technology it must now come as a considerable surprise to the American people to wake up and find that China has stolen its nuclear secrets, and that the sophisticated Chinese technology for weaponry trained on the United States was down loaded from Los Alemos Laboratories in New Mexico and other US nuclear research sites.

THE ROLE OF THE EUROPEAN UNION

"Europe offers the opportunities; there is nothing remotely comparable outside" - Sir George Gardiner

Because of its size and the immense value of its trade, The European Union has grown in stature and has already become a world power. The new post of a European Union Foreign and Security Chief is intended to set a common European policy in dealing with the rest of the world.

Respect for human rights is one of the basic conditions of membership of the European Union and forms an integral part of Community law. The European Court of Justice has developed these rights by drawing on constitutional traditions common to member states and international Conventions for the protection of human rights to which member states are signatories or have collaborated. The European Court of Justice has said in a number of cases that although the European Convention on Human Rights is not directly a part of Community law, the principles on which that Convention is based must also be taken into consideration in EU law: see *Case 130/75 Vivien Prais v. Council* [1976] ECR 1589, paras.8, 16; *Case 222/84 Johnston v. Chief Constable of the Royal Ulster Constabulary* [1986] ECR 1651 para.18; *Case C-260/89 Elliniki Radiophonia Tileorassi AE v. Dimotiki Etairia Plirofissis* [1991] ECR I-2925 para.41. It is also a requirement that EU Agreements with third countries must contain a clause defining human rights in recognition of the fact that considerations of trade, however important, do not predominate over the imperatives of liberty and justice. An important precedent for a common European position in foreign affairs was set in 1991 by the European Community "Guidelines on the Recognition of New States in Eastern Europe and in the Soviet Union".

Considerable concern about human rights in Tibet and China has been shown by the European Parliament. Between 1993 and 1999 44 Resolutions on Tibet put down in the European Parliament have included:

> European Parliament Resolution on Tibet (14 October 1987);
> Council of Europe Parliamentary Assembly, Written Declaration No.173 on the Situation in Tibet and National Independence (21 October 1988);
> European Parliament Resolution on Human Rights in Tibet (15 March 1989);
> European Parliament Resolution on Human Rights in China and Tibet (September 1991);
> European Parliamentary Motion for a Resolution of the Situation in Tibet (1992);
> European Parliamentary Resolution on Repression in Tibet and the Exclusion of the Dalai Lama from the World Conference on Human Rights (24 June, 1993);
> European Parliamentary Resolution on Detention of Tibetans, Gendun, Rinchen, Lobsang, Yontan and Damchoe Pemo and other Violations of Human Rights in Tibet (16 September 1993);
> European Parliamentary Resolution on Panan Rural Integrated Project (17 May 1995);

European Parliamentary Resolution on the Situation in Tibet and the Disappearance of the six year-old Panchen Lama (13 July 1995);

European Parliamentary Resolution on the Selection of the Panchen Lama and Religious Freedom in Tibet (14 December 1995);

European Parliamentary Resolution on Human Rights in China and Tibet (18 April, 1996);

European Parliamentary Resolution on Human Rights in Tibet (23 May, 1996);

European Parliamentary Resolution on Human Rights in Tibet (14 March 1997).

MEPs have persistently urged the Chinese Government to negotiate with the Dalai Lama and expressed its grave concern at the violations of fundamental human rights of the Tibetan people.

EU Parliamentary Resolution (1992) urged "the resumption of negotiations between the Tibetan Government in exile and the Chinese authorities ... the consideration in these negotiations of genuine self-determination and, as a first step and sign of goodwill, recommends the incorporation of all Tibetan territories into a single administrative and political unit," i.e. the Tibet Autonomous Region and the Tibetan Autonomous Prefectures in Qinghai, Gansu, Sichuan and Yunnan provinces. EU Parliamentary Resolution 17 May 1995 called on the EU Commission to re-deploy resources from the Panam Project to aid which will better serve the Tibetan people and called on the European Union Commission to make the granting of aid to China conditional on the Chinese Government showing respect for fundamental human rights and freedoms, particularly in Tibet. Resolution 13 July 1993 also reaffirmed the illegal nature of the invasion and occupation of Tibet, expressed its support for the Tibetan people and calls on the European Parliament to establish permanent contacts with the Tibetan Government in exile. EU Parliamentary Resolution 14 December 1995 urged the Chinese Government to respect the wishes of the Tibetan people by accepting the child Panchen Lama and called upon the representatives of the Council and the Commission to exert strong diplomatic or other pressure on the Chinese authorities "to put an end to their unacceptable treatment of the Tibetan people" and urges that the final decision to proceed with the EU Panam project should not be taken until such time as the requests in the Resolution are met.

The European Parliament not only presses for dialogue with China about human rights abuses. The concern of MEPs is that EU-funded or supported projects should serve the interests of the Tibetan people and not Han Chinese immigrants and that aid to China should be linked to reform.

Elsewhere within the European Union member states, particularly France and Germany where support for Tibet is strong, there has been considerable parliamentary activity. There have been two German Parliament pro-Tibet resolutions, the West German Parliament Resolution on Tibet (1987) and the German Parliament Resolution on Tibet (1966). In France, 200 French Parliamentarians signed an Appeal for Tibet (1996). In Belgium, there have been two Resolutions on Tibet, in the House of Representatives (1994) and the

Chamber of Deputies (1996). In Italy, the 1989 Italian Parliament Commission of Foreign Affairs Motion on Tibet. In Austria the 1992 Report of the Austrian Delegation of Legal experts to China. There have also been resolutions by the Parliament of Liechtenstein (Welcome to the Dalai Lama (1996) and Chambers of Deputies of Luxembourg Resolution (1996)). Regional autonomous parliaments in Europe have also shown considerable interest in Tibet, for example the Basque Autonomous Country Parliament Resolution on Tibet (1995) and the Nordic Saami Parliaments Statement on Tibet (1996).

Until 1996 the European Union supported an annual attempt led by the United States condemning China's human rights abuses at the Human Rights Commission in Geneva. But in 1996 China broke off dialogue on human rights with the EU after EU support for the human rights resolution. Sir Leon Brittan, Vice-President of the EU Commission, then complained that his mission to promote trade would be easier without irritating human rights abuses condemnations of China. In 1997 both Germany and France secured important contracts with China. Later that year the EU Council of Ministers decided at the Turin summit to support the human rights resolution but in the following year there was no common position as France, Germany, Greece, Italy and Spain withdrew their traditional support for the motion. In 1998 with Britain holding the presidency of the EU Council of Ministers, European Union support for the resolution was withdrawn. In March 1998 China allowed a tightly controlled EU mission at ambassadorial level represented by Britain, Luxembourg, Austria and the EU (the so called "EU Troika visit") into Tibet to investigate Human Rights. The Troika saw what the Chinese authorities wanted them to see and published their findings in a bland uncritical report. On 22 March 1999 The EU Council of Ministers decided to continue a human rights dialogue with China rather than support a resolution at the 55th UN Commission for Human Rights in Geneva.

The European Union has already joined China, Russia and the United States as a world super power. It is the world's largest trading unit. In the past it has been both a supporter of China and a critic, endeavouring to link trade and aid to human rights. The legislative importance of the European Parliament has been increased by "conciliation", the last phase in the co-decision procedure introduced in 1992 by Maastricht and strengthened by the Amsterdam Treaty. When a proposal is presented by the Commission co-decision provides for two "shuttles" between the European Parliament and the Council in which both institutions express their opinion. Should there be disagreement, a process involving negotiation through the Conciliation State (composed of 15 representatives of the Council and 15 MEPs) takes place with the Commission acting as conciliators. As the European Parliament continues to develop real powers and a common foreign policy takes shape there will be a new opportunity for the west to take up the issue of Tibet and to deal with China in strength instead of as hitherto weakened by self-interested individual member states competing for trade.

A NEW START

"Time and patience brings roses" - Slovakian Proverb

After the large-scale 1959 uprising in protest against the Chinese invaders the Dalai Lama and one hundred thousand Tibetans fled across the Himalayas to India and other neighbouring countries and since then, with world-wide support, the Tibetans have established forty six refugee settlements in India and Nepal with a population of 70,000 whilst a further 50,000 refugees live in other scattered communities. It is estimated that some 6,000 Tibetans live outside South East Asia. In Dharamsala the Dalai Lama formed a government in exile and in 1991 published a democratic Constitution and Charter for Tibetans in exile. Under his leadership the traditions of Tibetan society are preserved in exile through re-built monastic institutions, schools, hospitals, orphanages, craft co-operatives, farming communities, institutions for the preservation of Tibetan music and drama. But the majority six million Tibetans, who are the future hope, remain in the Autonomous Region of Tibet and the annexed provinces of Kham and Amdo.

The Dalai Lama has tried to negotiate with China and has stated that he does not seek independence from China if Tibet is granted real autonomy. He has even said that he will use his moral authority with the Tibetan people so that they renounce their aspirations for independence.

When delivering the Nobel Peace Prize Lecture in Oslo on 10 December 1989 the Dalai Lama declared: "Because violence breeds more violence and suffering our struggle must continue non-violently and without hatred. We shall try to put an end to our people's suffering, not to make others suffer. Ruthless politics is against human nature. I feel that the humanitarian perspective is about to gain the upper hand."

Elaborating on his Strasbourg proposal that the whole of Tibet (U-Tsang, Kham and Amdo) would become self-governing on the restoration of peace and human rights in Tibet the Dalai Lama said:

"The Five Point Peace Plan ... calls for (1) Transformation of the whole of Tibet, including the eastern provinces of Kham and Amdo, into a Zone of Ahimsa (non-violence); (2) Abandonment of China's population transfer policy; (3) Respect for the Tibetan people's fundamental human rights and democratic freedoms; (4) Restoration and protection of Tibet's natural environment; and (5) Commencement of earnest negotiations on the future status of Tibet and of relations between the Tibetan and Chinese peoples. In the Strasbourg address I proposed that Tibet become a fully self-governing political entity.

"... It is my dream that the entire Tibetan plateau should become a free refuge where humanity and nature can live in peace and in harmonious balance. It would be a place where people from all over the world could come to seek the true meaning of peace within themselves, away from the tensions and pressures of much of the rest of the world. Tibet could indeed become a creative centre for the promotion and development of peace.

The following are the key elements of the proposed

Zone of Ahimsa:

- the entire Tibetan plateau would be demilitarized;
- the manufacture, testing, and stock-piling of nuclear weapons and other armaments on the Tibetan plateau would be prohibited;
- the Tibetan plateau would be transformed into the world's largest natural park or biosphere. Strict laws would be enforced to protect wildlife and plant life; the exploitation of natural resources would be carefully regulated so as not to damage relevant ecosystems; and a policy of sustainable development would be adopted in popular areas;
- the manufacture and use of nuclear power and other technologies which produce hazardous waste would be prohibited;
- national resources and policy would be directed towards the active promotion of peace and environmental protection. Organizations dedicated to the furtherance of peace and to the protection of all forms of life would find a hospitable home in Tibet;
- the establishment of international and regional organizations for the promotion and protection of human rights would be encouraged in Tibet."

Yet the reaction of the Chinese Government to the Dalai Lama's modest proposal was their assertion that they have "sacred sovereignty" over Tibet and will not allow independence in any form. On 2 September 1991, the Kashag (Tibetan Cabinet) issued a statement that in view of the

Chinese response Tibet was no longer pursing the Strasbourg proposal. Negotiations between Beijing and Dharamsala have now broken down and ended in stalemate.

Since the violence of the Cultural Revolution ended, China's policy has changed to more selective persecution: to a discrete war against dissidents in the guise of a "strike hard", anti-crime campaign. The Chinese Government now admits to having made mistakes in the past and it says new policies have been introduced, Tibetans have been brought into local government of the Tibet Autonomous Region, a few temples have been restored and Tibet has been opened up to controlled tourism. But China's disdain for human rights continues. In September/October 1987 and again in March 1990 the Tibetan people demonstrated for independence from China, claiming lack of religious freedom. Despite Article 35 (freedom of speech and demonstration) and Article 36 (freedom of religious beliefs) of China's Constitution and Article 11 of the Autonomous Region Constitution the demonstrations were savagely repressed by the People's Armed Police and The Public Security Bureau.

Interviewed in November 1997, President Lee Teng-hui of Taiwan called China essentially "a culture", not a necessarily a country, and noted there had been long periods of disunity in Chinese history. He said there were two governments of China, the "Republic of China on Taiwan" and "the People's Republic of China". Should Beijing forces attack Taiwan, he said "Washington was bound to provide weapons under the US-Taiwan Relations Act although supplying troops would ... be a decision for the United States". He rejected Beijing's description of Taiwan as "a renegade province". In relation to unification he said: "For that to happen, first China would have to become a free democratic socially just country. Dialogue between the two countries would be very important. But how should the reunification take shape? A commonwealth? A federation? There could even be two capitals. No one can predict this now". China in response abusively branded Lee Teng-hui "a deformed test-tube baby" and threatened to invade Taiwan.

The Preliminary Report of the International Commission of Jurists, "The Question of Tibet and the Rule of Law" published in 1959 concluded with a grim warning which is equally valid today:

"... the events in Tibet constitute *prima facie* a threat to and a breach of the fundamental legal principles which the International Commission of Jurists stands for and endeavours to promote and protect. From the present report there emerges also, it is submitted, a *prima facie* case of the worse type of imperialism and colonialism, coming precisely from the very people who claim to fight against it. A solution of this problem , through the United Nations or by any other peaceful means, remains to be found.

"The danger in such cases as that of Tibet is a feeling of impotence and powerless overcoming people in the face of a *fait accompli* - a mixture of indifference, lack of moral courage and determination.

"It is important to remember that in our world of today wanton and widespread violations of basic human rights can affect international peace and the stability of the entire world and the security of every individual. What happened in Tibet yesterday may happen in our own countries to-morrow. The force of public opinion, however, cannot be disregarded: ideas will penetrate where bullets will not ..."

What is it about China that so mesmerises the West that China is allowed to act with impunity. The United Nations authority calling for implementation of Tibet's right to self-determination as contained in UN General Assembly Resolution No.1723, passed 20 December 1961, and respect for human rights in Tibet, has been contemptuously ignored by China. The mandate of the UN Special State on Decolonisation should have been extended long ago to include Tibet. No sanctions economic or otherwise have been applied against China for defying United Nations instructions, and apart from the United States no major world power has recognized the Dalai Lama and his representatives as the legitimate government of an independent Tibet.

Yet China's communism is hardly a success. Away from the glitter of the big cities, China is still very poor and backward. Despite over half a century of communism China's living standards generally are desperately low. As the GDP table below shows, China's estimated *per capita* gross domestic product for 1998 was only $880, only $50 more than Zimbabwe ($750). This because China's poorly run state industries are loss making, its bureaucracy bloated, its officials corrupt. Despite an official 13% unemployed statistic, unemployment in Shanghai is estimated to be 20% and in Chengdu possibly as much as 28%. The state is no longer prepared to underwrite social security benefits. And so its hard-line communist rulers have been forced to invent a socialist market economy system to perpetuate their hold on power. The Chinese Communist Party Constitution (see Appendix, document 17) amended 22 September 1997 explains: "Reform and opening to the outside world are the only way to liberate and develop the productive forces. It is necessary to fundamentally reform the economic structure impeding the development of the productive forces and to institute a system of socialist market economy. Corresponding to this, reform should be carried out to the political structure and other fields. Opening includes opening to the outside world and inside in an all-round way. Efforts should be made to develop economic and technological exchanges and co-operation with foreign countries; use more foreign funds, resources and technology in a better way ..."

Gross Domestic Product Table-1998 (per capita) showing China sixth from bottom in the world economy league with China, Taiwan and Hong Kong high-lighted

	GPD (national gross)	GDP (per capita)	Population	GDP (growth)	Inflation
Japan	$4,545.0bn	$35,906	125.9m	2.2%	1.1%
Switzerland	$246.0bn	$34,750	7.1m	2.2%	1.0%
Norway	$151.0bn	$34,130	4.4m	4.1%	2.2%
Denmark	$176.5bn	$33,370	5.3m	2.6%	2.7%
Singapore	$101.3bn	$32,020	3.0m	5.2%	2.3%
USA	$8,431.4bn	$31,230	270.0m	2.5%	2.7%
Hong Kong	**$195.0bn**	**$29,890**	**6.3m**	**4.5%**	**7.5%**
Germany	$2,159bn	$26,400	81.8m	3.1%	1.9%

Holland	$395.2bn	$25,330	15.5m	3.3%	2.5%
Sweden	$568.5bn	$24,520	8.9m	3.4%	2.3%
France	$1,374.8bn	$23,910	58.4m	3.0%	1.6%
Austria	$142.9bn	$23,810	8.1m	2.6%	1.9%
Finland	$114.9bn	$22,354	5.1m	3.5%	1.6%
UK	$1,317bn	$22,300	59.1	2.1%	2.9%
Belgium	$220.4bn	$21,610	10.2m	2.7%	2.1%
Australia	$424.3bn	$21,380	18.7m	3.8%	1.8%
Italy	$1,225bn	$21,380	57.3m	2.8%	2.4%
Canada	$648.3bn	$21,220	30.6m	3.4%	2.1%
Ireland	$68.3bn	$18,620	3.7m	5.3%	2.7%
New Zealand	$68.9bn	$18,520	3.6m	3.3%	1.5%
Israel	$101.1bn	$16,940	5.7m	2.5%	8.5%
Spain	$568.5bn	$14,440	39.3m	3.2%	2.3%
Taiwan	**$310.4bn**	**$14,250**	**21.4m**	**6.2%**	**3.3%**
Greece	$124.3bn	$11,830	10.5m	3.0%	4.9%
S. Korea	$542.2bn	$11,700	45.5m	5.8%	4.5%
Portugal	$109.8bn	$11,170	9.9m	3.2%	2.6%
Argentina	$337.0bn	$9,510	34.7m	5.0%	1.6%
Saudi Arabia	$148.1bn	$7,470	18.5m	2.0%	4.0%
Chile	$87.3bn	$5,875	14.4m	6.5%	4.6%
Brazil	$803.4bn	$4,970	147.8m	3.8%	7.0%
CzechRep	$48.4bn	$4,680	10.3m	3.3%	8.5%
Mexico	$443.1bn	$4,505	95.1m	4.5%	13.0%
Venezuela	$110.2bn	$4,505	21.9m	6.5%	28.1%
Lebanon	$16.9bn	$4,390	3.6m	3.5%	6.0%
Hungary	$45.3bn	$4,470	10.1m	4.4%	16.0%
Malaysia	$87.1bn	$4,000	20.7m	3.8%	4.3%
Poland	$138.2bn	$3,570	38.7m	5.3%	13.7%
S. Africa	$139.0bn	$3,535	37.9m	3.2%	7.0%
Slovakia	$17.7bn	$3,278	5.4m	3.2%	8.0%
Russia	£475.0bn	$3,240	146.7m	2.0%	14.0%
Estonia	$4.7bn	$3,240	1.5m	4.1%	9.6%
Turkey	$186.2bn	$2,880	62.6m	5.7%	89.6%
Lithuania	$9.9bn	$2,680	3.7m	4.0%	8.1%

Columbia	$106.3bn	$2,570	39.5m	3.9%	17.5%
Latvia	$6.0bn	$2,450	2.4m	5.0%	8.5%
Thailand	$149.7bn	$2,440	60.1m	1.4%	6.7%
Jordan	$8.7bn	$1,830	4.4m	6.0%	3.4%
Romania	$40.0bn	$1,780	22.5m	4.0%	45.0%
Bulgaria	$13.7bn	$1,654	8.3m	3.5%	25.0%
Algeria	$48.1bn	$1,570	29.2m	4.5%	10.0%
Kazakstan	$24.0bn	$1,475	16.5m	4.0%	17.5%
Egypt	$93.6bn	$1,460	61.5m	5.4%	6.6%
Iran	$81.5bn	$1,250	62.4m	2.3%	20.0%
Philippines	$87.0bn	$1,200	72.6m	3.5%	6.0%
Iraq	$30.4bn	$1,300	22.4m	12.0%	65.0%
Indonesia	$233.5bn	$1,150	196.9m	4.8%	11.0%
Ukraine	$54.5bn	$1,073	51.8m	1.0%	16.4%
China	**$1,098.0bn**	**$880**	**1.22bn**	**8.0%**	**7.0%**
Zimbabwe	$9.4bn	$750	11.8m	3.1%	25.0%
Pakistan	$69.2bn	$490	133.0m	3.6%	11.8%
India	$412.4bn	$420	954.5m	5.4%	9.5%
Nigeria	$40.7bn	$380	101.8m	4.4%	25.0%
Vietnam	$27.0bn	$340	75.5m	6.5%	11.0%

Thus, per capita, China is one of the world's poorest countries although by GDP ($1,098.01bn) China is currently seventh behind Italy ($1,225bn); UK ($1,317bn); France ($1,374bn); Germany ($2,159bn); Japan ($4,545bn); USA ($8,431bn). With the GDP of Hong Kong and Macao, China is now ahead of Italy, the UK and France. But China's wealth is spread unevenly and thinly. China has the world's largest population (1.3 billion people comprising 20% of the world's population). Chinese official statistics indicate that 10 million people have been laid off from state enterprises in a country where there is virtually no social security. An additional 120 million former peasants are thought to be roaming the cities looking for work or working on casual labouring jobs. Deng

Xiaoping changed China's policy because he realised China was at breaking point. China aims to solve its problems by encouraging foreign investment, creating special growth areas and encouraging migration to its new colonies particularly Tibet where there has been a massive influx of Han Chinese. China also casts envious eyes on tiny Taiwan with its massive GDP. China's intentions on re-unification with Taiwan are made clear in the preamble to the Chinese Constitution (see Appendix, document 15).

The Chinese leaders know only too well that it has to improve living standards to contain social unrest particularly outside special growth areas. The question is whether the free world should help China overcome its economic difficulties without strings? Do ethics come in before profit and if so what ethical considerations are relevant? Should trade and the supply of technology be linked to the question of Tibet and human rights in Tibet and China? Without rapid economic growth the People's Republic of China risks increased civil unrest and possible disintegration. The free world is far from powerless. Support for the Chinese economy may be the free world's opportunity to do something. As the Dalai Lama said on 2 April 1998:

> "... a free and democratic China is not only advantageous to China, but is important to the rest of the world as well. Therefore it makes sense to engage with China. It would be useless to isolate China. China must be brought into the international circle. For this to be achieved, China must be sincere, with a spirit of true friendship and have pure and clear intentions. The lies and mistakes of the past

should be settled clearly and in a friendly spirit. Concealing the truth about China and insincere flattery have no place. They will not help the image of China. The way to resolve these issues is with respect and sincerity. To quote two Tibetan expressions 'the closer the friend, the more faults he will point out' and 'one never hears praise and appreciation from a true friend'. Therefore, to be a true friend of China, mistakes must be pointed out sincerely. It is important that the world knows the truth ..."

Without respect for human rights by and all nations big and small, and long overdue reform of the United Nations so that its resolutions are respected and enforced, the prospects for the twenty first century seem no better than the dismal twentieth. The decolonising remit of the United Nations must be extended to compel self-determination for all territories acquired by force. Once the European Union begins to have a common foreign policy perhaps the European Union should replace Britain and France on the Security Council and the veto of the five permanent members of the Security Council abolished. If China is not prepared to grant Tibet the right to determine its own future and show respect for human rights, its leaders must be told that their dream of creating a socialist capitalist society by opening China to world trade will not be supported by the rest of the world it relies on to sustain it. In the new millennium access to international trade must be linked to human rights and trade and respect for human rights must become inseparable.

China has become entrenched in Tibet. The stench of the

cultural revolution lingers there as China's hard line government seems unwilling to give up Tibet or modify its policies an inch to reach agreement with the Tibetan Government in exile. The Chinese Government's obsession with Chinese nationalism which it sees as the only way of preventing China breaking up is the cause of its hostility to Tibetan Buddhism and the Dalai Lama. Yet it is this obsessive hold on empire which fans nationalistic opposition to Beijing. China mistakenly believes, as the flight of the Karmapa Lama has shown, that opposition to its occupation will fade in time and that it need do no more than wait for the Dalai Lama, who will be 65 on 6 June 2000, to die, because the weakness of the Dalai Lama system is the long interregnum between adult Dalai Lamas, even an immediate reincarnation involves years of wait before a successor is old enough to reign. Inevitably China would forbid the search for the fifteenth Dalai Lama in Tibet just as they tried in the case of the Panchen Lama.

The Dalai Lama has said that his wish is to return to Tibet to join a monastery and become a simple monk. Although he has set up a democratically elected government in exile he does not seek to impose his government on Tibet. In Tibet he envisages a democratically elected government with candidates from within Tibet and the government in exile. The Dalai Lama has even said that Han Chinese settlers can stay in Tibet if they wish. A settlement could be accomplished by resuscitating the broken-back 1951, 17-point Agreement which promised to respect the religious beliefs, customs and habits of the Tibetan people and which guaranteed not to alter the political system in Tibet before the invasion. But without fundamental change in Beijing there is no prospect of a settlement or, as things stand of even resuscitating talks.

A settlement requires give and take on both sides. "One China, Two Systems" seems to work in Hong Kong. Why not "One China, Three Systems". Tibet denied genuine autonomy because China's leaders believe China is in danger of break-up like the old Soviet Union. But the astute would realise that break-up is inevitable if China continues to resist change.

The Chinese people need to be assured that people in the west are their friends. China's leaders need to understand that all states, however mighty, are not above international law and the fundamental human rights laid down in United Nations covenants and that these rights are universal and not subject to alterations to suit the regime in China. If China does not listen it cannot expect to receive unconditional or any economic support from the west. If China wishes to sustain major participation in world trade it must accept the fundamental principle that Tibet has the right to self-determination. For a start China should not be allowed to join the World Trade Organization without agreeing to allow Tibet to decide its own future. Similarly, international aid and investment in China must be linked to human rights. No one wants trade sanctions or to see China isolated, but China has most to lose. It is time for the United States and the European Union to say to China, enough is enough, sit down and start genuine talks about the future of Tibet or bring the consequences upon yourself. It is time for the international community to recognize the right of the Tibetan people to self-determination.

ENVOY

I started this book in 1998. Since then, there have been a number of developments, some depressing, some hopeful. The deployment of NATO against the evil ethnic cleansers of Kosovo seemed to signal the start of a more effective international response to human rights violators. The decision in the Pinochet case means that there is no immunity from prosecution. At the beginning of this year the incredible news that the Karmapa, whom China believed was its puppet, had fled across the Himalayas and joined the Dalai Lama in exile brought hope to all Tibetans. In Taiwan the recent victory of Chen Shui Bian's Democratic Progressive Party is a clear rejection by Taiwan of the "one country, two systems" model for unification. But the immediate political augurs are dark. After President Zemin left London in triumph having been feted by the Blair Government, repression was stepped up in Tibet and elsewhere in China. There have been arrests and recent reports of the death of a Tibetan in custody. To its shame in November 1999 the Chinese Government shut down an orphanage in Lhasa paid for by western charities, over 70 children rescued from the streets have disappeared and the staff have been arrested. In China thousands of members of the Falun Gong were detained and held without trial on Zemin's return. Doubtless Zemin was encouraged by the way the Blair Government handles peaceful demonstrations and policing.

Yet I believe that Tibet will be free. I believe democracy will eventually come to China. In his final days the dictator knows only repression. There will be a struggle for democracy and freedom in Tibet and China but it must be a non-violent struggle. The four weapons against China's leaders are truth, shaming, the use of information technology and globalization. There is a true story that a Chinese tour guide in Tibet broke down and wept when a westerner told her what the Chinese Government had done in Tibet. She said she never knew. She said she had been taught by the Chinese Government that they were "helping" the Tibetan people.

The role of the Tibetan Government in Exile is crucial. For half a century single-handedly the Dalai Lama has kept alive the cause of Tibetan independence. The case for independence must not be compromised and thrown away for ever by a meaningless compromise on autonomy. Somehow there needs to be a referendum for all Tibetan people on independence or autonomy. China in the meantime thinks that the Tibetan freedom movement will die out after the Dalai Lama's death. Crucially the Government in Exile's democratic institutions needed to be further developed, so that authority is handed down to democratically elected lay leaders and it becomes irrelevant who succeeds the Dalai Lama as spiritual leader.

The question of Tibet has special significance for the British people. What happened to Tibet is the direct result of British interference in Tibet and the rest of China when Great Britain had an empire. Yet now we have a government that thinks that trade is the be all and end all. And when this so-called trade is examined it only shows that billions of pounds of British taxpayers money is flowing into China. Tibet's fight is our fight. It concerns the British people. It concerns all people in the world who believe in freedom and decent values.

APPENDIX

Index to Documents

Document 1: Convention between Great Britain and China relating to Sikkim and Tibet - signed at Calcutta March 17, 1890.

Document 2: Regulations regarding Trade, Communication and Pasturage, appended to the Convention between Great Britain and China of March 17, 1890 relative to Sikkim and Tibet - signed at Darjeeling, December 5, 1893.

Document 3: Convention between Great Britain and Tibet - signed at Lhasa, September 7, 1904.

Document 3a: Declaration appended to the Lhasa Convention.

Document 4: Convention between Great Britain and China respecting Tibet - signed at Beijing, April 27, 1906.

Document 5: Convention between Great Britain and Russia relating to Persia, Afghanistan and Tibet - signed at St Petersburg, August 31, 1907.

Document 6: Agreement between Great Britain, China and Tibet amending Tibet Trade Regulations of December 5, 1893 - signed at Calcutta April 20, 1908.

Document 7: Agreement between the Chinese and Tibetan Governments of August 12, 1912.

Document 8: Agreement between the Chinese and Tibetan Governments of December 14, 1912.

Document 9: Tibetan Declaration of Independence, 8th month of the water ox year (1913).

Document 10: Simla Convention between Great Britain, China and Tibet, July 3, 1914.

Document 11: Anglo-Tibetan Trade Regulations - signed at Simla, July 3, 1914.

Document 12: Agreement for the Restoration of Peaceful Relations and the Delimitation of a Provisional Frontier between China and Tibet of August 19, 1918.

Document 13: Supplementary Agreement Regarding Mutual Withdrawal of Troops and Cessation of Hostilities between Chinese and Tibetans of October 10, 1918.

Document 14: Agreement on Measures for the Peaceful Liberation of Tibet (17-point Agreement) of May 23, 1951.

Document 15: Constitution of the People's Republic of China, adopted 4 December 1982, as amended 12 April 1988, 15 February 1993, 15 March 1999.

Document 16: Law of the People's Republic of China on Regional National Autonomy 1984.

Document 17: Chinese Communist Party Constitution as amended September 18, 1997.

Document 18: United States Foreign Relations Authorization Act 1996 and 1997 (excerpt) HR 1561.

Document 19: House of Commons Debate on Tibet, April 1, 1998.

DOCUMENT 1

Convention

between Great Britain and China, relating to Sikkim and Tibet - signed at Calcutta, March 17, 1890

(Ratifications exchanged at London, August 27, 1890)

Whereas Her Majesty the Queen of the United Kingdom of Great Britain and Ireland, Empress of India, and His Majesty the Emperor of China, are sincerely desirous to maintain and perpetuate the relations of friendship and good understanding which now exist between their respective Empires; and whereas recent occurrences have tended towards a disturbance of the said relations, and it is desirable to clearly define and permanently settle certain matters connected with the boundary between Sikkim and Tibet, Her Britannic Majesty and His Majesty the Emperor of China have resolved to conclude a Convention on this subject, and have, for this purpose, named Plenipotentiaries, that is to say:

Her Majesty the Queen of Great Britain and Ireland, his Excellency the Most Honourable Henry Charles Keith Petty Fitzmaurice, G.M.S.I., G.C.M.G., G.M.I.E., Marquess of Landsdowne, Viceroy and Governor-General of India;

And His Majesty the Emperor of China, his Excellency Sheng Tai, Imperial Associate Resident in Tibet, Military Deputy Lieutenant-Governor;

Who, having met and communicated to each other their full powers, and finding these to be in proper form, have agreed upon the following Convention in eight Articles:

Art. 1. The boundary of Sikkim and Tibet shall be the crest of the mountain-range separating the waters flowing into the Sikkim

Teesta and its affluents from the waters flowing into the Tibetan Mochu and northwards into other rivers of Tibet. The line commences at Mount Gipmochi on the Bhutan frontier, and follows the above-mentioned water-parting to the point where it meets Nepal territory.

II. It is admitted that the British Government, whose Protectorate over the Sikkimstate is hereby recognized, has direct and exclusive control over the internal administration of foreign relations of that state, and except through and with the permission of the British Government neither the ruler of the state nor any of its officers shall have official relations of any kind, formal or informal, with any other country.

III. The government of Great Britain and Ireland and the government of China engage reciprocally to respect the boundary as defined in Article I, and to prevent acts of aggression from their respective sides of the frontier.

IV. The question of providing increased facilities for trade across the Sikkim-Tibet frontier will hereafter be discussed with a view to a mutually satisfactory arrangement by the High Contracting Powers.

V. The question of pasturage on the Sikkim side of the frontier is reserved for further examination and future adjustment.

VI. The High Contracting Powers reserve for discussion and arrangement the method in which official communications between the British authorities in India and the authorities in Tibet shall be conducted.

VII. Two joint Commissioners shall, within six months from the ratification of this Convention, be appointed, one by the British government in India, the other by the Chinese Resident in Tibet. The said Commissioners shall meet and discuss the questions which, by the last three preceding Articles, have been reserved.

VII. The present Convention shall be ratified, and the ratifications shall be exchanged in London as soon as possible after the date of the signature thereof.

In witness whereof the respective negotiators have signed the same, and affixed thereunto the seals of their arms.

Done in quadruplicate in Calcutta, this 17th day of March, in the year of our Lord 1890, corresponding with the Chinese date, the 27th day of the second moon of the 16th year of Kuang Hsü.

(L. S.) LANSDOWNE.
(L. S.) Signature of the Chinese Plenipotentiary.

DOCUMENT 2

Regulations

regarding Trade, Communication, and Pasturage, appended to the Convention between Great Britain and China of March 17, 1890 relative to Sikkim and Tibet - Signed at Darjeeling, December 5, 1893

1. A trade mart shall be established at Yatung on the Tibetan side of the frontier, and shall be open to all British subjects for purposes of trade from the 1st day of May, 1894. The government of India shall be free to send officers to reside at Yatung to watch the conditions of British trade at that mart.

2. British subjects trading at Yatung shall be at liberty to travel freely to and fro between the frontier and Yatung, to reside at Yatung, and to rent houses and godowns for their own accommodation, and the storage of their goods. The Chinese Government undertake that suitable buildings for the above purposes shall be provided for British subjects, and also that a special and fitting residence shall be provided for the officer or officers appointed by the government of India under Regulation 1 to reside at Yatung. British subjects shall be at liberty to sell their goods to whomsoever they please, to purchase native commodities in kind or in money, to hire transport of any kind, and in general to conduct their business transactions in conformity with local usage, and without any vexatious restrictions. Such British subjects shall receive efficient protection for their persons and property. At Lang-jo and Ta-chun, between the frontier and Yatung, where rest-houses have been built by the Tibetan authorities, British subjects can break their journey in consideration of a daily rent.

3. Import and export trade in the following articles - arms, ammunition, military stores, salt, liquors, and intoxicating or narcotic drugs, may, at the option of either government, be entirely prohibited, or permitted only on such conditions as either government, on their own side, may think fit to impose.

4. Goods, other than goods of the descriptions enumerated in Regulation 3, entering Tibet from British India, across the Sikkim-Tibet frontier, or *vice versa*, whatever their origin, shall be exempt from duty for a period of five years, commencing from the date of the opening of Yatung to trade; but after the expiration of this term, if found desirable, a Tariff may be mutually agreed upon and enforced.

Indian tea may be imported into Tibet at a rate of duty not exceeding that at which Chinese tea is imported into England, but trade in Indian tea shall not be engaged in during the five years for which other commodities are exempt.

5. All goods on arrival at Yatung, whether from British India or from Tibet, must be reported at the Custom station there for examination, and the report must give full particulars of the description, quantity, and value of the goods.

6. In the event of trade disputes arising between British and Chinese or Tibetan subjects in Tibet, they shall be inquired into and settled in personal conference by the Political Officer for Sikkim and the Chinese Frontier Officer. The object of personal conference being to ascertain facts and do justice, where there is a divergence of views, the law of the country to which the defendant belongs shall guide.

7. Despatches from the government of India to the Chinese Imperial Resident in Tibet shall be handed over by the Political Officer for Sikkim to the Chinese Frontier Officer, who will forward them by special courier.

Despatches from the Chinese Imperial Resident in Tibet to the government of India will be handed over by the Chinese Frontier Officer to the Political Officer for Sikkim, who will forward them as quickly as possible.

8. Despatches between the Chinese and Indian officials must be treated with due respect, and couriers will be assisted in passing to and fro by the officers of each government.

9. After the expiration of one year from the date of the opening of Yatung, such Tibetans as continue to graze their cattle in Sikkim will be subject to such regulations as the British Government may from time to time enact for the general conduct of grazing in Sikkim. Due notice will be given of such regulations.

General Articles

1. In the event of disagreement between the Political Officer for Sikkim and the Chinese Frontier Officer, each official shall report the matter to his immediate superior, who in turn, if a settlement is not arrived at between them, shall refer such matter to their respective governments for disposal.

2. After the lapse of five years from the date on which these Regulations shall come into force, and on six months' notice given by either party, these Regulations shall be subject to revision by Commissioners appointed on both sides for this purpose, who shall be empowered to decide on and adopt such amendments and extensions as experience shall prove to be desirable.

3. It having been stipulated that Joint Commissioners should be appointed by the British and Chinese Governments under Articles VII of the Sikkim-Tibet Convention to meet and discuss, with a view to the final settlement of the questions reserved under Articles IV, V, and VI of the said Convention; and the Commissioners thus appointed having met and discussed the questions referred to, namely, trade, communication, and pasturage, have been further appointed to sign the agreement in nine Regulations and three General Articles now arrived at, and to declare that the said nine Regulations and the three General Articles form part of the Convention itself.

In witness whereof the respective Commissioners have hereto subscribed their names.

Done in quadruplicate at Darjeeling, this 5th day of December, in the year 1893, corresponding with the Chinese date, the 28th day of the 10th moon of the 19th year of Kuang Hsü.

(L. S.) A. W. Paul, *British Commissioner.*
(L. S.) HO CHANG-JUNG,
   JAMES H. HART, *Chinese Commissioners.*

DOCUMENT 3

Convention

between Great Britain and Tibet - Signed at Lhasa, September 7, 1904

Whereas doubts and difficulties have arisen as to the meaning and validity of the Anglo-Chinese Convention of 1890, and the Trade Regulations of 1893, and as to the liabilities of the Tibetan Government under these agreements; and whereas recent occurrences have tended towards a disturbance of the relations of friendship and good understanding which have existed between the British Government and the government of Tibet; and whereas it is desirable to restore peace and amicable relations, and to resolve and determine the doubts and difficulties as aforesaid, the said governments have resolved to conclude a Convention with these objects, and the following Articles have been agreed upon by Colonel F.E. Younghusband, C.I.E., in virtue of full powers vested in him by His Britannic Majesty's Government, and on behalf of that said government, and Lo-Sang Gyal-Tsen, the Ga-den Ti-Rimpoche, and the representatives of the Council, of the three monasteries Se-ra, Dre-pung, and Ga-den, and of the ecclesiastical and lay officials of the National Assembly on behalf of the government of Tibet:

Art. I. The government of Tibet engages to respect the Anglo-Chinese Convention of 1890, and to recognize the frontier between Sikkim and Tibet, as defined in Article 1 of the said Convention, and to erect boundary pillars accordingly.

II. The Tibetan Government undertakes to open forthwith trade marts to which all British and Tibetan subjects shall have free right of access at Gyangtse and Gartok, as well as at Yatung.

The Regulations applicable to the trade mart at Yatung, under the Anglo-Chinese Agreement of 1893, shall, subject to such amendments as may hereafter be agreed upon by common consent between the British and Tibetan Governments, apply to the marts above mentioned.

In addition to establishing trade marts at the places mentioned, the Tibetan Government undertakes to place no restrictions on the trade by existing routes, and to consider the question of establishing fresh trade marts under similar conditions if development of trade requires it.

III. The question of the amendment of the Regulations of 1893 is reserved for separate consideration, and the Tibetan Government undertakes to appoint fully authorized delegates to negotiate with representatives of the British Government as to the details of the amendments required.

IV. The Tibetan Government undertakes to levy no dues of any kind other than those provided for in the tariff to be mutually agreed upon.

V. The Tibetan Government undertakes to keep the roads to Gyangtse and Gartok from the frontier clear of all obstruction and in a state of repair suited to the needs of the trade, and to establish at Yatung, Gyangtse, and Gartok, and at each of the other trade marts that may hereafter be established, a Tibetan Agent who shall receive from the British Agent appointed to watch over British trade at the marts in question any letter which the latter may desire to send to the Tibetan or to the Chinese authorities. The Tibetan Agent shall also be responsible for the due delivery of such communications and for the transmission of replies.

VI. As an indemnity to the British Government for the expense incurred in the dispatch of armed troops to Lhasa, to exact reparation for breaches of Treaty obligations, and for the insults offered to and attacks upon the British Commissioner and his following and escort, the Tibetan Government engages to pay a sum of £500,000 - equivalent to 75 lakhs of rupees - to the British Government.

The indemnity shall be payable at such place as the British Government may from time to time, after due notice, indicate, whether in Tibet or in the British districts of Darjeeling or

Jalpaiguri, in seventy-five annual instalments of one lakh of rupees each on 1st January in each year, beginning from 1st January, 1906.

VII. As security for the payment of the above-mentioned indemnity, and for the fulfilment of the provisions relative to trade marts specified in Articles II, III, IV and V, the British Government shall continue to occupy the Chumbi Valley until the indemnity has been paid, and until the trade marts have been effectively opened for three years, whichever date may be the later.

VIII. The Tibetan Government agrees to raise all forts and fortifications and remove all armaments which might impede the course of free communication between the British frontier and the towns of Gyangtse and Lhasa.

IX. The government of Tibet engages that, without the previous consent of the British Government -

(a) No portion of Tibetan territory shall be ceded, sold, leased, mortgaged or otherwise given for occupation, to any foreign Power;
(b) No such Power shall be permitted to intervene in Tibetan affairs;
(c) No Representations or Agents of any foreign Power shall be admitted to Tibet;
(d) No concessions for railways, roads, telegraphs, mining, or other rights, shall be granted to any foreign Power, or the subject of any foreign Power. In the event of consent to such Concessions being granted, similar to equivalent Concessions shall be granted to the British Government;
(e) No Tibetan revenues, whether in kind or in cash, shall be pledged or assigned to any foreign Power, or to the subject of any foreign Power.

X. In witness whereof the Negotiators have signed the same, and affixed thereunto the seals of their arms.

Done in quintuplicate at Lhasa, this 7th day of September, in the year of our Lord, 1904, corresponding with the Tibetan date, the 27th of the seventh month of the Wood Dragon year.

F. E. YOUNGHUSBAND,
Colonel,
British Commissioner.

(Tibet Frontier
Commission)

(Seal of British
Commissioner)

(Seal of Dalai Lama
affixed by the
Ga-den Ti-Rimpoche)

| (Seal of Council) | (Seal of Dre-pung Monastery) | (Seal of Sera Monastery) | (Seal of Ga-den Monastery) | (Seal of National Assembly) |

In proceedings to the signature of the Convention, dated this day the Representatives of Great Britain and Tibet declare that the English text shall be binding.

AMPTHILL,
Viceroy and Governor-General of India

This Convention was ratified by the Viceroy and Governor-General of India in Council at Simla on the 11th day of November, 1904. (See document 3a, *post*).

S. M. FRASER,
Secretary to the Government of India,
Foreign Department.

DOCUMENT 3a

Declaration Signed by His Excellency the Viceroy and Governor-General of India, and Appended to the Ratified Convention of 7th September, 1904

His Excellency the Viceroy and Governor-General of India, having ratified the Convention which was concluded at Lhasa on 7th September, 1904, by Colonel Younghusband, C. I. E. , British Commissioner for Tibet Frontier Matters, on behalf of His Britannic Majesty's Government; and by Lo-Sang Gyal-Tsen, the Ga-den Ti-Rimpoche, and the representatives of the Council, of the three monasteries Sera, Dre-pung and Ga-den, and of the ecclesiastical and lay officials of the National Assembly, on behalf of the government of Tibet, is pleased to direct as an act of grace that the sum of money which the Tibetan Government have bound themselves under the terms of Articles VI of the said Convention to pay to His Majesty's Government as an indemnity for the expenses incurred by the latter in connection with the despatch of armed forces to Lhasa, be reduced from Rs. 75,000,000 to Rs. 25,000,000; and to declare that the British occupation of the Chumbi Valley shall cease after the due payment of three annual instalments of the said indemnity as fixed by the said Articles, provided, however, that the trade-marts as stipulated in Articles II of the Convention shall have been effectively opened for three years as provided in Article VI of the Convention; and that, in the meantime, the Tibetans shall have faithfully complied with the terms of the said Convention in all other respects.

DOCUMENT 4

Convention

between Great Britain and China respecting Tibet - Signed at Peking, April, 27 1906

(Ratifications exchanged at London July 23, 1906)

Whereas His Majesty the King of Great Britain and Ireland and of the British Dominions beyond the Seas, Emperor of India, and His Majesty the Emperor of China are sincerely desirous to maintain and perpetuate the relations of friendship and good understanding which now exist between their respective Empires;

And whereas the refusal of Tibet to recognize the validity of or to carry into full effect the provisions of the Anglo-Chinese Conventions of March 17, 1890 and Regulations of December 5, 1893 placed the British Government under the necessity of taking steps to secure their rights and interests under the said Convention and Regulations;

And whereas a Convention of ten Articles was signed at Lhasa on September 7, 1904 on behalf of Great Britain and Tibet, and was ratified by the Viceroy and Governor-General of India on behalf of Great Britain on November 11, 1904, a declaration on behalf of Great Britain modifying its terms under certain conditions being appended thereto;

His Britannic Majesty and His Majesty the Emperor of China have resolved to conclude a Convention on this subject and have for this purpose named Plenipotentiaries, that is to say:

His Majesty and the King of Great Britain and Ireland:

Sir Ernest Mason Satow, Knight Grand Cross of the Most Distinguished Order of Saint Michael and Saint George, His said Majesty's Envoy Extraordinary and Minister Plenipotentiary to His Majesty the Emperor of China;

And His Majesty the Emperor of China:

His Excellency Tong Shoa-yi, His said Majesty's High

Commissioner Plenipotentiary and a Vice-President of the Board of Foreign Affairs; who having communicated to each other their respective full powers and finding them to be in good and true form have agreed upon and concluded the following Convention in six Articles:

Art. I. The Convention concluded on September 7, 1904 by Great Britain and Tibet, the texts of which in English and Chinese are attached to the present Convention as an annex, is hereby confirmed, subject to the modification stated in the declaration appended thereto, and both of the High Contracting Parties engage to take at all times such steps as may be necessary to secure the due fulfilment of the terms specified therein.

II. The government of Great Britain engages not to annex Tibetan territory or to interfere in the administration of Tibet. The government of China also undertakes not to permit any other foreign state to interfere with the territory or internal administration of Tibet.

III. The Concessions which are mentioned in Articles IX (d) of the Convention concluded on September 7, 1904 by Great Britain and Tibet are denied to any state or to the subject of any state other than China, but it has been arranged with China that at the trade marts specified in Article II of the aforesaid Convention Great Britain shall be entitled to lay down telegraph lines connecting with India.

IV. The provisions of the Anglo-Chinese Convention of 1890 and Regulations of 1893 shall, subject to the terms of this present Convention and annex thereto, remain in full force.

V. The English and Chinese texts of the present Convention have been carefully compared and found to correspond but in the event of there being any difference of meaning between them the English text shall be authoritative.

VI. This Convention shall be ratified by the Sovereigns of both countries and ratifications shall be exchanged at London within three months after the date of signature by the Plenipotentiaries of both Powers.

In token whereof the respective Plenipotentiaries have signed and sealed this Convention, four copies in English and four in Chinese.

Done at Peking this twenty-seventh day of April, one thousand nine hundred and six, being the fourth day of the fourth month of the thirty-second year of the reign of Kuang Hsü.

(L. S.) ERNEST SATOW
(Signature and Seal of the Chinese Plenipotentiary)

ANNEX

Convention between the governments of Great Britain and Tibet signed at Lhasa on the 7th September, 1904.

Declaration signed by His Excellency the Viceroy and Governor-General of India on behalf of the British Government and appended to the ratified Convention of the 7th September, 1904.

Exchange of Notes between Great Britain and China respecting the Non-employment of Foreigners in Tibet.

Peking, April 27, 1906.

(1.) - Tong Shoa-yi to Sir E. Satow.

April 27, 1906

Your Excellency,

With reference to the Convention relating to Tibet which was signed today by your Excellency and myself on behalf of our respective governments, I have the honour to declare formally that the government of China undertakes not to employ any one not a

Chinese subject and not of Chinese nationality in any capacity whatsoever in Tibet.

I avail, &c.

TONG SHOA-YI

(2.) - Sir E. Satow to Tong Shoa-yi.

Peking, April 27, 1906

Your Excellency,

I have the honour to acknowledge the receipt of your Excellency's note of this day's date, in which you declare formally, with reference to the Convention relating to Tibet which was signed today by your Excellency and myself on behalf of our respective governments, that the government of China undertakes not to employ any one not a Chinese subject and not of Chinese nationality in any capacity whatsoever in Tibet.

I avail, &c.

ERNEST SATOW

DOCUMENT 5

Convention Between Great Britain and Russia, 1907

His Majesty the King of the United Kingdom of Great Britain and Ireland and of the British Dominions beyond the Seas, Emperor of India, and His Majesty the Emperor of All the Russians, animated by the sincere desire to settle by mutual agreement different questions concerning the interests of their states on the Continent of Asia, have determined to conclude agreements destined to prevent all cause of misunderstanding between Great Britain and Russia in regard to the questions referred to, and have nominated for this purpose their respective Plenipotentiaries, to wit:

His Majesty the King of the United Kingdom of Great Britain and Ireland and of the British Dominions beyond the Seas, Emperor of India, the Right Honourable Sir Arthur Nicolson, His Majesty's Ambassador Extraordinary and Plenipotentiary to His Majesty the Emperor of All the Russias;

His Majesty the Emperor of All the Russias, the Master of his Court Alexander Iswolsky, Minister for Foreign Affairs;

Who, having communicated to each other their full powers, found in good and due form, have agreed on the following:

Arrangement Concerning Tibet

The governments of Great Britain and Russia recognizing the suzerain rights of China in Tibet, and considering the fact that Great Britain, by reason of her geographical position, has a special interest in the maintenance of the *status quo* in the external relations of Tibet, have made the following Arrangement:

Article I. - The two High Contracting Parties engage to respect the territorial integrity of Tibet and to abstain from all interference in its internal administration.

Article II. - In conformity with the admitted principle of the suzerainty of China over Tibet, Great Britain and Russia engage not to enter into negotiations with Tibet except through the intermediary of the Chinese Government. This engagement does not exclude the direct relations between British Commercial Agents and the Tibetan authorities provided for in Article V of the Convention between Great Britain and Tibet of the 7th September, 1904, and confirmed by the Convention between Great Britain and China of 27th April, 1906; nor does it modify the engagements entered into by Great Britain and China in Article I of the said Convention of 1906.

It is clearly understood that Buddhists, subjects of Great Britain or of Russia, may enter into direct relations on strictly religious matters with the Dalai Lama, and the other representatives of Buddhism in Tibet; the government of Great Britain and Russia engage as far as they are concerned, not to allow those relations to infringe the stipulations of the present Arrangement.

Article III. - The British and Russian Governments respectively engage not to send Representatives to Lhasa.

Article IV. - The two High Contracting Parties engage neither to seek nor to obtain, whether for themselves or their subjects, any Concessions for railways, roads, telegraphs, and mines, or other rights in Tibet.

Article V. - The two governments agree that no part of the revenues of Tibet, whether in kind or in cash, shall be pledged or assigned to Great Britain or Russia or to any of their subjects.

Annex to the Arrangement Between Great Britain and Russia concerning Tibet

Great Britain reaffirms the Declaration, signed by His Excellency the Viceroy and Governor-General of India and appended to the ratification of the Convention of the 7th September, 1904, to the effect that the occupation of the Chumbi Valley by British forces shall cease after the payment of three annual instalments of the indemnity of 2,500,000 rupees, provided that the trade-marts mentioned in Article II of that Convention have been effectively opened for three years, and that in the meantime the Tibetan authorities have faithfully complied in all respects with the terms of the said Convention of 1904. It is clearly understood that if the occupation of the Chumbi Valley by the British forces has, for any reason, not been terminated at the time anticipated in the above Declaration, the British and Russian Governments will enter upon a friendly exchange of views on this subject.

DOCUMENT 6

Agreement
between Great Britain, China and Tibet amending Trade Regulations in Tibet, of December 5, 1893 - Signed at Calcutta April 20, 1908

(Ratifications exchanged at Peking, October 14, 1908)

TIBET TRADE REGULATIONS

Preamble

Whereas by Article I of the Convention between Great Britain and China on the 27th April, 1906, that is the 4th day of the 4th moon of the 32nd year of Kwang Hsü, it was provided that both the High Contracting Parties should engage to take at all times such steps as might be necessary to secure the due fulfilment of the terms specified in the Lhasa Convention of the 7th September, 1904, between Great Britain and Tibet, the text of which in English and Chinese was attached as an annex to the above-named Convention;

And whereas it was stipulated in Article III of the said Lhasa Convention that the question of the amendment of the Tibet Trade Regulations which were signed by the British and Chinese Commissioners on the 5th day of December, 1893, should be reserved for separate consideration, and whereas the amendment of these Regulations is now necessary;

His Majesty the King of the United Kingdom of Great Britain and Ireland and of the British Dominions beyond the Seas, Emperor of India, and His Majesty the Emperor of the Chinese Empire have for this purpose named as their Plenipotentiaries, that is to say:

His Majesty the King of Great Britain and Ireland and of the British Dominions beyond the Seas, Emperor of India: Mr. E. C. Wilton, C.M.G.;

His Majesty the Emperor of the Chinese Empire; His Majesty's Special Commissioner Chang Yin Tang;

And the High Authorities of Tibet have named as their fully

authorized representative to act under the directions of Chang Tachen and take part in the negotiations, the Tsarong Shape, Wang-Chuk Gyalpo.

And whereas Mr. E.C. Wilton and Chang Tachen have communicated to each other since their respective full powers and have found them to be in good and true form and have found the authorization of the Tibetan Delegate to be also in good and true form, the following amended Regulations have been agreed upon:

1. The Trade Regulations of 1893 shall remain in force in so far as they are not inconsistent with these Regulations.

2. The following places shall form, and be included within,` the boundaries of the Gyantse mart:

(a) The line begins at the Chumig Dangsang (Chhu-Mig-Dangs-Sangs) north-east of the Gyantse Fort, and thence it runs in a curved line, passing behind the Pekor Chode (Dpal-Hkhor-Choos-Sde), down to Chag-Dong-Gang (Phyag-Gdong-Sgang); thence passing straight over the Nyan Chu, it reaches the Zamsa (Zam-Srag).

(b) From the Zamsa the line continues to run, in a south-eastern direction, round to Lachi-To (Gla-Dykii-Stod), embracing all the farms on its way, viz. , the Lahong, the Hogtso (Hog-Mtsho), the Tong-Chung-Shi (Grong-Chhung-Gshis), and the Rabgang (Rab-Sgang), &c.

(c) From Lachi-To the line runs to the Yutog (Gyu-Thog), and thence runs straight, passing through the whole area of Gamkar-Shi (Ragal-Mkhar-Gshis), to Chumig Dangsang.

As difficulty is experienced in obtaining suitable houses and godowns at some of the marts, it is agreed that British subjects may also lease lands for the building of houses and godowns at the marts, the locality for such buildings sites to be marked out specially at each mart by the Chinese and Tibetan authorities in consultation with the British Trade Agent. The British Trade

Agents and British subjects shall not build houses and godowns except in such localities, and this arrangement shall not be held to prejudice in any way the administration of the Chinese and Tibetan local authorities over such localities, or the right of British subjects to rent houses and godowns outside such localities for their own accommodation and the storage of their goods.

British subjects desiring to lease building sites shall apply through the British Trade Agent to the municipal office at the mart for a permit to lease. The amount of rent, or the period or conditions of the lease, shall then be settled in a friendly way by the lessee and the owner themselves. In the event of a disagreement between the owner and lessee as to the amount of rent or the period or conditions of the lease, the case will be settled by the Chinese and Tibetan authorities, in consultation with the British Trade Agent. After the lease is settled, the sites shall be verified by the Chinese and Tibetan officers of the municipal office conjointly with the British Trade Agent. No building is to be commenced by the lessee on a site before the municipal office has issued him a permit to build, but it is agreed that there shall be no vexatious delays in the issue of such permit.

3. The administration of the trade marts shall remain with the Tibetan officers, under the Chinese officers' supervision and directions.

The Trade Agents at the marts and Frontier Officers shall be of suitable rank, and shall hold personal intercourse and correspondence one with another on terms of mutual respect and friendly treatment.

Questions which cannot be decided by agreement between the Trade Agents and the local authorities shall be referred for settlement to the government of India and the Tibetan High Authorities at Lhasa. The purpose of a reference by the government of India will be communicated to the Chinese Imperial Resident at Lhasa. Questions which cannot be decided by agreement between the government of India and the Tibetan High

Authorities at Lhasa shall, in accordance with the terms of Article I of the Peking Convention of 1906, be referred for settlement to the governments of Great Britain and China.

4. In the event of disputes arising at the marts between British subjects and persons of Chinese and Tibetan nationalities, they shall be inquired into and settled in personal conferences between the British Trade Agent at the nearest mart and the Chinese and Tibetan authorities of the Judicial Court at the mart, the object of personal conference being to ascertain facts and to do justice. Where there is a divergence of view the law of the country to which the defendant belongs shall guide. In any of such mixed cases, the officer or officers of the defendant's nationality shall preside at the trial, the officer or officers of the plaintiff's country merely attending to watch the course of the trial.

All questions in regard to rights, whether of property or person, arising between British subjects, shall be subject to the jurisdiction of the British authorities.

British subjects who may commit any crime at the marts or on the routes to the marts shall be handed over by the local authorities to the British Trade Agent at the mart nearest to the scene of offence, to be tried and punished according to the laws of India, but such British subjects shall not be subjected by the local authorities to any ill-usage in excess of necessary restraint.

Chinese and Tibetan subjects, who may be guilty of any criminal act towards British subjects at the marts or on the routes thereto, shall be arrested and punished by the Chinese and Tibetan authorities according to law.

Justice shall be equitably and impartially administered on both sides.

Should it happen that Chinese or Tibetan subjects bring a criminal complaint against a British subject before the British Trade Agent, the Chinese or Tibetan authorities shall have the right to send a representative, or representatives, to watch the course of trial in the British Trade Agent's Court. Similarly, in cases in which a British subject has reason to complain of a Chinese or Tibetan subject in the Judicial Court at the mart, the British Trade agent shall have the right to send a representative to the Judicial Court to watch the course of trial.

5. The Tibetan authorities, in obedience to the instructions of the Peking Government, having a strong desire to reform the judicial system of Tibet, and to bring it into accord with that of Western nations, Great Britain agrees to relinquish her rights of extra-territoriality in Tibet, whenever such rights are relinquished in China, and when she is satisfied that the state of the Tibetan laws and the arrangements for their administration and other considerations warrant her in so doing.

6. After the withdrawal of the British troops, all the rest-houses, eleven in number, built by Great Britain upon the routes leading from the Indian frontier to Gyantse, shall be taken over at original cost by China and rented to the government of India at a fair rate. One-half of each rest-house will be reserved for the use of the British officials employed on the inspection and maintenance of the telegraph lines from the marts to the Indian frontier and for the storage of their materials, but the rest-houses shall otherwise be available for occupation by British, Chinese, and Tibetan officers of respectability who may proceed to and from the marts.

Great Britain is prepared to consider the transfer to China of the telegraph lines from the Indian frontier to Gyantse when the telegraph lines from China reach that mart, and in the meantime Chinese and Tibetan messages will be duly received and transmitted by the line constructed by the government of India.

In the meantime China shall be responsible for the due protection of the telegraph lines from the marts to the Indian frontier, and it is agreed that all persons damaging the lines or interfering in any way with them or with the officials engaged in the inspection or maintenance thereof shall at once be severely punished by the local authorities.

7. In law suits involving cases of debt on account of loans,

commercial failure, and bankruptcy, the authorities concerned shall grant a hearing and take steps necessary to enforce payment; but, if the debtor plead poverty and be without means, the authority concerned shall not be held responsible for the said debts, nor shall any public or official property be distrained upon in order to satisfy these debts.

8. The British Trade Agents at the various trade marts now or hereafter to be established in Tibet may make arrangements for the carriage and transmission of their posts to and from the frontier of India. The couriers employed in conveying these posts shall receive all possible assistance from the local authorities whose districts they traverse and shall be accorded the same protection as the persons employed in carrying the despatches of the Tibetan authorities. When efficient arrangements have been made by China in Tibet for a postal service, the question of the abolition of the Trade Agents' couriers will be taken into consideration by Great Britain and China. No restrictions whatever shall be placed on the employment by British officers and traders of Chinese and Tibetan subjects in any lawful capacity. The persons so employed shall not be exposed to any kind of molestation or suffer any loss of civil rights to which they may be entitled as Tibetan subjects, but they shall not be exempted from all lawful taxation. If they be guilty of any criminal act, they shall be dealt with by the local authorities according to law without any attempt on the part of their employer to screen or conceal them.

9. British officers and subjects, as well as goods, proceeding to the trade marts, must adhere to the trade routes from the frontier of India. They shall not, without permission, proceed beyond the marts, or to Gartok from Yatung and Gyantse, or from Gartok to Yatung and Gyantse, by any route through the interior of Tibet, but natives of the Indian frontier, who have already by usage traded and resided in Tibet, elsewhere than at the marts shall be at liberty to continue their trade, in accordance with the existing practice, but when so trading or residing they shall remain, as heretofore,

amenable to the local jurisdiction.

10. In cases where officials or traders, *en route* to and from India or Tibet, are robbed of treasure or merchandise, public or private, they shall forthwith report to the police officers, who shall take immediate measures to arrest the robbers and hand them to the local authorities. The local authorities shall bring them to instant trial, and shall also recover and restore the stolen property. But if the robbers flee to places out of the jurisdiction and influence of Tibet, and cannot be arrested, the police and the local authorities shall not be held responsible for such losses.

11. For public safety, tanks or stores of kerosene oil or any other combustible or dangerous articles in bulk must be placed far away from inhabited placed at the marts.

British or Indian merchants wishing to build such tanks or stores may not do so until, as provided in Regulation 2, they have made application for a suitable site.

12. British subjects shall be at liberty to deal in kind or in money, to sell their goods to whomsoever they please, to purchase native commodities from whomsoever they please, to hire transport of any kind, and to conduct in general their business transactions in conformity with local usage and without any vexations restrictions or oppressive exactions whatever.

It being the duty of the police and local authorities to afford efficient protection at all times to the persons and property of the British subjects at the marts, and along the routes to the marts, China engages to arrange effective police measures at the marts and along the routes to the marts. On due fulfilment of these arrangements, Great Britain undertakes to withdraw the Trade Agents' guards at the marts and to station no troops in Tibet, so as to remove all cause for suspicion and disturbance among the inhabitants. The Chinese authorities will not prevent the British Trade Agents holding personal intercourse and correspondence with the Tibetan officers and people.

Tibetan subjects trading, travelling, or residing in India shall receive equal advantages to those accorded by this Regulation to British subjects in Tibet.

13. The present Regulations shall be in force for a period of ten years reckoned from the date of signature by the two Plenipotentiaries as well as by the Tibetan Delegate; but if no demand for revision be made by either side within six months after the end of the first ten years, then the Regulations shall remain in force for another ten years from the end of the first ten years; and so it shall be at the end of the each successive ten years.

14. The English, Chinese, and Tibetan texts of the present Regulations have been carefully compared, and, in the event of any question arising as to the interpretation of these Regulations, the sense as expressed in the English text shall be held to be the correct sense.

15. The ratification of the present Regulations under the hand of His Majesty the King of Great Britain and Ireland, and of His Majesty the Emperor of the Chinese Empire, respectively, shall be exchanged at London and Peking within six months from the date of signature.

In witness whereof the two Plenipotentiaries and the Tibetan Delegate have signed and sealed the present Regulations.

Done in quadruplicate at Calcutta this 20th day April, in the year of our Lord 1908, corresponding with the Chinese date, the 20th day of the 3rd moon of the 34th year of Kuang Hsü.

    (L. S.)   E. C. Wilton
                    British Commissioner

                      Signature of
    (L. S.)   Chang Yin Tang,
                      Chinese Special Commissioner.

                      Signature of
    (L. S.)   Wang Chuk Gyalpo,
                      Tibetan Delegate.

DOCUMENT 7

Agreement Between the Chinese and Tibetans

12 August, 1912

Translation of the Tibetan version

The representatives of the Chinese and the Tibetans met together in the presence of the Gorkha witnesses to discuss the three-point proposals, approved by the Dalai Lama in his answer to the letter submitted by Ambans Len and Chung on the 29th day of the 6th month. On the 30th the parties carefully discussed the matter and decided to have the three-point proposals drawn up in the Chinese, Tibetan and Nepali languages, and to sign and seal them.

Point I. All the arms and equipment including field guns and Maxim guns in the possession of the Chinese at Dabshi and Tseling in Lhasa shall be sealed in the presence of the representatives of the two sides and witnesses and entrusted to the custody of the government of Tibet. Before the departure of the Chinese officials and soldiers from Tibet, all the arms and equipment shall be removed to the Yabshi Lang Dun house within fifteen days; the bullets and gunpowder shall be collected and deposited in the Doring house. All the arms and ammunition shall be removed to the Doring house on the expiry of the fifteen-day limit, and the witnessing Gorkha envoy shall arrange to guard the house.

Point II. The Chinese officials and soldiers shall leave Tibet within fifteen days. According to the dates given by them for their departure in three batches, Tibetans will depute an official to accompany the different batches and will arrange to supply the necessary pack animals and riding ponies. The Tibetans will supply against adequate payment and according to local rates foodstuffs such as rice, flour, tsampa, meat, butter and tea to the Chinese at the halting stages up to the frontier, through the Tibetans escorting them. There shall not be any delay in supplying pack animals and riding ponies on the way. The Chinese shall not take by force any pack of riding animals beyond the frontier.

Point III. The two representatives shall remove all Chinese officials and soldiers from the Yapshi house and the Tibetan soldiers from the Doring house tomorrow in order to keep the arms and ammunition in these houses.

All the arms and ammunition belonging to the Chinese Government at Dabshi and Tseling in Lhasa, including those in the possession of the Chinese private traders from China, shall, according to the letter of the 29th day of the 6th month from Ambans Len and Chung, be produced before the representatives of the two parties and witnesses on the 1st day of the 7th month together with an inventory. No part of these arms and ammunition shall be given away, sold, hidden or thrown away. Ambans Lea and Chung for their protection shall, as suggested by the witnesses, be allowed to retain sixty rifles and ammunition. All other arms and equipment shall be kept in the Doring and Yabshi houses, which shall be scaled by the two representatives and the witnesses. The two representatives and witnesses shall arrange to place guards as stated above. After all arms, equipment, field-guns, and Maxim guns from Lhasa, Dabshi, and Tseling and from the Chinese Government and private traders have been collected, they shall be deposited, without giving away, selling, hiding, or leaving out any. A list will be made of the arms genuinely belonging to the private Chinese traders, and the representatives and the witnesses shall discuss matters concerning their return to them.

This agreement, signed and sealed by the two parties and witnessed this day, will be considered void in the event of any party infringing any of its provisions.

> Joint seal of the Dalai Lamas's representatives:
> Sertsa Thitul and Tsedon Tangyal
> Seals of the representatives of Ambans Len and Chung:
> Luchang Krang Lungrin
> Yulji Lu Langrin
> U Yon Krephu Hai Kru

DOCUMENT 8

Agreement of the Chinese and the Tibetans
14 December, 1912

(translation of the Nepalese version)

On account of the fighting between the Chinese and the Tibetans, the representatives of the Chinese and of the Tibetans met together in the presence of the Nepalese representative as a witness, and in his office, in order to satisfy the respective parties. The representatives discussed the matters which were in dispute, and finally decided as follows.

1. First, to count consecutively all the arms which had been stored in Yapshi house, to see whether the number of arms stored there is correct. After this, to set apart from the arms which were kept in Yapshi house, and also from the arms which are to be collected hereafter, and to hand over to the Tibetans, the Tibetan prong-guns, the newly manufactured five-shot magazine U-shang guns, and the Nu-chhau-u or Martini-Henri guns which bear Tibetan marks. The cannon, and all the big and small guns (without bolts), and the powder, and the cartridges, which belong to the Chinese, shall be kept in the Sho store room. The (door of the) store room shall be sealed by the representatives of the Chinese, Tibetans and Nepalese, and it shall be guarded by the Nepalese until the Chinese have crossed the Tromo (Chumbi Valley) frontier. After this the Nepalese shall hand over the sealed (store room) to (the custody of) the Tibetans, and shall obtain proper receipt from them.

2. Until the Chinese leave Lhasa, the Tibetans shall send Tibetan merchants daily with sufficient food to sell to the Chinese. Should any Chinese require to go towards the Tibetan side, he shall receive a letter from Tungling, and should any articles have been left with the Tibetans, the owners, whether Tibetan or Chinese, can take them.

3. The Tibetans shall arrange to supply riding ponies and transport to the (Chinese) officials and soldiers during their march

according to the list. The Tibetans shall supply riding ponies and transport to the (Chinese) traders and subjects, on payment of 10 thankas for each riding pony and 6 thankas for each transport animal from one jong to the next jong, i.e., at each of the changing places for animals.

4. The Tungling and the (Chinese) officials and soldiers and subjects will start from here (Lhasa) on the 8th of this month (December 16th, 1913). They will not molest the Tibetan subjects, nor loot their property on the way, and they (Chinese) will return direct (to China) via India without delaying on their way.

5. Should any arms and ammunition other than bolts be found among the baggage of the Chinese at the place of inspection, the Tibetan Government will take possession of them.

6. The Tibetans will supply on proper payment sufficient food for the Chinese at halting places and stages on their way.

7. The Tibetans have promised not to injure the lives or loot the property of Tungling, or of the Chinese officials and soldiers, traders and subjects, who are leaving Tibet, or of the Chinese traders and subjects living in Tibet.

8. The houses in the neighbourhood of the Yamen are to be handed over to the Tibetans. The wooden boxes, and utensils, according to the list written in a book, will be kept in a separate house, the door of which shall be sealed by the representatives of the Chinese and Tibetans. The Tibetans will look after the house.

9. As regards the monks of the Tengyeling monastery. At the time when the first agreement was made, His Holiness the Dalai Lama promised to protect the lives of the monks should they behave well. The representatives undertake to observe this promise.

DOCUMENT 9

Tibetan Declaration of Independence 1913

I, The Dalai Lama, most omniscient possessor of the Buddhist faith, whose title was conferred by the Lord Buddha's command from the glorious land of India, speaks to you as follows:

I am speaking to all classes of Tibetan people. Lord Buddha, from the glorious country of India, prophesied that the reincarnations of Avalokiteśvara, through successive rulers from the early religious kings to the present day, would look after the welfare of Tibet.

During the time of Genghis Khan and Altan Khan of the Mongols, the Ming dynasty of the Chinese, and the Ch'ing dynasty of the Manchus, Tibet and China co-operated on the basis of benefactor and priest relationship. A few years ago, the Chinese authorities in Szechuan and Yunnan endeavoured to colonize our territory. They brought large numbers of troops into central Tibet on the pretext of policing the trade marts. I therefore, left Lhasa with my ministers for the Indo-Tibetan border, hoping to clarify to the Manchu Emperor by wire that the existing relationship between Tibet and China had been that of patron and priest and had not been based on the subordination of one to the other. There was no other choice for me but to cross the border, because Chinese troops were following with the intention of taking me alive or dead.

On my arrival in India, I dispatched several telegrams to the Emperor; but his reply to my demands was delayed by corrupt officials at Peking. Meanwhile, the Manchu Empire collapsed. The Tibetans were encouraged to expel the Chinese from central Tibet. I, too, returned safely to my rightful and sacred country, and I am now in the course of driving out the remnants of Chinese troops from Do Kham in eastern Tibet. Now, the Chinese intention of colonizing Tibet under the patron-priest relationship has faded like a rainbow in the sky. Having once again achieved for ourselves a period of happiness and peace, I have now allotted to all of you the following duties to be carried out without negligence;

(1) Peace and happiness in this world can only be maintained by preserving the faith of Buddhism. It is, therefore, essential to preserve all Buddhist institutions in Tibet, such as the Jokhang temple and Ramoche in Lhasa, Samye, and Traduk in southern Tibet, and the three great monasteries, etc.

(2) The various Buddhist sects in Tibet should be kept in a distinct and pure form. Buddhism should be taught, learned, and meditated upon properly. Except for special persons, the administrators of monasteries are forbidden to trade, loan money, deal in any kind of livestock, and/or subjugate another's subjects.

(3) The Tibetan Government's civil and military officials, when collecting taxes or dealing with their subject citizens, should carry out their duties with fair and honest judgment so as to benefit the government without hurting the interests of the subject citizens. Some of the central government officials posted at Ngari Korsum in western Tibet, and Do Kham in eastern Tibet, are coercing their subject citizens to purchase commercial goods at high prices and have imposed transportation rights exceeding the limit permitted by the government. Houses, properties, and lands belonging to subject citizens have been confiscated on the pretext of minor breaches of the law. Furthermore, the amputation of citizens' limbs has been carried out as a form of punishment. Henceforth, such severe punishments are forbidden.

(4) Tibet is a country with rich natural resources; but it is not scientifically advanced like other lands. We are a small, religious, and independent nation. To keep up with the rest of the world, we must defend our country. In view of past invasions by foreigners, our people may have to face certain difficulties, which they must disregard. To safeguard and maintain the independence of our country, one and all should voluntarily work hard. Our subject citizens residing near the borders should be alert and keep the government informed by special messenger of any suspicious developments. Our subjects must not create major clashes between two nations because of minor incidents.

(5) Tibet, although thinly populated, is an extensive country. Some local officials and landholders are jealously obstructing other people from developing vacant lands, even though they are not doing so themselves. People with such intentions are enemies of the state and our progress. From now on, no one is allowed to obstruct anyone else from cultivating whatever vacant lands are available. Land taxes will not be collected until three years have passed; after that the land cultivator will have to pay taxes to the government and to the landlord every year, proportionate to the rent. The land will belong to the cultivator.

Your duties to the government and to the people will have been achieved when you have executed all that I have said here. This letter must be posted and proclaimed in every district of Tibet, and a copy kept in the records of the offices in every district.

From the Potala Palace. (Seal of the Dalai Lama)
(8th day of the month of the Water ox year (1913))

DOCUMENT 10

Simla Convention between Great Britain, China and Tibet - 1914 (N.B. not ratified by China)

His Majesty the King of the United Kingdom of Great Britain and Ireland and of the British Dominions beyond the Seas, Emperor of India, His Excellency the President of the Republic of China, and His Holiness the Dalai Lama of Tibet, being sincerely desirous to settle by mutual agreement various questions concerning the interests of their several states on the Continent of Asia, and further to regulate the relations of their several governments, have resolved to conclude a Convention on this subject and have nominated for this purpose their respective Plenipotentiaries, that is to say:

His Majesty the King of the United Kingdom of Great Britain and Ireland and of the British Dominions beyond the Seas, Emperor of India, Sir Arthur Henry McMahon, Knight Grand Cross of the Royal Victorian Order, Knight Commander of the Most Eminent Order of the Indian Empire, Companion of the Most Exalted Order of the Star of India, Secretary to the government of India, Foreign and Political Department;

His Excellency the President of the Republic of China, Monsieur Ivan Chen, Officer of the Order of the China HO;

His Holiness the Dalai Lama of Tibet, Lonchen Ga-den Shatra Pal-jor Dorje; who having communicated to each other their respective full powers and finding them to be in good and due form have agreed upon and concluded the following Convention in eleven Articles:

Article 1

The Conventions specified in the Schedule to the present Conventions shall, except in so far as they may have been modified by, or may be inconsistent with or repugnant to, any of the provisions of the present Convention, continue to be binding upon the High Contracting Parties.

Article 2

The governments of Great Britain and China recognizing that Tibet is under the suzerainty of China, and recognizing also the autonomy of Outer Tibet, engage to respect the territorial integrity of the country, and to abstain from interference in the administration of Outer Tibet (including the selection and installation of the Dalai Lama), which shall remain in the hands of the Tibetan Government at Lhasa.

The government of China engages not to convert Tibet into a Chinese province. The government of Great Britain engages not to annex Tibet or any portion of it.

Article 3

Recognizing the special interest of Great Britain, in virtue of the geographical position of Tibet, in the existence of an effective Tibetan Government, and in the maintenance of peace and order in the neighbourhood of the frontiers of India and adjoining states, the government of China engages, except as provided in Articles 4 of this Convention, not to send troops into Outer Tibet, nor to station civil or military officers, not to establish Chinese colonies in the country. Should any such troops or officials remain in Outer Tibet at the date of the signature of this Convention, they shall be withdrawn within a period not exceeding three months.

The government of Great Britain engages not to station military or civil officers in Tibet (except as provided in the Convention of September 7, 1904, between Great Britain and Tibet) nor troops (except the Agents' escorts), nor to establish colonies in that country.

Article 4

The foregoing Article shall not be held to preclude the continuance of the arrangement by which, in the past, a Chinese high official with suitable escort has been maintained at Lhasa, but it is hereby provided that the said escort shall in no circumstances exceed 300 men.

Article 5

The governments of China and Tibet engage that they will not enter into any negotiations or agreements regarding Tibet with one another, or with any other Power, excepting such negotiations and agreements between Great Britain and Tibet as are provided for by the Convention of September 7, 1904, between Great Britain and Tibet and the Convention of April 27, 1906, between Great Britain and China.

Article 6

Article III of the Convention of April 27, 1906, between Great Britain and China is hereby cancelled, and it is understood that in Article IX(d) of the Convention of September 7, 1904, between Great Britain and Tibet the term "Foreign Power" does not include China.

Not less favourable treatment shall be accorded to British commerce than to the commerce of China or the most favoured nation.

Article 7

(a) The Tibet Trade Regulations of 1893 and 1908 are hereby cancelled.

(b) The Tibetan Government engages to negotiate with the British Government new Trade Regulations for Outer Tibet to give effect to Articles II, IV and V of the Convention of September

7, 1904, between Great Britain and Tibet without delay; provided always that such Regulations shall in no way modify the present Convention except with the consent of the Chinese Government.

Article 8

The British Agent who resides at Gyantse may visit Lhasa with his escort whenever it is necessary to consult with the Tibetan Government regarding matters arising out of the Convention of September 7, 1904, between Great Britain and Tibet, which it has been found impossible to settle at Gyantse by correspondence or otherwise.

Article 9

For the purpose of the present Convention the borders of Tibet, and the boundary between Outer and Inner Tibet, shall be as shown in red and blue respectively on the map attached hereto.

Nothing in the present Convention shall be held to prejudice the existing rights of the Tibetan Government in Inner Tibet, which include the power to select and appoint the high priests of monasteries and to retain full control in all matters affecting religious institutions.

Article 10

The English, Chinese and Tibetan texts of the present Convention have been carefully examined and found to correspond, but in the event of there being any difference of meaning between them the English text shall be authoritative.

Article 11

The present Convention will take effect from the date of signature.

In token whereof the respective Plenipotentiaries have signed and sealed this Convention, three copies in English, three in Chinese and three in Tibetan.

Done at Simla this third day of July A. D. , one thousand nine hundred and fourteen, corresponding with the Chinese date, the third day of the seventh month of the third year of the Republic, and the Tibetan date, the tenth day of the fifth month of the Wood Tiger year.

Initial of the Lonchen Shatra.	(Initialled) A. H. M.
Seal of the	Seal of the
Lonchen Shatra.	British Plenipotentiary

Schedule

1. Convention between Great Britain and China relating to Sikkim and Tibet, signed at Calcutta the 17th March 1890.

2. Convention between Great Britain and Tibet, signed at Lhasa the 7th September 1904.

3. Convention between Great Britain and China respecting Tibet, signed at Peking the 27th April 1906.

The notes exchanged are to the following effect -

1. It is understood by the High Contracting Parties that Tibet forms part of Chinese territory.

2. After the selection and installation of the Dalai Lama by the Tibetan Government, the latter will notify the installation to the Chinese Government whose representative at Lhasa will then formally communicate to His Holiness the titles consistent with his

dignity, which have been conferred by the Chinese Government.

3. It is also understood that the selection and appointment of all offices in Outer Tibet will rest with the Tibetan Government.

4. Outer Tibet shall not be represented in the Chinese Parliament or in any other similar body.

5. It is understood that the escorts attached to the British Trade Agencies in Tibet shall not exceed seventy-five per centum of the escort of the Chinese Representative at Lhasa.

6. The government of China is hereby released from its engagements under Article III of the Convention of March 17, 1890, between Great Britain and China to prevent acts of aggression from the Tibetan side of the Tibet-Sikkim frontier.

7. The Chinese high official referred to in Article 4 will be free to enter Tibet as soon as the terms of Article 3 have been fulfilled to the satisfaction of representatives of the three signatories to this Convention, who will investigate and report without delay.

Initial + of Lonchen Shatra.	(Initialled) A. H. M.
Seal of the	Seal of the
Lonchen Shatra.	British Plenipotentiary

DOCUMENT 11

Anglo-Tibetan Trade Regulations - 1914
(N.B. not ratified by China)

Whereas by Article 7 of the Convention concluded between the governments of Great Britain, China and Tibet on the third day of July, A. D. , 1914, the Trade Regulations of 1893 and 1908 were cancelled and the Tibetan Government engaged to negotiate with the British Government new Trade Regulations for Outer Tibet to give effect to Articles II, IV and V of the Convention of 1904;

His Majesty the King of the United Kingdom of Great Britain and Ireland, and of the British Dominions beyond the Seas, Emperor of India, and His Holiness the Dalai Lama of Tibet have for this purpose named as their Plenipotentiaries, that is to say:

His Majesty the King of Great Britain and Ireland and of the British Dominions beyond the Seas, Emperor of India, Sir A.H. McMahon, G.C.V.O., K.C.I.E., C.S.I.:

His Holiness the Dalai Lama of Tibet - Lonchen Ga-den Shatra Pal-jor Dorje;

And whereas Sir A. H. McMahon and Lonchen Ga-den Shatra Pal-jor Dorje have communicated to each other since their respective full powers and have found them to be in good and true form, the following Regulations have been agreed upon:

I. The area falling within a radius of three miles from the British Trade Agency site will be considered as the area of such Trade Mart.

It is agreed that British subjects may lease lands for the building of houses and godowns at the Marts. This arrangement shall not be held to prejudice the right of British subjects to rent houses and godowns outside the Marts for their own accommodation and the storage of their goods. British subjects desiring to lease building sites shall apply through the British Trade Agent to the Tibetan Trade Agent. In consultation with the British Trade Agent the Tibetan Trade Agent will assign such or other suitable building sites without unnecessary delay. They shall fix the terms of the leases in conformity with the existing laws and rates.

II. The administration of the Trade Marts shall remain with the Tibetan authorities, with the exception of the British Trade Agency sites and compounds of the rest-houses, which will be under the exclusive control of the British Trade Agents.

The Trade Agents at the Marts and Frontier Officers shall be of suitable rank, and shall hold personal intercourse and correspondence with one another on terms of mutual respect and friendly treatment.

III. In the event of disputes arising at the Marts or on the routes to the Marts between British subjects and subjects of other nationalities, they shall be enquired into and settled in personal conference between the British and Tibetan Trade Agents at the nearest Mart. Where there is a divergence of view the law of the country to which the defendant belongs shall guide.

All questions in regard to rights, whether of property or person, arising between British subjects, shall be subject to the jurisdiction of the British Authorities.

British subjects, who may commit any crime at the Marts or on the routes to the Marts shall be handed over by the Local Authorities to the British Trade Agent at the Mart nearest to the scene of the offence, to be tried and punished according to the laws of India, but such British subjects shall not be subjected by the Local Authorities to any ill-usage in excess of necessary restraint.

Tibetan subjects, who may be guilty of any criminal act towards British subjects, shall be arrested and punished by the Tibetan Authorities according to law.

Should it happen that a Tibetan subject or subjects bring a criminal complaint against a British subject or subjects before the British Trade Agent, the Tibetan Authorities shall have the right to send a representative or representatives of suitable rank to attend the trial in the British Trade Agent's Court. Similarly in cases in which a British subject or subjects have reason to complain against a Tibetan subject or subjects, the British Trade Agent shall have the right to send a representative or representatives to the Tibetan Trade Agent's Court to attend the trial.

IV. The government of India shall retain the right to maintain the telegraph lines from the Indian frontier to the Marts. Tibetan messages will be duly received and transmitted by these lines. The Tibetan Authorities shall be responsible for the due protection of the telegraph lines from the Marts to the Indian frontier, and it is agreed that all persons damaging the lines or interfering with them in any way or with the officials engaged in the inspection or maintenance thereof shall at once be severely punished.

V. The British Trade Agents at the various Trade Marts now or hereafter to be established in Tibet may make arrangements for the carriage and transport of their posts to and from the frontier of India. The couriers employed in conveying these posts shall receive all possible assistance from the Local Authorities, whose districts they traverse, and shall be accorded the same protection and facilities as the persons employed in carrying the despatches of the Tibetan Government.

No restrictions whatever shall be placed on the employment by British officers and traders of Tibetan subjects in any lawful capacity. The persons so employed shall not be exposed to any kind of molestation or suffer any loss of civil rights, to which they may be entitled as Tibetan subjects, but they shall not be exempted from lawful taxation. If they be guilty of any criminal act, they shall be dealt with by the Local Authorities according to law without any attempt on the part of their employer to screen them.

VI. No rights of monopoly as regards commerce or industry shall be granted to any official or private company, institution, or individual in Tibet. It is of course understood that companies and individuals; who have already received such monopolies from the Tibetan Government previous to the conclusion of this agreement, shall retain their rights and privileges until the expiry of the period fixed.

VII. British subjects shall be at liberty to deal in kind or in money, to sell their goods to whomsoever they please, to hire transport of any kind, and to conduct in general their business transactions in conformity with local usage and without any vexation, restrictions or oppressive exactions whatever. The Tibetan Authorities will not hinder the British Trade Agents or other British subjects from holding personal intercourse or correspondence with the inhabitants of the country.

It being the duty of the Police and the Local Authorities to afford efficient protection at all times to the persons and property of the British subjects at the Marts and along the routes to the Marts, Tibet engages to arrange effective Police measures at the Marts and along the routes to the Marts.

VIII. Import and export in the following Articles -

> arms, ammunition, military stores, liquors and intoxicating or narcotic drugs,

may at the option of either government be entirely prohibited, or permitted only on such conditions as either government on their own side may think fit to impose.

IX. The present Regulations shall be in force for a period of ten years reckoned from the date of signature by the two Plenipotentiaries; but, if no demand for revision be made on either side within six months after the end of the first ten years the Regulations shall remain in force for another ten years from the end of the first ten years; and so it shall be at the end of each successive ten years.

X. The English and Tibetan texts of the present Regulations have been carefully compared, but in the event of there being any difference of meaning between them the English text shall be authoritative.

XI. The present Regulations shall come into force from the date of signature.

Done at Simla this third day of July, A.D., one thousand nine hundred and fourteen, corresponding with the Tibetan date, the tenth day of the fifth month of the Wood-Tiger year.

Seal of the
Dalai Lama.

Signature of the Lochen Shatra.   A. Henry McMahon,
                                               British Plenipotentiary.

Seal of the   Seal of the
Lochen Shatra.   British Plenipotentiary.

Seal of the	Seal of the	Seal of the	Seal of the
Deprung	Sera	Gaden	National
Monastery	Monastery	Monastery	Assembly

DOCUMENT 12

Agreement for the Restoration of Peaceful Relations and the Delimitation of a Provisional Frontier Between China and Tibet
19 August, 1918

1. Whereas a state of hostilities arose last year between Chinese and Tibetans owing to an attack by Chinese troops on Tibetan troops on account of a trifling dispute near Leiwuchi and Chiamdo; and whereas the leaders on both sides are now desirous of a restoration of peaceful relations on the general basis of both sides retaining the territories they now occupy; and whereas the British Government has consented to mediate in the dispute; the following arrangement for complete cessation of hostilities has been agreed upon between the undersigned, namely, General Liu Tsanting, commanding the Chinese troops at Batang, and acting on behalf of China. The Kalon Lama, commanding the Tibetan troops on the frontier, and acting on behalf of Tibet, and Mr Eric Teichman, of His Britannic Majesty's Consular Service, acting on behalf of the British Government.

+ 2. This agreement is of a temporary nature and shall only remain in force until such time as the governments of China, Tibet, and Great Britain shall have arrived at a final and permanent tripartite settlement; but in the meantime it cannot be modified in any way except with the unanimous consent of all three contracting parties.

3. It is agreed that the provisional boundary line between Chinese and Tibetan controlled territory shall be as follows: The districts of Batang (Bean), Yenching (Tsakalo), Itun (Sanpa or Taso), Tejung (De-Rong), Litang (Lihua), Kantze, Nyarong (Chantui or Chanhua), Luho (Changku or Drango) (Traog-Go), Taofu (Taowu), Hokou (Nyachuka or Yachiang), Tachienlu (Dartsendo or Kangting), Tanpa (Romidrango) (Rong-Ming-Trag-Go), Lutingchiao (Jazamaka) (Chag-Sam-Ka), Chiulung (Jezerong) (Gya-Tso-Rong), Hsiangcheng (Tinghsiang) (Cha-Trong), and Taocheng (Taotria), and the country lying to the east of them, shall be under the control of the Chinese; no Tibetan troops or civil or milliary officials being permitted to reside therein; while the districts of

Riwoche (Leiwuchi), Enta (Ngenda), Chiamdo (Changtu), Draya (Chaya), Markam-Gartok (Chiangka or Ningching), Gonjo (Kungchueh), Sangen (Sangai or Wucheng), Tungpu (Teng-Pug), Tengko (Ten-Pug) Seshu (Shihchu), Derge (Teko), and Beyu (Paiyu), and the country lying to the west of them, shall be under the control of the Tibetans; no Chinese troops or civil or military officials being permitted to reside therein. As soon as the governments of China and Tibet shall have formally accepted this agreement, all the Tibetan troops and civil and military officials at present in Kantze and Nyarong (Chantui) districts shall be withdrawn; the Chinese civil and military authorities engaging not to oppress or in any way maltreat the natives of those parts, including the Lamas of Dargye Gomba and other monasteries, after the withdrawal of the Tibetan troops. The existing boundaries of Yunnan Province and of the Kokonor (i.e., the territory at present under the control of the Sining officials) shall remain for the present unchanged.

4. It is agreed that, apart from local constabulary necessary for the maintenance of law and order, no Tibetan troops shall be stationed to the east of the river Yangtze (Dre Chu or Chin Sha Chiang); and it is likewise agreed that, with the exception of one hundred local constabulary, the Chinese troops stationed on the south and north roads shall not cross to the West of the Yangtse and Yalung rivers respectively; both sides engaging to withdraw their troops in accordance with the above arrangements as soon as the governments of China and Tibet shall have formally accepted this agreement.

5. It is agreed that the control of all the monasteries in the above-mentioned Chinese governed districts, as well as the right of appointing high Lamas and other monastic functionaries, and the control of all matters appertaining to the Buddhist religion, shall be in the hands of the Dalai Lama; the Chinese authorities not interfering in any way therein; but the Lamas, on the other hand, shall not interfere in the territorial authority of the Chinese

officials.

6. The Chinese and Tibetan authorities on both sides of the border shall be responsible for and shall take all possible steps to prevent raids by members of their forces or by others under their respective jurisdictions across the temporary boundary line laid down in Article 3; and will render one another reciprocal assistance in the maintenance of order, suppression of brigandage, and apprehension of evil-doers. Peaceful traders and travellers, however, shall be permitted to cross the border without interference.

7. When the governments of China and Tibet shall have formally accepted this agreement, all the Chinese prisoners in the hands of Tibetans, and all the Tibetan prisoners in the hands of the Chinese, shall be released and permitted to return home if they so desire.

8. It is agreed that no Tibetans or Chinese will be punished or in any way maltreated for having adhered to or supported the Tibetan or Chinese cause in the past before the conclusion of this agreement, a general and complete amnesty in this respect coming into force immediately. The Tibetan and Chinese authorities further undertake that all Chinese in Tibetan controlled territory, and all Tibetans in Chinese controlled territory, whether lamas or laymen, agriculturalists, merchants, or others, shall be properly protected, well and fairly treated, and in no way oppressed.

9. In the event of any dispute arising between the Tibetan and Chinese authorities on the frontier after the conclusion of this agreement, there shall be no recourse to arms; but both sides agree to refer the matter in dispute to the British Consul for his arbitration. In order to enable the British Consul to carry out satisfactorily his duties of arbitrator and middleman under this agreement, the Chinese and Tibetan authorities engage to render him all possible assistance in visiting the frontier officials and travelling through the frontier districts.

10. Inasmuch as the natives of Eastern Tibet have suffered greatly of recent years from the large numbers of troops stationed

in the country, and since now that peace had been arranged under this agreement there is no longer any need for soldiers beyond those necessary for the maintenance of law and order, the Chinese and Tibetan authorities express their willingness to reduce their frontier garrisons; and in accordance with this policy it is agreed that not more than two hundred Chinese troops shall be stationed at Batang and Kantse, respectively, and that not more than two hundred Tibetan troops shall be stationed at Chiamdo and Gartok (Chiangka) respectively; but the authorities on either side shall be at liberty to take what military action they please in case of disturbances of the peace in their respective territories.

11. It is agreed that no Chinese troops shall be stationed in the districts known as Hsiangcheng (Tinghsiang) [Cha-Treng] and Nyarong (Chantui or Chanhua) so long as the natives of those regions remain peacefully within their own borders and abstain from raiding other parts, but in the event of their causing trouble the Tibetan authorities shall not interfere with any action the Chinese authorities may take.

12. When the governments of China and Tibet shall have formally accepted this agreement, its provisions shall be widely made known by proclamations in Tibetan and Chinese throughout the districts on both sides of the frontier with a view to pacifying the minds of the inhabitants of the border after the recent years of fighting and unrest.

13. Eighteen copies of this agreement having been drawn up and signed, six in Chinese, six in Tibetan, and six in English, each of the three signatories shall retain two Chinese, two Tibetan, and two English copies. As the British representative has acted as mediator in the matter the English text shall, in the event of disputes arising, be considered authoritative. Each signatory engages to report the provisions of this agreement to his government with the least possible delay for their approval. Both Chinese and Tibetan authorities engage not to move troops or open hostilities pending the receipt of the decisions of the three

governments.

Signed and sealed at Chiamdo, this Nineteenth Day of August, Nineteen Hundred and Eighteen.

Liu Tsan-Ting   *Eric Teichman*   *Chamba Denda*
   The Kalon Lama

DOCUMENT 13

Supplementary Agreement Regarding Mutual Withdrawal of Troops and Cessation of Hostilities Between Chinese and Tibetans

10 October 1918

Translation from Chinese and Tibetan texts

1. The Chinese and Tibetan leaders are equally desirous of peace. The Chinese troops will withdraw to Kantze. The Tibetan troops will withdraw to within the boundary of Dirge district. Both Chinese and Tibetans undertake not to advance their forces along either the Northern or Southern Roads and to cease all hostilities for a year from the date of the mutual withdrawal of troops pending the receipt of the decisions of the President of the Republic and the Dalai Lama regarding the Chiamdo negotiations.

2. This agreement only concerns the mutual withdrawal of troops and cessation of hostilities, and is not a definite settlement of the questions at issue.

3. The mutual withdrawal of troops to commence on October 17 (12th day of 9th Moon) and to be completed by October 31 (26th day of 9th Moon).

4. This agreement is concluded between Han Kuang-chun and the Chala Chief, special representatives of the Szechaun Frontier Commissioner, on the one hand, and the Kenchung Lama and Chungrang and Drentong Dapons, representing the Kalon Lama of Tibet, on the other, and is witnessed by Mr. Eric Teichman, British Vice-Consul, as middleman. The signatories engage to report the matter to their respective governments as soon as possible.

Signed and sealed by the Chinese, Tibetan, and British Representatives, at Rangbasta, October the 10th, 1918.

Additional Article

The Chinese troops shall withdraw to Kantze, but they shall be at liberty to occupy the strategic point of Beri - beyond which point, however, they must not advance during the cessation of hostilities.

(Signed by the three parties)

DOCUMENT 14

Agreement on Measures for the Peaceful Liberation of Tibet
(17-point Agreement of May 23, 1951)
(N.B.Repudiated by His Holiness, the Dalai Lama 20 June 1959)

The Tibetan nationality is one of the nationalities with a long history within the boundaries of China and, like many other nationalities, it has done its glorious duty in the course of the creation and development of the great Motherland. But, over the last 100 years or more, imperialist forces penetrated into China and in consequence also penetrated into the Tibetan region and carried out all kinds of deceptions and provocations. Like previous reactionary governments, the Kuomintang reactionary government continued to carry out a policy of oppression and sowing dissension among the nationalities, causing division and disunity among the Tibetan people. The local government of Tibet did not oppose the imperialist deception and provocation and adopted an unpatriotic attitude towards the great Motherland. Under such conditions the Tibetan nationality and people were plunged into the depths of enslavement and sufferings. In 1949 basic victory was achieved on a nation-wide scale in the Chinese people's war of liberation; the common domestic enemy of all nationalities - the Kuomingtang reactionary government - was overthrown and the common foreign enemy of all nationalities - the aggressive imperialist forces - was given out. On this basis the founding of the People's Republic of China (CPR) and of the CPG was announced.

In accordance with the Common Programme passed by the Chinese People's Political Consultative Conference (CPPCC), the CPG declared that all nationalities within the boundaries of the CPR are equal and that they shall establish unity and mutual aid and oppose imperialism and their own public enemies, so that the CPR will become a big family of fraternity and co-operation, composed of all its nationalities. Whithin the big family of all nationalities of the CPR, national regional autonomy shall be exercised in areas where national minorities are concentrated and all national minorities shall have freedom to develop their spoken and written languages and to preserve or reform their customs, habits and religious beliefs, and the CPG shall assist all national minorities to develop their political, economic, cultural, and educational construction work. Since then, all nationalities within the country - with the exception of those in the areas of Tibet and Taiwan - have gained liberation. Under the unified leadership of the CPG and the direct leadership of higher levels of people's governments, all national minorities have fully enjoyed the right of national equality and have exercised, or are exercising, national regional autonomy.

In order that the influences of aggressive imperialist forces in Tibet might be successfully eliminated, the unification of the territory and sovereignty of the CPR accomplished, and national defence safeguarded; in order that the Tibetan nationality and people might be freed and return to the big family of the CPR to enjoy the same rights of national equality as all other nationalities in the country and develop their political, economic, cultural and educational work, the CPG, when it ordered the People's Liberation Army (PLA) to march into Tibet, notified the local government of Tibet to send delegates to the central authorities to conduct talks for the conclusion of an agreement on measures for the peaceful liberation of Tibet. At the latter part of April 1951 the delegates with full powers of the local government of Tibet arrived in Peking. The CPG appointed representatives with full powers to conduct talks on a friendly basis with the delegates with full powers of the local government of Tibet. As a result of the talks both parties agreed to establish this agreement and ensure that it be carried into effect.

(1) The Tibetan people shall unite and drive out imperialist aggressive forces from Tibet; the Tibetan people shall return to the big family of the Motherland - the People's Republic of China.

(2) The local government of Tibet shall actively assist the PLA to enter the Tibet and consolidate the national defences.

(3) In accordance with the policy towards nationalities laid down in the Common Programme of the CPPCC, the Tibetan people have the right of exercising national regional autonomy under the unified leadership of the CPG.

(4) The central authorities will not alter the existing political system in Tibet. The central authorities also will not alter the established status, functions and powers of the Dalai Lama. Officials of various ranks shall hold office as usual.

(5) The established status, functions and powers of the Panchen Ngoerhtehni (Lama) shall be maintained.

(6) By the established status, functions and powers of the Dalai Lama and of the Panchen Ngoerhtehni are meant the status, functions and powers of the thirteenth Dalai Lama and of the ninth Panchen Ngoerhtehni when they were in friendly and amicable relations with each other.

(7) The policy of freedom of religious belief laid down in the Common Programme of the CPPCC shall be carried out. The religious beliefs, customs and habits of the Tibetan people shall be respected and lama monasteries shall be protected. The central authorities will not effect a change in the income of the monasteries.

(8) Tibetan troops shall be reorganized step by step into the PLA and become a part of the national defence forces of the CPR.

(9) The spoken and written language and school education of the Tibetan nationality shall be developed step by step in accordance with the actual condition of Tibet.

(10) Tibetan agriculture, livestock-raising, industry and commerce shall be developed step by step and the people's livelihood shall be improved step by step in accordance with the actual condition in Tibet.

(11) In matters related to various reforms in Tibet, there will be no compulsion on the part of the central authorities. The local government of Tibet should carry out reforms of its own accord, and, when the people raise demands for reform, they shall be

settled by means of consultation with the leading personnel of Tibet.

(12) In so far as former pro-imperialist and pro-Kuomintang officials resolutely sever relations with imperialism and the Kuomintang and do not engage in sabotage or resistance, they may continue to hold office irrespective of their past.

(13) The PLA entering Tibet shall abide by all the above mentioned policies and shall also be fair in all buying and selling and shall not arbitrarily take a needle or thread from the people.

(14) The CPG shall have centralized handling of all external affairs of the area of Tibet; and there will be peaceful co-existence with neighbouring countries and establishment and development of fair commercial and trading relations with them on the basis of equality, mutual benefit and mutual respect for territory and sovereignty.

(15) In order to ensure the implementation of this agreement, the CPG shall set up a Military and Administrative Committee and a Military Area HQ in Tibet and - apart from the personnel sent there by the CPG - shall absorb as many local Tibetan personnel as possible to take part in the work. Local Tibetan personnel taking part in the Military and Administrative Committee may include patriotic elements from the local government of Tibet, various districts and various principal monasteries; the name-list shall be set forth after consultation between the representatives designated by the CPG and various quarters concerned and shall be submitted to the CPG for appointment.

(16) Funds needed by the Military and Administrative Committee, the Military Area HQ and the PLA entering Tibet shall be provided by the CPG. The local government of Tibet should assist the PLA in the purchase and transport of food, fodder and other daily necessities.

(17) This agreement shall come into force immediately after signatures and seals are affixed to it.

Signed and sealed by delegates of the CPG with full powers: Chief Delegate - Li Wei-Han (Chairman of the Commission of Nationalities Affairs); Delegates - Chang Ching-wu, Chang Kuo-hua, Sun Chih-yuan. Delegates with full powers of the local government of Tibet: Chief Delegate - Kaloon Ngabou Ngawang Jigme (Ngabo Shape); Delegates - Dizasak Khemey Sonam Wangdi, Khentrung Thupten Tenthar, Khenchung Thupten Lekmuun, Rimshi Samposey Tenzin Thundup.

Beijing, 23rd May, 1951

DOCUMENT 15

Constitution of the People's Republic of China

(Adopted on December 4, 1982 by the Fifth National People's Congress of the People's Republic of China at its Fifth Session - Amendments, 12 April 1988, 29 March 1993 and 15 March 1999 in italics)

Table of Contents

Preamble

Chapter One:	General Principles
Chapter Two:	The Fundamental Rights and Duties of Citizens
Chapter Three:	The Structure of the State
Section I:	The National People's Congress
Section II:	The President of the People's Republic of China
Section III:	The State Council
Section IV:	The Central Military Commission
Section V:	The Local People's Congresses and the Local People's Governments at different Levels
Section VI:	The Organs of Self-Government of National Autonomous Areas
Section VII:	The People's Courts and the People's Procuratorates
Chapter Four:	The National Flag, the National Emblem and the Capital

Constitution of the People's Republic of China

Preamble

China is one of the countries with the longest histories in the world. The people of all nationalities in China have jointly created a splendid culture and have a glorious revolutionary tradition.

Feudal China was gradually reduced after 1840 to a semi-colonial and semi-feudal country. The Chinese people waged wave upon wave of heroic struggles for national independence and liberation and for democracy and freedom.

Great and earth-shaking historical changes have taken place in China in the 20th century.

The Revolution of 1911, led by Dr Sun Yat-sen, abolished the feudal monarchy and gave birth to the Republic of China. But the Chinese people had yet to fulfill their historical task of overthrowing imperialism and feudalism.

After waging hard, protracted and tortuous struggles, armed and otherwise, the Chinese people of all nationalities led by the Communist Party of China with Chairman Mao Zedong as its leader ultimately in 1949, overthrew the rule of imperialism, feudalism and bureaucrat-capitalism, won the great victory of the new-democratic revolution and founded the People's Republic of China. Thereupon the Chinese people took state power into their own hands and became masters of the country.

After the founding of the People's Republic, the transition of Chinese society from a new-democratic to a socialist society was effected step by step. The socialist transformation of the private ownership of the means of production was completed, the system of exploitation of man by man eliminated and the socialist system established. The people's democratic dictatorship led by the working class and based on the alliance of workers and peasants, which is in essence the dictatorship of the proletariat, has been consolidated and developed. The Chinese people and the Chinese People's Liberation Army have thwarted aggression, sabotage and armed provocations by imperialists and hegemonists, safeguarded China's national independence and security and strengthened its national defence. Major successes have been achieved in economic development. An independent and fairly comprehensive socialist system of industry has in the main been established. There has been a marked increase in agricultural production. Significant progress has been made in education, scientific, cultural and other undertakings, and socialist ideological education has yielded noteworthy results. The living standards of the people have improved considerably.

Both the victory of China's new democratic revolution and the successes of its socialist cause have been achieved by the Chinese people of all nationalities under the leadership of the Communist Party of China and the guidance of Marxism -Leninism and Mao Zedong Thought, and by upholding truth, correcting errors and overcoming numerous difficulties and hardships. *Our country will remain in the initial stage for a long time to come. The basic task of the nation is to concentrate its efforts on socialist modernisation along the road of building socialism with Chinese characteristics. Under the leadership of the CPC and the guidance of Marxism-Leninism-Mao Zedong Thought, Deng Xiaoping Thought, Chinese people of all nationalities will continue to adhere to the people's democratic dictatorship and follow the socialist road, persist in reform and opening up, steadily improving socialist institutions, develop socialist market economy develop the socialist legal system and work hard and self-reliantly to modernize industry, agriculture, national defence, and science and technology step by step to turn China into a prosperous, strong, democratic and culturally advanced socialist country.*

The exploiting classes as such have been eliminated in our country. However, class struggle will continue to exist within certain limits for a long time to come. The Chinese people must fight against those forces and elements, both at home and abroad, that are hostile to China's socialist system and try to undermine it.

Taiwan is part of the sacred territory of the People's Republic of China. It is the lofty duty of the entire Chinese people, including our compatriots in Taiwan, to accomplish the great task of reunifying the motherland.

In building socialism it is imperative to rely on the workers, peasant and intellectuals and unite with all the force that can be united. In the long years of revolution and construction, there has been formed under the leadership of the Communist Party of China a broad patriotic united front that is composed of democratic parties and people's organizations and embraces all socialist working people, all patriots who support socialism and all patriots who stand for reunification of the motherland. This united front will continue to be consolidated and developed. The Chinese People's Political Consultative Conference is a broadly representative organization of the united front, which has played a significant historical role and will continue to do so in the political and social life of the country, in promoting friendship with the people of other countries and in the struggle for socialist modernisation and for the reunification and unity of the country.

The system of multiparty cooperation and political consultation led by the CCP will exist and develop in China for a long time to come.

The People's Republic of China is a unitary multi-national state built up jointly by the people of all its nationalities. Socialist relations of equality, unity and mutual assistance have been established among them and will continue to be strengthened. In the struggle to safeguard the unity of the nationalities, it is necessary to combat big-national chauvinism, mainly Han chauvinism, and also necessary to combat local-national chauvinism. The state does its utmost to promote the common prosperity of all nationalities in the country.

China's achievements in revolution and construction are inseparable from support by the people of the world. The future of China is closely linked with that of the whole world. China adheres to an independent foreign policy as well as to the five principles of mutual respect for sovereignty and territorial integrity, mutual non-aggression, non-interference in each other's internal affairs, equality and mutual benefit, and peaceful coexistence in developing diplomatic relations and economic and cultural exchanges with other countries. China consistently opposes imperialism, hegemonism and colonialism, works to strengthen unity with the people of other countries, supports the oppressed nations and the developing countries in their just struggle to win and preserve national independence and develop their national economies, and strives to safeguard world peace and promote the cause of human progress.

This constitution affirms the achievements of the struggles of the Chinese people of all nationalities and defines the basic system and basic tasks of the state in legal form; it is the fundamental law of the state and has supreme legal authority. The people of all nationalities; all state organs, the armed forces, all political parties and public organizations and all enterprises and institutions in the country must take the Constitution as the basic standard of conduct, and they have the duty to uphold the dignity of the Constitution and ensure its implementation.

Chapter 1

General Principles

Article 1. The People's Republic of China is a socialist state under the people's democratic dictatorship led by the working class and based on the alliance of workers and peasants.

The socialist system is the basic system of the People's Republic of China. Sabotage of the socialist system by any organization or individual is prohibited.

Article 2. All power in the People's Republic of China belongs to the people.

The organs through which the people exercise state power are the National People's Congress and the local people's congresses at different levels.

The people administer state affairs and manage economic,

cultural and social affairs through various channels and in various ways in accordance with the law.

Article 3. The state organs of the People's Republic of China apply the principle of democratic centralism.

The National People's Congress and the local people's congresses at different levels are instituted through democratic election. They are responsible to the people and subject to their supervision.

All administrative, judicial and procuratorial organs of the state are created by the people's congresses to which they are responsible and under whose supervision they operate.

The division of functions and powers between the central and local state organs is guided by the principle of giving full play to the initiative and enthusiasms of the local authorities under the unified leadership of the central authorities.

Article 4. All nationalists in the People's Republic of China are equal. The state protects the lawful rights and interests of the minority nationalities and upholds and develops the relationship of equality, unity and mutual assistance among all of China's nationalities. Discrimination against and oppression of any nationality are prohibited, any acts that undermine the unity of the nationalities or instigate their secession are prohibited.

The state helps the areas inhabited by minority nationalities speed up their economic and cultural development in accordance with the peculiarities and needs of the different minority nationalities.

Regional autonomy is practised in areas where people of minority nationalities live in compact communities; in these areas organs of self-government are established for the exercise of the right of autonomy. All the national autonomous areas are inalienable parts of the People's Republic of China.

The people of all nationalities have the freedom to use and develop their own spoken and written languages, and to preserve or reform their own ways and customs.

Article 5. *The People's Republic of China shall be governed according to law and shall be built into a socialist country based on the rule of law.*

The state upholds the uniformity and dignity of the socialist legal systems.

No law or administrative or local rules and regulations shall contravene the Constitution.

All state organs, the armed forces, all political parties and public organizations and all enterprises and undertakings must abide by the Constitution and the law. All acts in violation of the Constitution and the law must be looked into.

No organization or individual may enjoy the privilege of being above the Constitution and the law.

Article 6. The basis of the socialist economic system of the People's Republic of China is socialist public ownership of the means of production, namely, ownership by the whole people and collective ownership by the working people.

The system of socialist public ownership supersedes the system of exploitation of man by man; it applies the principle of "from each according to his ability,to each according to his work."

In the initial stage of socialism, the country shall uphold the basic economic system in which the public ownership is dominant and diverse forms of ownership develop side by side, and it shall uphold the distribution system with distribution according to work remaining dominant and a variety of modes of distribution coexisting.

Article 7. The state *owned* economy *namely* the socialist economy under ownership by the whole people; it is the leading force in the national economy. The state ensures the consolidation and growth of the state *owned* economy.

Article 8. *The rural collective economic organizations shall implement a two-tier operations system that combines unified operations with independent operations on the basis of household contract operations and different cooperative economic forms in the rural areas - the producers, supply and marketing, credit, and consumers' cooperatives - are part of the socialist economy collectively owned by the working people. Working people who are all members of rural economic collectives have the right, within the limits prescribed by law, to farm plots of cropland and hilly land allotted for their private use, engage in household sideline production and raise privately owned livestock.*

The various forms of co-operative economy in the cities and towns, such a those in the handicraft, industrial, building, transport, commercial and service traders, all belong to the sector of socialist economy under collective ownership by the working people.

The state protects the lawful rights and interests of the urban and rural economic collectives and encourages, guides and helps the *growth* of the collective economy.

Article 9. Mineral resources, waters, forests, mountains, grassland, unreclaimed land, beaches and other natural resources are owned by the state, that is, by the whole people, with the exception of the forests, mountains, grassland, unreclaimed land and beaches that are owned by collectives in accordance with the law.

The state ensures the rational use of natural resources and protects rare animals and plants. The appropriation or damage of natural resources by any organization or individual by whatever means is prohibited.

Article 10. Land in the cities is owned by the state.

Land in the rural and suburban areas is owned by collectives except for those portions which belong to the state in accordance with the law; house sites and privately farmed plots of cropland *and hilly land* are also owned by collectives.

The state may in the public interest take over land for its use in accordance with the law.

No organization or individual may appropriate, buy, sell, lease or otherwise engage in the transfer of land by unlawful means. The right to the use of land may be transferred according to the law.

All organizations and individuals who use land must make rational use of the land.

Article 11. *The non-public sector of the economy comprising the individual and private sectors, operating within the limits prescribed by law is an important component of the socialist market economy.*

The state protects the lawful rights and interests of the non-public sector comprising the individual and private sectors. The state exercises guidance, supervision, and control over the individual and private sector of the economy.

Article 12. Socialist public property is sacred and inviolable.

The state protects socialist public property. Appropriation or damage of state or collective property by any organization or individual by whatever means is prohibited.

Article 13. The state protects the right of citizens to own lawfully earned income, savings, houses and other lawful property.

The state protects by law the right of citizens to inherit private property.

Article 14. The state continuously raises labour productivity, improves economic results and develops the productive forces by enhancing the enthusiasm of the working people, raising the level of their technical skill, disseminating advanced science and technology, improving the systems of economic administration and enterprise operation and management, instituting the socialist system of responsibility in various forms and improving organization of work.

The state practices strict economy and combats waste.

The state properly apportions accumulation and consumption, pays attention to the interests of the collective and the individual as well as of the state and, on the basis of expanded production, gradually improves the material and cultural life of the people.

Article 15. The state practices *a socialist market economy*. It ensures the proportionate and co-ordinated growth of the national economy through overall balancing by economic planning and the supplementary role of regulation by the market.
Disturbance of the orderly functioning of the social economy or disruption of the state economic plan by any organization or individual is prohibited.
The state strengthens economic legislation and perfects macro control The state prohibits, according to law, disturbance of society's economic order by any organization or individual.

Article 16. State enterprises have decision-making power in operation and management within the limits prescribed by law.
State-*owned* enterprises practise democratic management through congresses of workers and staff and in other ways in accordance with the law.

Article 17. Collective economic organizations have decision-making power in conducting economic activities, on condition that they abide by the relevant laws.
Collective economic organizations practise democratic management *elect and remove* managerial personnel and *decide* on major issues *in accordance with the law.*

Article 18. The People's Republic of China permits foreign enterprises, other foreign economic organizations and individual foreigners to invest in China and to enter into various forms of economic co-operation with Chinese enterprises and other economic organizations in accordance with the law of the People's

Republic of China.

All foreign enterprises and other foreign economic organizations in China, as well as joint ventures with Chinese and foreign investment located in China, shall abide by the law of the People's Republic of China. Their lawful rights and interests are protected by the law of the People's Republic of China.

Article 19. The state develops socialist educational undertakings and works to raise the scientific and cultural level of the whole nation.

The state runs schools of various types, makes primary education compulsory and universal, develops secondary, vocational and higher education and promotes pre-school education.

The state develops educational facilities of various types in order to wipe out illiteracy and provide political, cultural, scientific, technical and professional education for workers, peasants, state functionaries and other working people. It encourages people to become educated through independent study.

The state encourages the collective economic organizations, state enterprises and undertakings and other social forces to set up educational institutions of various types in accordance with the law.

The state promotes the nationwide use of **Putonghua** (Common Speech based on Beijing pronunciation).

Article 20. The state promotes the development of the natural and social sciences, disseminates scientific and technical knowledge, and commends and rewards achievements in scientific research as well as technological discoveries and inventions.

Article 21. The state develops medical and health services, promotes modern medicine and traditional Chinese medicine, encourages and supports the setting-up of various medical and health facilities by the rural economic collectives, state enterprises and undertakings and neighbourhood organizations, and promotes public health activities of a mass character, all to protect the people's health.

The state develops physical culture and promotes mass sports activities to build up the people's physique.

Article 22. The state promotes the development of literature and art, the press, broadcasting and television undertakings, publishing and distribution services, libraries, museums, cultural centres and other cultural undertakings, that serve the people and socialism, and sponsors mass cultural activities.

The state protects places of scenic and historical interest, valuable cultural monuments and treasures and other important items of China's historical and cultural heritage.

Article 23. The state trains specialized personnel in all fields who serve socialism, increases the number of intellectuals and creates conditions to give full scope to their role in socialist modernization.

Article 24. The state strengthens the building of socialist spiritual civilization through spreading education in high ideals and morality, general education and education in discipline and the legal system, and through promoting the formulation and observance of rules of conduct and common pledges by different sections of the people in urban and rural areas.

The state advocates the civic virtues of love of the motherland, of the people, of labour, of science and of socialism; it educates the people in patriotism, collectivism, internationalism and communism and in dialectical and historical materialism; it combats capitalist, feudal and other decadent ideas.

Article 25. The state promotes family planning so that population growth may fit the plan for economic and social development.

Article 26. The state protects and improves the living environment and the ecological environment, and prevents and remedies pollution and other public hazards.

The state organizes and encourages afforestation and the protection of forests.

Article 27. All state organs carry out the principle of simple and efficient administration, the system of responsibility for work and the system of training functionaries and appraising their work in order constantly to improve quality of work and efficiency and combat bureaucratism.

All state organs and functionaries must rely on the support of the people, keep in close touch with them, heed their opinions and suggestions, accept their supervision and work hard to serve them.

Article 28. The state maintains public order and suppresses treasonable and other *criminal activities that endanger national security*; it penalizes activities that endanger public security and disrupt the socialist economy *as well as* other criminal activities; and *it* punishes and reforms criminals.

Article 29. The armed forces of the People's Republic of China belong to the people. Their tasks are to strengthen national defence, resist aggression, defend the motherland, safeguard the people's peaceful labour, participate in national reconstruction, and work hard to serve the people.

The state strengthens the revolutionization, modernization and regularization of the armed forces in order to increase the national defence capability.

Article 30. The administrative division of the People's Republic of China is as follows:

(1) The country is divided into provinces, autonomous regions

and municipalities directly under the central government;
(2) Provinces and autonomous regions are divided into autonomous prefectures, counties, autonomous counties and cities;
(3) Counties and autonomous counties are divided into townships, nationality townships and towns.

Municipalities directly under the central government and other large cities are divided into districts and counties. Autonomous prefectures are divided into counties, autonomous counties, and cities.

All autonomous regions, autonomous prefectures and autonomous counties are national autonomous areas.

Article 31. The state may establish special administrative regions when necessary. The systems to be instituted in special administrative regions shall be prescribed by law enacted by the National People's Congress in the light of the specific conditions.

Article 32. The People's Republic of China protects the lawful rights and interests of foreigners within Chinese territory, and while on Chinese territory foreigners must abide by the law of the People's Republic of China.

The People's Republic of China may grant asylum to foreigners who request it for political reasons.

Chapter II

The Fundamental Rights and Duties of Citizens

Article 33. All persons holding the nationality of the People's Republic of China are citizens of the People's Republic of China.

All citizens of the People's Republic of China are equal before the law.

Every citizen enjoys the rights and at the same time must perform the duties prescribed by the Constitution and the law.

Article 34. All citizens of the People's Republic of China who have reached the age of 18 have the right to vote and stand for election, regardless of nationality, race, sex, occupation, family background, religious belief, education, property status, or length of residence, except persons deprived of political rights according to law.

Article 35. Citizen of the People's Republic of China enjoy freedom of speech, of the press, of assembly, of association, of procession and of demonstration.

Article 36. Citizens of the People's Republic of China enjoy freedom of religious belief.

No state organ, public organization or individual may compel citizens to believe in, or not to believe in, any religion; nor may they discriminate against citizens who believe in, or do not believe in, any religion.

The state protects normal religious activities. No one may make use of religion to engage in activities that disrupt public order, impair the health of citizens or interfere with the educational system of the state.

Religious bodies and religious affairs are not subject to any foreign domination.

Article 37. The freedom of person of citizens of the People's Republic of China is inviolable.

No citizen may be arrested except with the approval or by decision of a people's procuratorate or by decision of a people's court, and arrests must be made by a public security organ.

Unlawful deprivation or restriction of citizens' freedom of person by detention or other means is prohibited; and unlawful search of the person of citizens is prohibited.

Article 38. The personal dignity of citizens of the People's Republic of China is inviolable. Insult, libel, false charge or frame-up directed against citizens by any means is prohibited.

Article 39. The home of citizens of the People's Republic of China is inviolable, Unlawful search of, or intrusion into, a citizen's home is prohibited.

Article 40. The freedom and privacy of correspondence of citizens of the People's Republic of China are protected by law. No organization or individual may, on any ground, infringe upon the freedom and privacy of citizens' correspondence except in cases where, to meet the needs of state security or of investigation into criminal offences, public security or procuratorial organs are permitted to censor correspondence in accordance with procedures prescribed by law.

Article 41. Citizens of the People's Republic of China have the right to criticize and make suggestions to any state organ or functionary. Citizens have the right to make to relevant state organs complaints and charges against, or exposures of, any state organ or functionary for violation of the law or dereliction of duty; but fabrication or distortion of facts for the purpose of libel or frame-up is prohibited.

The state organ concerned must deal with complaints, charges or exposures made by citizens in a responsible manner after ascertaining the facts. No one may suppress such complaints, charges and exposures, or retaliate against the citizens making them.

Citizens who have suffered losses through infringement of their civic rights by any state organ or functionary have the right to compensation in accordance with the law.

Article 42. Citizens of the People's Republic of China have the right as well as the duty to work.

Using various channels, the state creates conditions for employment, strengthens labour protection, improves working conditions and, on the basis of expanded production, increases remuneration for work and social benefits.

Work is the glorious duty of every able-bodied citizen. All working people in state-*owned* enterprises and in urban and rural economic collectives should perform their tasks with an attitude consonant with their status as masters of the country. The state promotes socialist labour emulation, and commends and rewards model and advanced workers. The state encourages citizens to take part in voluntary labour.

The state provides necessary vocational training to citizens before they are employed.

Article 43. Working people in the People's Republic of China have the right to rest.

The state expands facilities for rest and recuperation of working people, and prescribes working hours and vacations for workers and staff.

Article 44. The state prescribes by law the system of retirement for workers and staff in enterprises and undertakings and for functionaries of organs of state. The livelihood of retired personnel is ensured by the state and society.

Article 45. Citizens of the People's Republic of China have the right to material assistance from the state and society when they are old, ill or disabled. The state develops the social insurance, social relief and medical and health services that are required to enable citizens to enjoy this right.

The state and society ensure the livelihood of disabled members of the armed forces, provide pensions to the families of martyrs and give preferential treatment to the families of military personnel.

The state and society help make arrangements for the work, livelihood and education of the blind, deaf-mutes and other handicapped citizens.

Article 46. Citizens of the People's Republic of China have the duty as well as the right to receive education.

The state promotes the all-round moral, intellectual and physical development of children and young people.

Article 47. Citizens of the People's Republic of China have the freedom to engage in scientific research, literary and artistic creation and other cultural pursuits. The state encourages and assists creative endeavours conducive to the interests of the people that are made by citizens engaged in education, science, technology, literature, art and other cultural work.

Article 48. Women in the People's Republic of China enjoy equal rights with men in all spheres of life, political, economic, cultural and social, including family life.

The state protects the rights and interests of women, applies the principle of equal pay for equal work for men and women alike and trains and selects cadres from among women.

Article 49. Marriage, the family and mother and child are protected by the state.

Both husband and wife have the duty to practise family planning.

Parents have the duty to rear and educate their minor children, and children who have come of age have the duty to support and assist their parents.

Violation of the freedom of marriage is prohibited. Maltreatment of old people, women and children is prohibited.

Article 50. The People's Republic of China protects the legitimate rights and interests of Chinese nationals residing abroad and protects the lawful rights and interests of returned overseas Chinese and of the family members of Chinese nationals residing abroad.

Article 51. The exercise by citizens of the People's Republic of China of their freedoms and rights may not infringe upon the interests of the state, of society and of the collective, or upon the lawful freedoms and rights of other citizens.

Article 52. It is the duty of citizens of the people's Republic of China to safeguard the unity of the country and the unity of all its nationalities.

Article 53. Citizens of the People's Republic of China must abide by the Constitution and the law, keep state secrets, protect public property and observe labour discipline and public order and respect social ethics.

Article 54. It is the duty of citizens of the People's Republic of China to safeguard the security, honour and interests of the motherland; they must not commit acts detrimental to the security, honour and interests of the motherland.

Article 55. It is the sacred obligation of every citizen of the People's

Republic of China to defend the motherland and resist aggression.

It is the honourable duty of citizens of the People's Republic of China to perform military service and join the militia in accordance with the law.

Article 56. It is the duty of citizens of the People's Republic of China to pay taxes in accordance with the law.

Chapter III

The Structure of the State

Section I The National People's Congress

Article 57. The National People's Congress of the People's Republic of China is the highest organ of state power. Its permanent body is the Standing Committee of the National People's Congress.

Article 58. The National People's Congress and its Standing Committee exercise the legislative power of the state.

Article 59. The National People's Congress is composed of deputies elected by the provinces, autonomous regions and municipalities directly under the central government, and by the armed forces. All the minority nationalities are entitled to appropriate representation.

Election of deputies to the National People's Congress is conducted by the Standing Committee of the National People's Congress.

The number of deputies to the National People's Congress and the manner of their election are prescribed by law.

Article 60. The National People's Congress is elected for a term of five years.

Two months before the expiration of the term of office of a National People's Congress, its Standing Committee must ensure that the election of deputies to the succeeding National People's Congress is completed. Should exceptional circumstances prevent such an election, it may be postponed by decision of a majority vote of more than two-thirds of all those on the Standing Committee of the current National People's Congress, and the term of office of the current National People's Congress may be extended. The election of deputies to the succeeding National People's Congress must be completed within one year after the termination of such exceptional circumstances.

Article 61. The National People's Congress meets in session once a year and is convened by its Standing Committee. A session of the National People's Congress may be convened at any time the Standing Committee deems this necessary, or when more than one-fifth of the deputies to the National People's Congress so propose.

When the National People's Congress meets, it elects a presidium to conduct its session.

Article 62. The National People's Congress exercises the following functions and powers:

(1) to amend the Constitution;
(2) to supervise the enforcement of the Constitution;
(3) to enact and amend basic statutes concerning criminal offences, civil affairs, the state organs and other matters;
(4) to elect the President and the Vice-President of the People's Republic of China;
(5) to decide on the choice of the Premier of the State Council upon nomination by the President of the People's Republic of China, and to decide on the choice of the Vice-Premiers, State Councillors, Ministers in charge of Ministries or

Commissions and the Auditor-General and the Secretary-General of the State Council upon nomination by the Premier;
(6) to elect the Chairman of the Central Military Commission and, upon nomination by the Chairman, to decide on the choice of all the others on the Central Military Commission;
(7) to elect the President of the Supreme People's Court;
(8) to elect the Procurator-General of the Supreme People's Procuratorate;
(9) to examine and approve the plan for national economic and social development and the report on its implementation;
(10) to examine and approve the state budget and the report on its implementation;
(11) to alter or annul inappropriate decisions of the Standing Committee of the National People's Congress;
(12) to approve the establishment of provinces, autonomous regions and municipalities directly under the central government;
(13) to decide on the establishment of special administrative regions and the systems to be instituted there;
(14) to decide on questions of war and peace; and
(15) to exercise such other functions and powers as the highest organ of state power should exercise.

Article 63. The National People's Congress has the power to recall or remove from office the following persons:

(1) the President and the Vice-President of the People's Republic of China;
(2) the Premier, Vice-Premiers, State Councillors, Ministers in charge of Ministries or Commissions and the Auditor-General and the Secretary-General of the State Council;
(3) the Chairman of the Central Military Commission and others on the Commission;

(4) the President of the Supreme People's Court; and
(5) the Procurator-General of the Supreme People's Procuratorate.

Article 64. Amendments to the Constitution are to be proposed by the Standing Committee of the National People's Congress or by more than one-fifth of the deputies to the National People's Congress and adopted by a majority vote of more than two-thirds of all the deputies to the congress.

Statutes and resolutions are adopted by a majority vote of more than one half of all the deputies to the National People's Congress.

Article 65. The Standing Committee of the National People's Congress is composed of the following:

the Chairman;
the Vice-Chairman;
the Secretary-General; and members.

Minority nationalities are entitled to appropriate representation on the Standing Committee of the National People's Congress.

The National People's Congress elects, and has the power to recall, all those on its Standing Committee.

No one on the Standing Committee of the National People's Congress shall hold any post in any of the administrative, judicial or procuratorial organs of the state.

Article 66. The Standing Committee of the National People's Congress is elected for the same term as the National People's Congress; it exercises its functions and powers until a new Standing Committee is elected by the succeeding National People's Congress.

The Chairman and Vice-Chairman of the Standing Committee shall serve no more than two consecutive terms.

Article 67. The Standing Committee of the National People's Congress exercises the following functions and powers:

(1) to interpret the Constitution and supervise its enforcement;
(2) to enact and emend statutes with the exception of those which should be enacted by the National People's Congress;
(3) to enact, when the National People's Congress is not in session, partial supplements and amendments to statutes enacted by the National People's Congress provided that they do not contravene the basic principles of these statutes;
(4) to interpret statues;
(5) to examine and approve, when the National People's Congress is not in session, partial adjustments to the plan for national economic and social development and to the state budget that prove necessary in the course of their implementation;
(6) to supervise the work of the State Council, the Central Military Commission, the Supreme People's Court and the Supreme People's Procuratorate;
(7) to annul those administrative rules and regulations, decisions or orders of the State Council that contravene the Constitution or the statutes;
(8) to annul those local regulations or decisions of the organs of state power of provinces, autonomous regions and municipalities directly under the central government that contravene the Constitution, the statutes or the administrative rules and regulations;
(9) to decide, when the National People's Congress is not in session, on the choice of Ministers in charge of Ministries or Commissions or the Auditor-General and the Secretary-General of the State Council upon nomination by the Premier of the State Council:
(10) to decide, upon nomination by the Chairman of the Central Military Commission, on the choice of others on the

Commission, when the National People's Congress is not in session;

(11) to appoint and remove Vice-Presidents and judges of the Supreme People's Court, members of its Judicial Committee and the President of the Military Court at the suggestion of the President of the Supreme People's Court;

(12) to appoint and remove Deputy Procurators-General and Procurators of the Supreme People's Procuratorate, members of its Procuratorial Committee and the Chief Procurator of the Military Procuratorate at the suggestion of the Procurator-General of the Supreme People's Procuratorate, and to approve the appointment and removal of the chief procurators of the people's procuratorates of provinces, autonomous regions and municipalities directly under the central government;

(13) to decide on the appointment and recall of plenipotentiary representatives abroad;

(14) to decide on the ratification and abrogation of treaties and important agreements concluded with foreign states;

(15) to institute systems of titles and ranks for military and diplomatic personnel and of other specific titles and ranks;

(16) to institute state medals and titles of honour and decide on their conferment;

(17) to decide on the granting of special pardons;

(18) to decide, when the National People's Congress is not in session, on the proclamation of a state of war in the event of an armed attack on the country or in fulfilment of international treaty obligations concerning common defence against aggression;

(19) to decide on general mobilization or partial mobilization;

(20) to decide on the enforcement of martial law throughout the country or in particular provinces, autonomous regions or municipalities directly under the central government; and

(21) to exercise such other functions and powers as the National

People's Congress may assign to it.

Article 68. The Chairman of the Standing Committee of the National People's Congress presides over the work of the Standing Committee and convenes its meetings. The Vice-Chairman and the Secretary-General assist in the work of the Chairman.

Executive meetings with the participation of the Chairman, Vice-Chairman and Secretary-General handle the important day-to-day work of the Standing Committee of the National People's Congress.

Article 69. The Standing Committee of the National People's Congress is responsible to the National People's Congress and reports on its work to the congress.

Article 70. The National People's Congress establishes a Nationalities Committee, a Law Committee, a Financial and Economic Committee, an Education, Science, Culture and Public Health Committee, a Foreign Affairs Committee, an Overseas Chinese Committee and such other special committees as are necessary. These special committees work under the direction of the Standing Committee of the National People's Congress when the congress is not in session.

The special committees examine discuss and draw up relevant bills and draft resolutions under the direction of the National People's Congress and its Standing Committee.

Article 71. The National People's Congress and its Standing Committee may, when they deem it necessary, appoint committees of inquiry into specific questions and adopt relevant resolutions in the light of their reports.

All organs of state, public organizations and citizens concerned are obliged to supply the necessary information to those committees of inquiry when they conduct investigations.

Article 72. Deputies to the National People's Congress and all those on its Standing Committee have the right, in accordance with procedures prescribed by law, to submit bills and proposals within the scope of the respective functions and powers of the National People's Congress and its Standing Committee.

Article 73. Deputies to the National People's Congress during its sessions, and all those on its Standing Committee during its meetings, have the right to address questions, in accordance with procedures prescribed by law, to the State Council or the Ministries and Commissions under the State Council, which must answer the questions in a responsible manner.

Article 74. No deputy to the National People's Congress may be arrested or placed on criminal trial without the consent of the Presidium of the current session of the National People's Congress or, when the National People's Congress is not in session, without the consent of its Standing Committee.

Article 75. Deputies to the National People's Congress may not be called to legal account for their speeches or votes at its meetings.

Article 76. Deputies to the National People's Congress must play an exemplary role in abiding by the Constitution and the law and keeping state secrets and, in production and other work and their public activities, assist in the enforcement of the Constitution and the law.
    Deputies to the National People's Congress should maintain close contact with the units which elected them and with the people, listen to and convey the opinions and demands of the people and work hard to serve them.

Article 77. Deputies to the National People's Congress are subject to the supervision of the units which elected them. The electoral units have the power, through procedures prescribed by law, to recall deputies whom they elected.

Article 78. The organization and working procedures of the National People's Congress and its Standing Committee are prescribed by law.

Section II

The President of the People's Republic of China

Article 79. The President and Vice-President of the People's Republic of China are elected by the National People's Congress.

Citizens of the People's Republic of China who have the right to vote and to stand for election and who have reached the age of 45 are eligible for election as President or Vice-President of the People's Republic of China.

The term of office of the President and Vice-President of the People's Republic of China is the same as that of the National People's Congress, and they shall serve no more than two consecutive terms.

Article 80. The President of the People's Republic of China, in pursuance of decisions of the National People's Congress and its Standing Committee, promulgates statutes; appoints and removes the Premier, Vice-Premiers, State Councillors, Ministers in charge of Ministries or Commissions, and the Auditor-General and the Secretary-General of the State Council; confers state medals and titles of honour; issues orders of special pardons; proclaims martial law; proclaims a state of war; and issues mobilization orders.

Article 81. The President of the People's Republic of China receives foreign diplomatic representatives on behalf of the People's Republic of China and, in pursuance of decision of the Standing

Committee of the National People's Congress, appoints and recalls plenipotentiary representatives abroad, and ratifies and abrogates treaties and important agreements concluded with foreign states.

Article 82. The Vice-President of the People's Republic of China assists in the work of the President.

The Vice-President of the People's Republic of China may exercise such parts of the functions and powers of the President as may be deputed by the President.

Article 83. The President and Vice-President of the People's Republic of China exercise their functions and powers until the new President and Vice-President elected by the succeeding National People's Congress assume office.

Article 84. In case the office of the President of the People's Republic of China falls vacant, the Vice-President succeeds to the office of President.

In case the office of the Vice-President of the People's Republic of China falls vacant, the National People's Congress shall elect a new Vice-President to fill the vacancy.

In the event that the offices of both the President and the Vice-President of the People's Republic of China fall vacant, the National People's Congress shall elect a new President and a new Vice-President. Prior to such election, the Chairman of the Standing Committee of the National People's Congress shall temporarily act as the President of the People's Republic of China.

Section III

The State Council

Article 85. The State Council, that is, the central people's government of the People's Republic of China is the executive body of the highest organ of state power; it is the highest organ of state administration.

Article 86. The State Council is composed of the following:

the Premier;
the Vice-Premiers;
the State Councillors;
the Ministers in charge of Ministries;
the Ministers in charge of Commissions;
the Auditor-General; and
the Secretary-General

The Premier has overall responsibility for the State Council. The Ministers have overall responsibility for the Ministries or Commissions under their charge.

The organization of the State Council is prescribed by law.

Article 87. The term of office of the State Council is the same as that of the National People's Congress.

The Premier, Vice-Premiers and State Councillors shall serve no more than two consecutive terms.

Article 88. The Premier directs the work of the State Council. The Vice-Premiers and State Councillors assist in the work of the Premier.

Executive meetings of the State Council are composed of the Premier, the Vice-Premiers, the State Councillors and the Secretary-General of the State Council.

The Premier convenes and presides over the executive meetings and plenary meetings of the State Council.

Article 89. The State Council exercises the following functions and powers:

(1) to adopt administrative measures, enact administrative rules and regulations and issue decisions and orders in accordance with the Constitution and the statutes;
(2) to submit proposals to the National People's Congress or its Standing Committee;
(3) to lay down the tasks and responsibilities of the Ministries and Commissions of the State Council, to exercise unified leadership over the work of the Ministries and Commissions and to direct all other administrative work of a national character that does not fall within the jurisdiction of the Ministries and Commissions;
(4) to exercise unified leadership over the work of local organs of state administration at different levels throughout the country, and to lay down the detailed division of functions and powers between the central government and the organs of state administration of provinces, autonomous regions and municipalities directly under the central government;
(5) to draw up and implement the plan for national economic and social development and the state budget;
(6) to direct and administer economic affairs and urban and rural development;
(7) to direct and administer affairs of education, science, culture, public health, physical culture and family planning;
(8) to direct and administer civil affairs, public security, judicial administration, supervision and other related matters;
(9) to conduct foreign affairs and conclude treaties and agreements with foreign states;
(10) to direct and administer the building of national defence;
(11) to direct and administer affairs concerning the nationalities, and to safeguard the equal rights of minority nationalities and the right of autonomy of the national autonomous areas;
(12) to protect the legitimate rights and interests of Chinese nationals residing abroad and protect the lawful rights and

interests of returned overseas Chinese and of the family members of Chinese nationals residing abroad;

(13) to alter or annul inappropriate orders, directives and regulations issued by the Ministries or Commissions;

(14) to alter or annul inappropriate decisions and orders issued by local organs of state administration at different levels;

(15) to approve the geographic division of provinces, autonomous regions and municipalities directly under the central government, and to approve the establishment and geographic division of autonomous prefectures, counties, autonomous counties and cities;

(16) to decide on the enforcement of martial law in parts of provinces, autonomous regions and municipalities directly under the central government;

(17) to examine and decide on the size of administrative organs and, in accordance with the law, to appoint, remove and train administrative officers, appraise their work and reward or punish them; and

(18) to exercise such other functions and powers as the National People's Congress or its Standing Committee may assign it.

Article 90. The Ministers in charge of Ministries or Commissions of the State Council are responsible for the work of their respective departments and convene and preside over ministerial meetings or commission meetings that discuss and decide on major issues in the work of their respective departments.

The Ministries and Commissions issue orders, directives and regulations within the jurisdiction of their respective departments and in accordance with the statutes and the administrative rules and regulations, decisions and orders issued by the State Council.

Article 91. The State Council establishes an auditing body to supervise through auditing the revenue and expenditure of all departments under the State Council and of the local governments at different levels, and those of the state financial and monetary organizations and of enterprises and undertakings.

Under the direction of the Premier of the State Council, the auditing body independently exercises its powers to supervise through auditing in accordance with the law, subject to no interference by any other administrative organ or any public organization or individual.

Article 92. The State Council is responsible, and reports on its work, to the National People's Congress or, when the National People's Congress is not in session, to its Standing Committee.

Section IV

The Central Military Commission

Article 93. The Central Military Commission of the People's Republic of China directs the armed forces of the country.

The Central Military Commission is composed of the following:

the Chairman;
the Vice-Chairmen; and
members.

The Chairman of the Central Military Commission has overall responsibility for the Commission.

The term of office of the Central Military Commission is the same as that of the National People's Congress.

Article 94. The Chairman of the Central Military Commission is responsible to the National People's Congress and its Standing Committee.

Section V

The Local People's Congresses and the Local People's Governments at Different Levels

Article 95. People's congresses and people's governments are established in provinces, municipalities directly under the central government, counties, cities, municipal districts, townships, nationality townships and towns.

The organization of local people's congresses and local people's governments at different levels is prescribed by law.

Organs of self-government are established in autonomous regions, autonomous prefectures and autonomous counties. The organization and working procedures of organs or self-government are prescribed by law in accordance with the basic principles laid down in Sections V and VI of Chapter Three of the Constitution.

Article 96. Local people's congresses at different levels are local organs of state power.

Local people's congresses at and above the country level establish Standing Committees.

Article 97. Deputies to the people's congresses of provinces, municipalities directly under the central government, and cities divided into districts are elected by the people's congresses at the next lower level; deputies to the people's congresses of counties, cities not divided into districts, municipal districts, townships, nationality townships and towns are elected directly by their constituencies.

The number of deputies to local people's congresses at different levels and the manner of their election are prescribed by law.

Article 98. The term of office of the people's congresses of provinces, municipalities directly under the central government cities *and municipal districts* is five years. The term of office of the people's congresses of townships, nationality townships and towns is three years.

Article 99. Local people's congresses at different levels ensure the observance and implementation of the Constitution, the statutes and the administrative rules and regulations in their respective administrative areas. Within the limits of their authority as prescribed by law, they adopt and issue resolutions and examine and decide on plans for local economic and cultural development and for the development of public services.

Local people's congresses at and above the county level examine and approve the plans for economic and social development and the budgets of their respective administrative areas, and examine and approve reports on their implementation. They have the power to alter or annul inappropriate decisions of their own Standing Committees.

The people's congresses of nationality townships may, within the limits of their authority as prescribed by law, take specific measures suited to the peculiarities of the nationalities concerned.

Article 100. The people's congresses of provinces and municipalities directly under the central government, and their Standing Committees, may adopt local regulations, which must not contravene the Constitution, the statutes and the administrative rules and regulations, and they shall report such local regulations to the Standing Committee of the National People's Congress for the record.

Article 101. At their respective levels, local people's congresses elect, and have the power to recall, governors and deputy governors, or mayors and deputy mayors, or heads and deputy heads of countries, districts, townships and towns.

Local people's congresses at and above the county level elect, and have the power to recall, presidents of people's courts and chief procurators of people's procuratorates at the corresponding level. The election or recall of chief procurators of people's procuratorates shall be reported to the chief procurators of the people's procuratorates at the next higher level for submission to the Standing Committees of the people's congresses at the corresponding level for approval.

Article 102. Deputies to the people's congresses of provinces, municipalities directly under the central government and cities divided into districts are subject to supervision by the units which elected them; deputies to the people's congresses of counties, cities not divided into districts, municipal districts, townships, nationality townships and towns are subject to supervision by their constituencies.

The electoral units and constituencies which elect deputies to local people's congresses at different levels have the power, according to procedures prescribed by law, to recall deputies whom they elected.

Article 103. The Standing Committee of a local people's congress at and above the county level is composed of a Chairman, Vice-Chairman and members, and is responsible, and reports on its work, to the people's congress at the corresponding level.

The local people's congress at and above the county level elects, and has the power to recall, anyone on the Standing Committee of the people's congress at the corresponding level.

No one on the Standing Committee of a local people's congress at and above the county level shall hold any post in state administrative, judicial and procuratorial organs.

Article 104. The Standing Committee of a local people's congress at and above the county level discusses and decides on major issues in all fields of work in its administrative area; supervises the work of the people's government, people's court and people's procuratorate at the corresponding levels; annuls inappropriate decisions and orders of the people's government at the corresponding level; annuls inappropriate resolutions of the people's congress at the next lower level; decides on the appointment and removal of functionaries of state organs within the limits of its authority as prescribed by law; and when the people's congress at the corresponding level is not in session, recalls individual deputies to the people's congress at the next higher level and elects individual deputies to fill vacancies in that people's congress.

Article 105. Local people's governments at different levels are the executive bodies of local organs of state power as well as the local organs of state administration at the corresponding level.
   Local people's governments at different levels practise the system of overall responsibility by governors, mayors, county heads, district heads, township heads and town heads.

Article 106. The term of office of local people's governments at different levels is the same as that of the people's congresses at the corresponding level.

Article 107. Local people's governments at and above the county level, within the limits of their authority as prescribed by law, conduct the administrative work concerning the economy, education, science, culture, public health, physical culture, urban and rural development, finance, civil affairs, public security, nationalities affairs, judicial administration, supervision and family planning in their respective administrative areas; issue decisions and orders; appoint, remove and train administrative functionaries, appraise their work and reward or punish them.
   People's governments of townships, nationality townships and

towns carry out the resolutions of the people's congress at the corresponding level as well as the decisions and orders of the state administrative organs at the next higher level and conduct administrative work in their respective administrative areas.

People's governments of provinces and municipalities directly under the central government decide on the establishment and geographic division of townships, nationality townships and towns.

Article 108. Local people's governments at and above the county level direct the work of their subordinate departments and of people's governments at lower levels, and have the power to alter or annul inappropriate decisions of their subordinate departments and people's governments at lower levels.

Article 109. Auditing bodies are established by local people's governments at and above the county level. Local auditing bodies at different levels independently exercise their power to supervise through auditing in accordance with the law and are responsible to the people's government at the corresponding level and to the auditing body at the next higher level.

Article 110. Local people's governments at different levels are responsible, and report on their work, to people's congresses at the corresponding level. Local people's governments at and above the county level are responsible, and report on their work, to the Standing Committee of the people's congress at the corresponding level when the congress is not in session.

Local people's governments at different levels are responsible, and report on their work, to the state administrative organs at the next higher level. Local people's governments at different levels throughout the country are state administrative organs under the unified leadership of the State Council and are subordinate to it.

Article 111. The residents' committees and villagers' committees establish among urban and rural residents on the basis of their place of residence are mass organizations of self-management at the grass-roots levels. The Chairman, Vice-Chairmen and members of each residents' or villagers' committee are elected by the residents. The relationship between the residents' and villagers' committees and the grass-roots organs of state power is prescribed by law.

The residents' and villagers' committees establish committees for people's mediation, public security, public health and other matters in order to manage public affairs and social services in their areas, mediate civil disputes, help maintain public order and convey residents' opinions and demands and make suggestions to the people's government.

Section VI

The Organs of Self-Government of National Autonomous Areas

Article 112. The organs of self-government of national autonomous areas are the people's congresses and people's governments of autonomous regions, autonomous prefectures and autonomous counties.

Article 113. In the people's congress of an autonomous region, prefecture or county, in addition to the deputies of the nationality or nationalities exercising regional autonomy in the administrative area, the other nationalities inhabiting the area are also entitled to appropriate representation.

The chairmanship and vice-chairmanships of the Standing Committee of the people's congress of an autonomous region, prefecture or county shall include a citizen or citizens of the nationality or nationalities exercising regional autonomy in the area concerned.

Article 114. The administrative head of an autonomous region, prefecture or county shall be a citizen of the nationality, or of one of the nationalities, exercising regional autonomy in the area concerned.

Article 115. The organs of self-government of autonomous regions, prefectures and counties exercise the functions and powers of local organs of state as specified in Section V of Chapter Three of the Constitution. At the same time, they exercise the power of autonomy within the limits of their authority as prescribed by the Constitution, the law of regional national autonomy and other laws, and implement the laws and policies of the state in the light of the existing local situation.

Article 116. People's congresses of national autonomous areas have the power to enact autonomy regulations and specific regulations in the light of the political, economic and cultural characteristics of the nationality or nationalities in the areas concerned. The autonomy regulations and specific regulations of autonomous regions shall be submitted to the Standing Committee of the National People's Congress for approval before they go into effect. Those of a autonomous prefectures and counties shall be submitted to the Standing Committees of the people's congresses of provinces or autonomous regions for approval before they go into effect, and they shall be reported to the Standing Committee of the National People's Congress for the record.

Article 117. The organs of self-government of the national autonomous areas have the power of autonomy in administering the finances of their areas. All revenues accruing to the national autonomous areas under the financial system of the state shall be managed and used by the organs of self-government of those areas on their own.

Article 118. The organs of self-government of the national autonomous areas independently arrange for and administer local economic development under the guidance of state plans.

In exploiting natural resources and building enterprises in the national autonomous areas, the state shall give due consideration to the interests of those areas.

Article 119. The organs of self-government of the national autonomous areas independently administer education, scientific, cultural, public health and physical culture affairs in their respective areas, protect and cull through the cultural heritage of the nationalities and work for the development and flourishing of their cultures.

Article 120. The organs of self-government of the national autonomous areas may, in accordance with the military system of the state and concrete local needs and with the approval of the State Council, organize local public security forces for the maintenance of public order.

Article 121. In performing their functions, the organs of self-government of the national autonomous areas, in accordance with the autonomy regulations of the respective areas, employ the spoken and written language or languages in common use in the locality.

Article 122. The state gives financial, material and technical assistance to the minority nationalities to accelerate their economic and cultural development.

The state helps the national autonomous areas train large numbers of cadres at different levels and specialized personnel and skilled workers of different professions and trades from among the nationality or nationalities in those areas.

Section VII

The People's Courts and the People's Procuratorates

Article 123. The people's courts in the People's Republic of China are the judicial organs of the state.

Article 124. The People's Republic of China establishes the Supreme People's Court and the local people's courts at different levels, military courts and other special people's courts.

The terms of office of the President of the Supreme People's Court is the same as that of the National People's Congress; the President shall serve no more than two consecutive terms.

The organization of people's courts is prescribed by law.

Article 125. All cases handled by the people's courts, except for those involving special circumstances as specified by law, shall be heard in public. The accused has the right of defence.

Article 126. The people's courts shall, in accordance with the law, exercise judicial power independently and are not subject to interference by administrative organs, public organizations or individuals.

Article 127. The Supreme People's Court is the highest judicial organ.

The Supreme People's Court supervises the administration of justice by the local people's courts at different levels and by the special people's court; people's courts at higher levels supervise the administration of justice by those at lower levels.

Article 128. The Supreme People's Court is responsible to the National People's Congress and its Standing Committee. Local people's courts at different levels are responsible to the organs of state power which created them.

Article 129. The people's procuratorates of the People's Republic of China are state organs for legal supervision.

Article 130. The People's Republic of China establishes the Supreme People's Procuratorate and the local people's procuratorates at different levels, military procuratorates and other special people's procuratorates.
　　The term of office of the Procurator-General of the Supreme People's Procuratorate is the same as that of the National People's Congress; the Procurator-General shall serve no more than two consecutive terms.
　　The organization of people's procuratorates is prescribed by law.

Article 131. People's procuratorates shall, in accordance with the law, exercise procuratorial power independently and are not subject to interference by administrative organs, public organizations or individuals.

Article 132. The Supreme People's Procuratorate is the highest procuratorial organ.
　　The Supreme People's Procuratorate directs the work of the local people's procuratorates at different levels and of the special people's procuratorates; people' procuratorates at higher levels direct the work of those at lower levels.

Article 133. The Supreme People's Procuratorate is responsible to the National People's Congress and its Standing Committee. Local people's procuratorates at different levels are responsible to the organs of state power at the corresponding levels which created them and to the people's procuratorates at the higher level.

Article 134. Citizens of all nationalities have the right to use the spoken and written languages of their own nationalities in court proceedings. The people's courts and people's procuratorates should provide translation for any party to the court proceedings who is not familiar with the spoken or written languages in common use in the locality.

In an area where people of a minority nationality live in a compact community or where a number of nationalities live together, hearings should be conducted in the language or languages in common use in the locality; indictments, judgments, notices and other documents should be written, according to actual needs, in the language or languages in common use in the locality.

Article 135. The people's courts, people's procuratorates and public security organs shall, in handling criminal cases, divide their functions, each taking responsibility for its own work, and they shall co-ordinate their efforts and check each other to ensure correct and effective enforcement of law.

Chapter IV

The National Flag, The National Emblem and the Capital

Article 136. The National flag of the People's Republic of China is a red flag with five stars.

Article 137. The national emblem of the People's Republic of China is Tian'anmen in the centre illuminated by five stars and encircled by ears of grain and a cogwheel.

Article 138. The capital of the People's Republic of China is Beijing.

DOCUMENT 16

Law of the People's Republic of China on Regional National Autonomy
1984

Republic of China on Regional National Autonomy is the basic law for the implementation of the system of regional national autonomy prescribed in the Constitution.

Chapter 1

General Principles

The People's Republic of China is a unitary multinational state created jointly by the people of all its nationalities. Regional national autonomy is the basic policy adopted by the Communist Party of China for the solution of the national question in China through its application of Marxism-Leninism; it is an important political system of the state. Regional national autonomy means that the minority nationalities, under unified state leadership, practise regional autonomy in areas where they live in concentrated communities and set up organs of self-government for the exercise of power of autonomy. Regional national autonomy embodies the state's full respect for and guarantee of the right of the minority nationalities to administer their internal affairs and its adherence to the principle of equality, unity and common prosperity for all its nationalities.

Regional national autonomy has played an enormous role in giving full play to the initiative of all nationalities as masters of the country, in developing among them a socialist relationship of equality, unity and mutual assistance, in consolidating the unification of the country and in promoting socialist construction in the national autonomous areas and the rest of the country. The system of regional national autonomy will have a still greater role to play in the country's socialist modernization in the years to come.

It has been proven by practice that adherence to regional national autonomy requires that the national autonomous areas be given effective guarantees for implementing state laws and policies in the light of existing local conditions; that large numbers of cadres at various levels and specialized personnel and skilled workers of various professions and trades be trained from among the minority nationalities; that the national autonomous areas strive to promote local socialist construction in the spirit of self-reliance and hard work and contribute to the nation's construction as a whole; and that the state strive to help the national autonomous areas speed up their economic and cultural development in accordance with the plans for national economic and social development. In the effort to maintain the unity of the nationalities, both big-nation chauvinism, mainly Han chauvinism, and local national chauvinism must be opposed.

Under the leadership of the Communist Party of China and the guidance of Marxism-Leninism and Mao Zedong Thought, the people of various nationalities in the autonomous areas shall, together with the people of the whole country, true to the people's democratic dictatorship and to the socialist road, concentrate their efforts on socialist modernization, speed up the economic and cultural development of the national autonomous areas, work towards their unity and prosperity and strive for the common prosperity of all nationalities and for the transformation of China into a socialist country with a high level of culture and democracy.

The Law of the People's Republic of China on Regional National Autonomy is the basic law for the implementation of the system of regional national autonomy prescribed in the Constitution.

Chapter I

General Principles

[Article 1] The Law of the People's Republic of China on Regional National Autonomy is formulated in accordance with the Constitution of the People's Republic of China.

[Article 2] Regional autonomy shall be practised in areas where minority nationalities live in concentrated communities. National autonomous areas shall be classified into autonomous regions, autonomous prefectures and autonomous counties.

All national autonomous areas are integral parts of the People's Republic of China.

[Article 3] Organs of self-government shall be established in national autonomous areas as local organs of state power at a particular level.

The organs of self-government of national autonomous areas shall apply the principle of democratic centralism.

[Article 4] The organs of self-government of national autonomous areas shall exercise the functions and powers of local organs of state as specified in Section 5 of Chapter III of the Constitution. At the same time, they shall exercise the power of autonomy within the limits of their authority as prescribed by the Constitution, by this Law and other laws, and implement the laws and policies of the state in the light of existing local conditions.

The organs of self-government of autonomous prefectures shall exercise the functions and powers of local state organs over cities divided into districts and cities with countries under their jurisdiction and, at the same time, exercise the power of autonomy.

[Article 5] The organs of self-government of national autonomous areas must uphold the unity of the country and guarantee that the Constitution and other laws are observed and implemented in these areas.

[Article 6] The organs of self-government of national autonomous areas shall lead the people of the various nationalities in a concentrated effort to promote socialist modernization.

On the principle of not contravening the Constitution and the laws, the organs of self-government of national autonomous areas shall have the power to adopt special policies and flexible measures in the light of local conditions to speed up the economic and cultural development of these areas.

Under the guidance of state plans and on the basis of actual conditions, the organs of self-government of national autonomous areas shall steadily increase labour productivity and economic results, develop social productive forces and gradually raise the material living standards of the people of the various nationalities.

The organs of self-government of national autonomous areas shall inherit and carry forward the fine traditions of national cultures, build a socialist society with an advanced culture and ideology and with national characteristics, and steadily raise the socialist consciousness and scientific and cultural levels of the people of the various nationalities.

[Article 7] The organs of self-government of national autonomous areas shall place the interests of the state as a whole above anything else and make positive efforts to fulfil the tasks assigned by state organs at higher levels.

[Article 8] State organs at higher levels shall guarantee the exercise of the power of autonomy by the organs of self-government of national autonomous areas and shall, in accordance with the characteristics and needs of these areas, strive to help them speed up their socialist construction.

[Article 9] State organs at higher levels and the organs of self-government of national autonomous areas shall uphold and develop the socialist relationship of equality, unity and mutual assistance among all of China's nationalities. Discrimination against and oppression of any nationality shall be prohibited; any act which undermines the unity of the nationalities or instigates national division shall also be prohibited.

[Article 10] The organs of self-government of national autonomous areas shall guarantee the freedom of the nationalities in these areas to use and develop their own spoken and written languages and their freedom to preserve or reform their own folkways and customs.

[Article 11] The organs of self-government of national autonomous areas shall guarantee the freedom of religious belief to citizens of the various nationalities.

No state organ, public organization or individual may compel citizens to believe in, or not to believe in, any religion, nor may they discriminate against citizens who believe in, or do not believe in, any religion.
The state shall protect normal religious activities. No one may make use of religion to engage in activities that disrupt public order, impair the health of citizens or interfere with the educational system of the state.
Religious bodies and religious affairs shall not be subject to any foreign domination.

Chapter II

Establishment of National Autonomous Areas and the Structure of the Organs of Self-Government

[Article 12] Autonomous areas may be established where one or more minority nationalities live in concentrated communities, in the light of local conditions such as the relationship among the various nationalities and the level of economic development, and with due consideration for historical background.

Within a national autonomous area, appropriate autonomous areas or nationality townships may be established where other minority nationalities live in concentrated communities.

Some residential areas and towns of the Han nationality or other nationalities may be included in a national autonomous area in consideration of actual local conditions.

[Article 13] With the exception of special cases, the name of a national autonomous area shall be composed of that name of the locality and the name of the nationality and the administrative status, in that order.

[Article 14] The establishment of a national autonomous area, the delineation of its boundaries and the elements of its name shall be proposed by the State organ at the next higher level jointly with the State organ in the relevant locality, after full consultation with representatives of the relevant nationalities, before they are submitted for approval according to the procedures prescribed by law.

Once defined, the boundaries of a national autonomous area may not be altered without authorization. When an alteration is found necessary, it shall be proposed by the relevant department of the State organ at the next higher level after full consultation with the organ of self-government of the national autonomous areas before it is submitted to the State Council for approval.

[Article 15] The organs of self-government of national autonomous areas shall be the people's congresses and people's governments of autonomous regions, autonomous prefectures and autonomous counties.

The people's governments of national autonomous areas shall be responsible to and report on their work to the people's congresses at corresponding levels and to the administrative organs of the State at the next higher level. When the people's congresses at corresponding levels are not in session, they shall be responsible to and report on their work to the Standing Committees of these people's congresses. The people's governments of all national autonomous areas shall be administrative organs of the State under the unified leadership of the State Council and shall be subordinate to it.

The organization and work of the organs of self-government of national autonomous areas shall be specified in these areas' regulations on the exercise of autonomy or separate regulation, in accordance with the Constitution and other laws.

[Article 16] In the people's congress of a national autonomous area, in addition to the deputies from the nationality exercising regional autonomy in the administrative area, the other nationalities inhabiting the area are also entitled to appropriate representation.

The number and proportion of deputies to the people's congress of a national autonomous area from the nationality exercising regional autonomy and from the other minority nationalities shall be decided upon by the Standing Committee of the people's congress of a province or an autonomous region, in accordance with the principles prescribed by law, and shall be reported to the

Standing Committee of the National People's Congress for the record.

Among the Chairman and Vice-Chairmen of the Standing Committee of the people's congress of a national autonomous area shall be one or more citizens of the nationality exercising regional autonomy in the area.

[Article 17] The Chairman of an autonomous region, the prefect of an autonomous prefecture or the head of an autonomous county shall be a citizen of the nationality exercising regional autonomy in the area concerned. Other posts in the people's government of an autonomous region, an autonomous prefecture or an autonomous county should, whenever possible, be assumed by people of the nationality exercising regional autonomy and of other minority nationalities in the area concerned.

The people's governments of national autonomous areas shall apply the system of giving overall responsibility to the Chairman of an autonomous region, the prefect of an autonomous prefecture or the head of an autonomous county, who shall direct the work of the people's government at their respective levels.

[Article 18] The cadres in the departments under the organs of self-government of a national autonomous area should, whenever possible, be chosen from among citizens of the nationality exercising regional autonomy and of the other minority nationalities in the area.

Chapter III

The Power of Autonomy of
The Organs of Self-Government

[Article 19] The people's congresses of national autonomous areas shall have the power to enact regulations on the exercise of autonomy and separate regulations in the light of the political, economic and cultural characteristics of the nationality or nationalities in the areas concerned. The regulation on the exercise of autonomy and separate regulations of autonomous regions shall be submitted to the Standing Committee of the National People's Congress for approval before they go into effect. The regulations on the exercise of autonomy and separate regulations of autonomous prefectures and autonomous counties shall be submitted to the Standing Committees of the people's congresses of provinces or autonomous regions for approval before they go into effect, and they shall be reported to the Standing Committee of the National People's Congress for the record.

[Article 20] If a resolution, decision, order or instruction of a State organ at a higher level does not suit the conditions in a national autonomous area, the organ of self-government of the area may either implement it with certain alterations or cease implementing it after reporting to and receiving the approval of the State organ at a higher level.

[Article 21] While performing its functions, the organ of self-government of a national autonomous area shall, in accordance with the regulations on the exercise of autonomy of the area, use one or several languages commonly used in the locality; where several commonly used languages are used for the performance of such functions, the language of the nationality exercising regional autonomy may be used as the main language.

[Article 22] In accordance with the needs of socialist construction, the organs of self-government of national autonomous areas shall take various measures to train large numbers of cadres at different levels and various kinds of specialized personnel, including scientists, technicians and managerial executives, as well as skilled workers from among the local nationalities, giving full play to their roles, and shall pay attention to the training of cadres at various levels and specialized and technical personnel of various kinds from among the women of minority nationalities.

The organs of self-government of national autonomous areas may adopt special measures to provide preferential treatment and encouragement to specialized personnel joining in the various kinds of construction in these areas.

[Article 23] When recruiting personnel, enterprises and institutions in national autonomous areas shall give priority to minority nationalities and may enlist them from the population of minority nationalities in rural and pastoral areas. When recruiting personnel from the population of minority nationalities in rural and pastoral areas, autonomous prefectures and autonomous counties must report to and secure the approval of the people's governments of the provinces or autonomous regions.

[Article 24] The organs of self-government of national autonomous areas may, in accordance with the military system of the State and practical local needs and with the approval of the State Council, organize local public security forces for the maintenance of public order.

[Article 25] Under the guidance of State plans, the organs of self-government of national autonomous areas shall independently arrange for and administer local economic development.

[Article 26] Under the guidance of State plans, the organs of self-government of national autonomous areas shall work out the guidelines, policies and plans for economic development in the light of local characteristics and needs.

[Article 27] Given the prerequisite of adherence to the principles of socialism, the organs of self-government of national autonomous areas shall, in accordance with legal stipulations and in the light of the characteristics of local economic development, rationally readjust the relations of production and reform the structure of economic administration.

In accordance with legal stipulations, the organs of self-government of national autonomous areas shall define the ownership of, and the right to use, the pastures and forests within these areas.

[Article 28] In accordance with legal stipulations the organs of self-government of national autonomous areas shall manage and protect the natural resources of these areas.

The organs of self-government of national autonomous areas shall protect and develop grasslands and forests and organize and encourage the planting of trees and grass. Destruction of grasslands and forests by any organization or individual by whatever means shall be prohibited.

In accordance with legal stipulations and unified State plans, the organs of self-government of national autonomous areas may give priority to the rational exploitation and utilization of the natural resources that the local authorities are entitled to develop.

[Article 29] Under the guidance of State plans, the organs of self-government of national autonomous areas shall independently arrange local capital construction projects according to their financial and material resources and other specific local conditions.

[Article 30] The organs of self-government of national autonomous areas shall independently administer the enterprises and institutions under local jurisdiction.

[Article 31] The organs of self-government of national autonomous areas shall independently arrange for the use of industrial, agricultural and other local and special products after fulfilling the quotas for State purchase and for State distribution at a higher level.

[Article 32] In accordance with State provisions, the organs of self-government of national autonomous areas may pursue foreign economic and trade activities and may, with the approval of the State Council, open foreign trade ports.

National autonomous areas adjoining foreign countries may develop border trade with the approval of the State Council.

While conducting foreign economic and trade activities, the organs of self-government of the national autonomous areas shall enjoy preferential treatment by the State with regard to the proportion of foreign exchange retained by them and in other respects.

[Article 33] The finance of a national autonomous area constitutes a particular level of finance and is a component of State finance.

The organs of self-government of national autonomous areas shall have the power of autonomy in administering the finances of their areas. All revenues accruing to the national autonomous areas under the financial system of the State shall be managed and used by the organs of self-government of these areas on their own.

The revenues and expenditures of national autonomous areas shall be specified by the State Council on the principle of giving preferential treatment to such areas.

In accordance with stipulations concerning the State financial system, if the revenues of a national autonomous area exceed its expenditures, a fixed amount of the surplus shall be delivered to the financial department at a higher level. Once fixed, the amount to be delivered may remain unchanged for several years. If the expenditures of a national autonomous area exceed its revenues, a subsidy shall be granted by the financial department at a higher level.

A national autonomous area shall, in accordance with State stipulations, lay aside a reserve fund for expenditure in its budget. The proportion of the reserve fund in its budget shall be higher than that in the budgets of other areas.

While implementing its fiscal budget, the organ of self-government of a national autonomous area shall arrange for the use of extra income and savings from expenditure at its own discretion.

[Article 34] In accordance with the principles set by the State and in the light of local conditions, the organs of self-government of national autonomous areas may work out supplementary provisions and concrete procedures with regard to the standards of expenditure, the sizes of the staff and the quotas of work for their respective areas. The supplementary provisions and concrete procedures worked out by autonomous regions shall be reported to the State Council for the record; those worked out by autonomous prefectures and autonomous counties shall be reported to the people's governments of the relevant provinces or autonomous regions for approval.

[Article 35] While implementing the tax laws of the State, the organs of self-government of national autonomous areas may grant tax exemptions or reductions for certain items of local financial income which should be encouraged or given preferential consideration in taxation, in addition to items on which tax reduction or exemption requires unified examination and approval by the State. The decisions of autonomous prefectures and autonomous counties on tax reduction and exemption shall be reported to the people's governments of the relevant provinces or autonomous regions for approval.

[Article 36] In accordance with the guidelines of the State on education and with the relevant stipulations of the law, the organs of self-government of national autonomous areas shall decide on plans for the development of eduction in these areas, on the establishment of various kinds of schools at different levels, and on their educational system, forms, curricula, the language used in jurisdiction and enrolment procedures.

[Article 37] The organs of self-government of national autonomous areas shall independently develop education for the nationalities by eliminating illiteracy, setting up various kinds of schools, spreading compulsory primary education, developing secondary education and establishing specialized schools for the nationalities, such as teachers' schools, secondary technical schools, national schools and institutes of nationalities to train specialized personnel from among the minority nationalities.

The organs of self-government of national autonomous areas may set up public primary schools and secondary schools, mainly boarding schools and schools providing subsidies, in pastoral areas and economically underdeveloped, sparsely populated mountain areas inhabited by minority nationalities.

Schools where most of the students come from minority nationalities should, whenever possible, use textbooks in their own languages and use these languages as the media of instruction. Classes for the teaching of Chinese (the Han language) shall be opened for senior grades of primary schools or for secondary schools to popularize Putonghua, the common speech based on Beijing pronunciation.

[Article 38] The organs of self-government of national autonomous areas shall independently develop literature, art, the press, publishing, radio broadcasting, the film industry, television and other cultural undertakings in forms and with characteristics unique to the nationalities.

The organs of self-government of national autonomous areas shall collect, sort out, translate and publish books of the nationalities and protect the scenic spots and historical sites in their areas, their precious cultural relics and their other important historical and cultural legacies.

[Article 39] The organs of self-government of national autonomous areas shall make independent decisions on local plans for developing science and technology and spreading knowledge of science and technology.

[Article 40] The organs of self-government of national autonomous areas shall make independent decision on plans for developing local medical and health services and for advancing both modern medicine and the traditional medicine of the nationalities.

The organs of self-government of national autonomous areas shall see to a more effective prevention and treatment of endemic diseases, provide better protection for the health of women and children, and improve sanitary conditions.

[Article 41] The organs of self-government of national autonomous areas shall independently develop sports, promote the traditional sports of the nationalities and improve the physical fitness of the people of the various nationalities.

[Article 42] The organs of self-government of the national autonomous areas shall strive to develop exchanges and cooperation with other areas in education, science and technology, culture and art, public health, sports, etc.

In accordance with relevant State provisions, the organs of self-government of autonomous regions and autonomous prefectures may conduct exchanges with foreign countries in education, science and technology, culture and art, public health, sports, etc.

[Article 43] In accordance with legal stipulations, the organs of self-government of national autonomous areas shall work out measures for control of the transient population.

[Article 44] In accordance with legal stipulation, the organs of self-government of national autonomous areas shall, in the light of local conditions, work out measures for family planning.

[Article 45] The organs of self-government of national autonomous areas shall protect and improve the living environment and the ecological environment and shall prevent and control pollution and other public hazards.

Chapter IV

The People's Courts and People's Procuratorates of National Autonomous Areas

[Article 46] The people's courts and people's procuratorates of national autonomous areas shall be responsible to the people's congresses at corresponding levels and their Standing Committees. The people's procuratorates of national autonomous areas shall also be responsible to the people's procuratorates at higher levels.

The administration of justice by the people's courts of national autonomous areas shall be supervised by the Supreme People's Court and by people's courts at higher levels. The work of the people's procuratorates of national autonomous areas shall be directed by the Supreme People's Procuratorate and by people's procuratorates at higher levels.

Members of the leadership and of the staff of the people's court and of the people's procuratorate of a national autonomous area shall include people from the nationality exercising regional autonomy in that area.

[Article 47] In the prosecution and trial of cases, the people's courts and people's procuratorates of national autonomous areas shall use the language commonly used in the locality. They shall guarantee that citizens of the various nationalities enjoy the right to use the spoken and written languages of their own nationalities in court proceedings. The people's courts and people's procuratorates should provide translation for any party to the court proceedings who is not familiar with the spoken or written languages commonly used in the locality. Legal documents should be written, according to actual needs, in the language or languages commonly used in the locality.

Chapter V

Relations Among Nationalities Within a National Autonomous Area

[Article 48] The organ of self-government of a national autonomous area shall guarantee equal rights for the various nationalities in the area.

The organ of self-government of a national autonomous area shall unite the cadres and masses of the various nationalities and give full play to their initiative in a joint effort to develop the area.

[Article 49] The organ of self-government of a national autonomous area shall persuade and encourage cadres of the various nationalities to learn each other's spoken and written languages. Cadres of Han nationality should learn the spoken and written languages of the local minority nationalities. While learning and using the spoken and written languages of their own nationalities, cadres of minority nationalities should also learn putonghua and the written Chinese (Han) language commonly used throughout the country.

Awards should be given to State functionaries in national

autonomous areas who can use skilfully two or more spoken or written languages that are commonly used in the locality.

[Article 50] The organ of self-government of a national autonomous area shall help other minority nationalities living in concentrated communities in the area establish appropriate autonomous area or nationality townships.

The organ of self-government of a national autonomous area shall help the various nationalities in the area develop their economic, educational, scientific, cultural, public health and physical culture affairs.

The organ of self-government of a national autonomous area shall give consideration to the characteristics and needs of nationalities living in settlements scattered over the area.

[Article 51] In dealing with special issues concerning the various nationalities within its area, the organ of self-government of a national autonomous area must conduct full consultation with their representatives and respect their opinions.

[Article 52] The organ of self-government of a national autonomous area shall guarantee that citizens of the various nationalities in the area enjoy the rights of citizens prescribed in the Constitution and shall educate them in the need to perform their duties as citizens.

[Article 53] The organ of self-government of a national autonomous area shall promote the civic virtues of love of the motherland, of the people, of labour, of science and of socialism and conduct education among the citizens of the various nationalities in the area in patriotism, communism and State policies concerning the nationalities. The cadres and masses of the various nationalities must be educated to trust, learn from and help one another and to respect the spoken and written languages, folkways and customs and religious beliefs of one another in a joint effort to safeguard the unification of the country and the unity of all the nationalities.

Chapter VI
Leadership and Assistance from State Organs at Higher Levels

[Article 54] The resolutions, decisions, orders and instructions concerning national autonomous areas adopted by State organs at higher levels should suit the conditions in these areas.

[Article 55] State organs at higher levels shall provide financial, material and technical assistance to national autonomous areas to accelerate their economic and cultural development.

In making plans for national economic and social development, State organs at higher levels should take into consideration the characteristics and needs of national autonomous areas.

[Article 56] The State shall set aside special funds to help national autonomous areas develop their economy and culture.

The special funds set aside by the State and its provisional grants to the nationalities may not be deducted, withheld or misappropriated by any State agency, nor may they be used to substitute for the normal budgetary revenues of national autonomous areas.

[Article 57] In accordance with the State policy for trade with the minority nationalities, State organs at higher levels shall give consideration to the commercial, supply and marketing, and medical and pharmaceutical enterprises in national autonomous areas.

[Article 58] State organs at higher levels shall rationally review or readjust the base figures for the financial revenues and expenditure of national autonomous areas.

[Article 59] While distributing the means of production and means of subsistence, State organs at higher levels shall give consideration to the needs of national autonomous areas.

While making plans for the State purchase of industrial and agriculture products and other local and special products of national autonomous areas and for State distribution of such products at a higher level, State organs at higher levels shall give consideration to the interests of the national autonomous areas and the producers, and set reasonable figures for State distribution at a higher level or a reasonable ratio between the amount to be purchased and the amount to be kept.

[Article 60] In matters of investment, loans and taxation and in production, supply, transportation and sales, State organs at higher levels shall help national autonomous areas in the rational exploitation of local resources to develop local industry, transportation and energy and to advance and improve the production of goods specially needed by minority nationalities and of traditional handicrafts.

[Article 61] State organs at higher levels shall enlist and support economically developed areas in pursuing economic and technological cooperation with national autonomous areas to help the latter areas raise their level of operation and management and their level of production technology.

[Article 62] While exploiting resources and undertaking construction in national autonomous areas, the State shall give consideration to the interests of these areas, make arrangements favourable to the economic construction there and pay proper attention to the productive pursuits and the life of the minority nationalities there.

Enterprises and institutions affiliated to State organs at higher levels but located in national autonomous areas shall give priority to local minority nationalities when recruiting personnel.

Enterprises and institutions affiliated to State organs at higher levels but located in national autonomous areas shall respect the power of autonomy of the local organs of self-government and accept their supervision.

[Article 63] Without the consent of the organ of self-government of a national autonomous area, no State agency at a higher level may change the affiliation of an enterprise under the administration of the local government.

[Article 64] State organs at higher levels shall help national autonomous areas train, from among local nationalities, large numbers of cadres at various levels and specialized personnel and skilled workers of different professions and trades; in accordance with local needs and in various forms, they shall send appropriate numbers of teachers, doctors, scientists and technicians as well as managerial executives to work in national autonomous areas and provide them with proper benefits.

[Article 65] State organs at higher levels shall help national autonomous areas speed up the development of education and raise the scientific and cultural levels of the people of local nationalities.

The State shall set up institutes of nationalities and, in other institutions of higher education nationality-orientated classes and preparatory classes that enrol only students from minority nationalities. Preferred enrolment and preferred assignment of jobs may also be introduced. In enrolment, institutions of higher education and secondary technical schools shall appropriately set lower standards and requirements for the admission of students from minority nationalities.

[Article 66] State organs at higher levels shall intensify education among cadres and masses of the various nationalities in the government's policies concerning nationalities and frequently review the observance and implementation of these policies and relevant laws.

Chapter VII

Supplementary Provisions

[Article 67] This Law has been adopted by the National People's Congress and shall go into effect on October 1, 1984.

DOCUMENT 17

Chinese Communist Party Constitution

Beijing, 22nd September 1982: The Constitution of the Chinese Communist Party [CCP] (partly amended by the 15th CCP National Congress and adopted on 18th September 1997)

General Programme

The Chinese Communist Party [CCP] is the vanguard of the Chinese working class, the faithful representative of the interests of the people of all nationalities in China, and the core leading China's socialist cause. The party's ultimate goal is to materialize a communist social system. The CCP takes Marxism-Leninism-Mao Zedong Thought and Deng Xiaoping Theory as its guide to action.

Marxism-Leninism has revealed the universal law on the historical development of human society, analysed the insurmountable contradictions inherent in the capitalist system, and pointed out that socialist society is bound to replace capitalist society and ultimately develop into communist society. The history of more than a century since the publication of the "Communist Manifesto" proves the correctness of the theory on scientific socialism and the strong vitality of socialism. Socialism essentially means to emancipate and develop the productive forces, to eliminate exploitation and polarization, and to ultimately realise common prosperity. The development and perfection of the socialist system is a protracted historical process. Despite twists, turns, and relapses in the course of development, the inevitable replacement of capitalism by socialism is an irreversible general trend in the history of social development. Socialism is bound to gradually triumph along the paths suited to the specific conditions of each country and chosen by its people of their own free will.

The Chinese communists, with Comrade Mao Zedong as their chief representative, created Mao Zedong Thought by integrating the universal principles of Marxism-Leninism with the concrete practice of the Chinese revolution. Mao Zedong Thought is the application and development of Marxism-Leninism in China; it is a theoretical principle concerning the Chinese revolution and construction and a summation of experience that have been proved correct by practice; it is the crystallization of the CCP's collective wisdom.

The CCP led the people of all nationalities throughout the country in waging their prolonged revolutionary struggle against imperialism, feudalism, and bureaucratic capitalism, winning victory in the new democratic revolution and establishing the PRC [People's Republic of China], a people's democratic dictatorship. After the founding of the People's Republic, it led them in smoothly carrying out socialist transformation, completing the transition from new democracy to socialism, establishing the socialist system, and developing socialist economy, politics and culture.

Since the third plenary session of the 11th CCP Central Committee, Chinese communists, with Comrade Deng Xiaoping as the main representative, have summed up positive and negative experience since the founding of New China; emancipated the mind; sought truth from facts; shifted the centre of the whole party's work to economic construction; carried out reform and opening up; opened up the new period of the development of the socialist cause; gradually formulated the line, principles, and policies of building socialism with Chinese characteristics; expounded the basic issues concerning building, strengthening, and developing socialism in China; and founded the Deng Xiaoping Theory. The Deng Xiaoping Theory is a product of integrating Marxist-Leninist basic law with contemporary China's practice and the features of the times, the inheritance and development of Mao Zedong Thought under the new historical conditions, a new stage of the development of Marxism in China, Marxism of contemporary China, and a crystallization of the CCP's collective wisdom. It has led China's socialist modernization drive to continue to advance.

Currently China is in the initial stage of socialism. This stage is a historical stage that cannot be skipped in building socialist modernization in China, a country that is economically and culturally backward. China will be in this stage for more than 100 years. In carrying out socialist construction in China, we must proceed from the country's national conditions and take the socialist path with Chinese characteristics. In the current stage, Chinese society's major contradictions are those between the people's increasing material and cultural needs and the backward social production. Due to domestic factors and international influence, class struggle has existed within a certain scope for a long time and, under certain conditions, may intensify; however, it is no longer the major contradiction. The fundamental task of China's socialist construction is to further liberate and develop productive forces, gradually realise socialist modernization, and, to attain these objectives, to reform the production relationships and the factors and links in the superstructure that are not in line with the development of productive forces. We must adhere to the ownership structure, with public ownership of capital goods as the main body, that allows economies of all sectors to simultaneously exist; implement the distribution system with distribution according to labour as the main body, and with other distribution forms as a supplement; encourage some localities and people to become better off first; gradually eliminate poverty; achieve common prosperity; and, on the basis of production development and increased social wealth, satisfy the people's increasing material and cultural needs. In doing work in all fields, we should regard "conducive to developing the productive forces of our socialist society, increasing the overall strength of our socialist country, and improving the people's living standards" as the general point of departure and criterion of examination. The strategic objective of China's economic development is to quadruple the country's 1980 GNP at the end of this century, and enable the per capita GNP to reach a medium-developed country's level in the middle of the next century.

The CPP's basic line for the initial stage of socialism is to lead and unite the people of all nationalities throughout the country to carry out economic construction as the central task, to uphold the four cardinal principles, to persevere in reform and opening to the outside world, and to strive to build our country into a prosperous, powerful, democratic, and civilized socialist modern country through self-reliance and arduous efforts.

In leading the socialist cause, the CCP must persist in regarding economic construction as its central task, and all other work must be subordinated to and serve the central task. It is necessary to seize the opportunity to speed up development, to give full play to the role of science and technology as the primary productive force, to raise efficiency, quality, and speed by relying on scientific and technological progress and improving workers' quality, and to strive to push economic construction forward.

The foundation for our country is to uphold the four cardinal principles - upholding the socialist road, the people's democratic dictatorship, leadership of the CCP, and Marxism-Leninism-Mao Zedong Thought. In the whole process of socialist modernization, it is imperative to uphold the four cardinal principles and oppose bourgeois liberalization.

Reform and opening to the outside world are the only way to liberate and develop the productive forces. It is necessary to fundamentally reform the economic structure impeding the development of the productive forces and to institute a system of socialist market economy. Corresponding to this, reform should be carried out in the political structure and other fields. Opening includes opening to the outside and inside in an all-round way. Efforts should be made to develop economic and technological exchanges and co-operation with foreign countries; use more foreign funds, resources, and technology in a better way; and draw on and assimilate all the achievements of civilization created by mankind, including developed Western countries' advanced methods of operation and management reflecting the law of modern production. In carrying out reform and opening to the outside, we should boldly explore, do pioneering work, and blaze new trails in practice.

The CCP leads the people, as they build a material civilization, in striving to build a socialist spiritual civilization. The building of socialist spiritual civilization provides the powerful mental impetus and intellectual support for economic construction, reform, and opening to the outside world, and helps create a favourable social environment. Major efforts should be made to promote education, science, and culture, and it is necessary to respect knowledge and trained personnel; to raise the ideological, moral, scientific, and cultural quality of the whole nation; to develop fine traditional national culture; and to bring about a thriving and developed socialist culture. It is essential to educate party members and the masses of people in the party's basic line, patriotism, collectivism, and socialist ideology, and to enhance their spirit of national dignity, confidence, and self-improvement. Efforts should also be made to educate party members in lofty communist ideals, to resist the corrosive influence of decadent capitalist and feudalist ideas, to eliminate all ugly social phenomena, and to encourage the Chinese people to have lofty ideals, moral integrity, education, and a sense of discipline.

The CCP leads the people in developing socialist democracy, perfecting the socialist legal system, and consolidating the people's democratic dictatorship. It upholds the system of people's congresses, the system of multi-party cooperation under the leadership of the Communist Party, and the system of political consultation. It greatly supports the people in becoming masters of their own country and takes concrete steps to protect the people's right to run the affairs of State and society, and to manage economic and cultural undertakings. It establishes and perfects the system and process for democratic decision-making and democratic supervision. It strengthens State legislation and law implementation work and gradually guides various undertakings into a legal framework. It enhances comprehensive management of public order and maintains long-term social stability. It resolutely cracks down on criminal acts and criminal elements that jeopardize State security and interests, and who endanger social stability and economic development. It makes a strict distinction and correctly handles the contradictions between us and enemies and the contradictions among the people, which are two different kinds of contradictions of different nature.

The CCP upholds its leadership over the People's Liberation Army [PLA] and other people's armed forces, strives to strengthen the building of PLA, and fully gives play to the PLA's role in consolidating national defence, in defending the motherland, and in taking part in socialist modernization construction.

The CCP upholds and promotes relations of equality, unity, and mutual assistance among all nationalities in their country. It persists in implementing and constantly improving the system of regional autonomy for minority nationalities. It makes great efforts to train and promote minority cadres, and assists in the development of the economy and culture in areas inhabited by minority nationalities with a view to bringing about common prosperity and progress for all nationalities.

The CCP unites with all workers, peasants, and intellectuals, and with all the democratic parties, non-party democrats, and patriotic forces of all nationalities in China in further expanding and fortifying the broadest possible patriotic united front embracing all socialist working people and all patriots who support socialism, or who support the reunification of the motherland. It is necessary to constantly strengthen the unity of all people in the nation, including the unity of our compatriots in Taiwan, Hong Kong, Macao, and overseas Chinese, and accomplish the great task of reunifying the motherland according to the policy of "one country, two systems".

The CCP stands for the vigorous development of relations with foreign countries and exerts efforts to create a favourable international environment for our country's reform, opening to the outside world, and modernization construction. In international affairs, it adheres to the peaceful foreign policy of independence, maintains our country's independence and sovereignty, opposes hegemony and power politics, safeguards world peace, and promotes human progress. It stands for the development of State relations between China and other countries on the basis of the five principles of mutual respect for sovereignty and territorial integrity, mutual non-aggression, non-interference in each other's internal affairs, equality and mutual benefit, and peaceful co-existence. It constantly develops our country's good-neighbourly and friendly relations with peripheral countries, and enhances unity and co-operation with developing countries. It also develops relations with communist parties and other political parties in other countries on the principle of independence, complete equality, mutual respect, and non-interference in each other's internal affairs.

In order to lead Chinese people of all nationalities in attaining the great goal of socialist modernization, the CCP must closely follow the party's basic line, strengthen party building, persist in strict management of the party, carry forward its fine traditions and work style, enhance its fighting capacity, and build the party into a strong core that leads all people in the nation to constantly advance along the road of socialism with Chinese characteristics. The following four basic requirements must be met in party building:

First, it is necessary to adhere to the party's basic line. The entire party should use the theory of building socialism with Chinese characteristics and the party's basic line to unify thinking and actions and to adhere unfailingly to it for a long time. We should unify reform and opening up with the four cardinal principles, comprehensively implement the party's basic line, and oppose all erroneous tendencies of "leftist" and rightist deviation; while keeping vigilance against rightist deviation, main attention should be paid to guarding against "leftist" deviation. Building of various levels of leading bodies should be stepped up. Cadres who have done outstanding jobs and are trusted by the masses in the course of reform, opening, and socialist modernization construction should be promoted. Hundreds and millions of successors to the cause of socialism should be trained and nurtured. All party organizations must ensure the implementation of the party's basic line.

Second, it is necessary to persist in mind emancipation and seeking truth from facts. The party's ideological line is to proceed from reality in all things, to integrate theory with practice, to seek truth from facts, and to verify and develop truth through practice. In accordance with this ideological line, the entire party must make vigorous explorations, conduct bold experiments, work creatively, constantly study the new situation, sum up new experiences, solve new problems, and enrich and develop Marxism through practice.

Third, it is necessary to serve the people wholeheartedly. The party has no special interests of its own apart from the interests of the working class and the broadest masses of the people. It always gives first priority to the masses' interests, shares weal and woe with them, maintains the closest ties with them, and never allows party members to deviate and ride roughshod over them. The party practices the mass line in its work. While it does all things for the masses, it too relies on all things from the masses. As the party is sprung from the masses, it must return to the fold. It also converts its correct policy into the masses' voluntary actions. The issues of party style and the ties between the party and the masses are two issues that concern the life and death of the party. The party steadfastly opposes corruption and always works to improve party style and build a clean government.

Fourth, adherence to democratic centralism. Democratic centralism is the integration of centralism based on democracy and democracy under the guidance of centralism. It is the party's basic organizational principle as well as the application of the mass line in the conduct of party activities. Full play should be given to democracy within the party, and the initiative and creativity of party committees at all levels and the broad ranks of party members should be brought into full play. It is necessary to exercise correct centralism to ensure unity of action throughout the ranks, and the prompt and effective implantation of decisions. It is necessary to strengthen a sense of organization and discipline, and see to it that everyone is equal before party discipline. In its internal political life, the party conducts criticism and self-criticism in the correct way, waging ideological struggles over matters of principle, upholding truth, and rectifying mistakes. It is necessary to work to develop a political situation in which we have both centralism and democracy, both discipline and freedom, both unity of will and personal ease of mind and liveliness.

Party leadership consists mainly of political, ideological, and organizational leadership. The party must adapt to the needs of reform, opening up, and socialist modernization, and step up and improve its leadership. It must concentrate on leadership over economic construction, and organize and co-ordinate the forces of all quarters to carry out its work around economic construction with concerted efforts. The party must practice democratic and scientific decision-making, formulate and implement correct lines, principles, and policies; do its organizational, propaganda, and educational work well; and make sure that all party members play their exemplary vanguard role. It must conduct its activities within the limits permitted by the Constitution and the law. It must see to it that the legislative, judicial, and administrative organs of the state and the economic, cultural, and people's organizational work actively and with initiative, independently, responsibly, and in harmony. It must strengthen leadership over the trade unions, the Communist Youth League, the Women's Federation, and other mass organizations, and give full scope to their roles. The party must adapt to the developments and changes of the situation, constantly improve its leadership style and method, and raise its leadership level. Its members must work in close co-operation with the masses of non-party people in the common effort to build socialism with Chinese characteristics.

Chapter I: Membership

Article 1. Any Chinese worker, peasant, member of the armed forces, intellectual or any other revolutionary who has reached the age of 18, who accepts the party's programme and Constitution, and is willing to join and work actively in one of the party organizations, carry out the party's decisions, and pay membership dues regularly may apply for membership of the CCP.

Article 2. Members of the CCP are vanguard fighters of the Chinese working class imbued with communist consciousness.

Members of the CCP must serve the people wholeheartedly, dedicate their whole lives to the realization of communism, and be ready to make any personal sacrifices.

Members of the CCP are at all times ordinary members of the working people. Communist Party members must not seek personal gain or privileges beyond the personal benefits, job functions and powers as provided for by the relevant laws and policies.

Article 3. Party members must fulfil the following duties:

(1) Conscientiously study Marxism-Leninism-Mao Zedong Thought and Deng Xiaoping Theory as well as the party's line, principles, policies, and resolutions; study essential knowledge concerning the party; and acquire general, scientific, and professional knowledge in an effort to improve their ability to serve the people.
(2) Unfailingly implement the party's basic line, principles, and

policies; take the lead in participating in reform, opening up, and socialist modernizations; encourage the masses to work hard for economic development and social progress; and play an exemplary vanguard role in production and other work, study, and social activities.

(3) Adhere to the principle that the interests of the party and people stand above everything, subordinate their personal interests to the interests of the party and people; be the first to bear hardships and the last to enjoy comforts; work selflessly for the public interest and make more contributions.

(4) Conscientiously observe party discipline and the laws of the State, rigorously guard party and State secrets, execute the party's decisions, accept any job, and actively fulfil any task assigned them by the party.

(5) Uphold the party's solidarity and unity; be loyal to and honest with the party and match words with deeds; firmly oppose all factional organizations and small-group activities, and oppose double-dealing and scheming of any kind.

(6) Earnestly practice criticism and self-criticism, be bold in exposing and correcting shortcomings and mistakes in work, and resolutely fight negative and decadent phenomena.

(7) Maintain close ties with the masses, propagate the party's views among them, consult with them when problems arise, keep the party informed of their views and demands in good time, and defend their legitimate interests.

(8) Develop new socialist habits, advocate communist ethics, and step forward in times of difficulty and danger, fighting bravely and defying death for the defence of the country and the interests of the people.

Article 4. Party members enjoy the following rights:

(1) To attend pertinent party meetings and read pertinent party documents, and to benefit from the party's education and training.
(2) To participate in discussion at party meetings and in party newspapers and journals on questions concerning the party's policies.
(3) To make suggestions and proposals regarding the work of the party.
(4) To make well-grounded criticism of any party organization or member at party meetings; to present information or charges against any party organization or member concerning violation of discipline and of the law to the party in a responsible way, and to demand disciplinary measures against such a member, or to demand the dismissal or replacement of any cadre who is incompetent.
(5) To vote, elect and stand for election.
(6) To attend, with the right of self-defence, discussions held by party organizations to decide on disciplinary measure to be taken against themselves or to appraise their work and behaviour, while other party members may also bear witness or argue on their behalf.
(7) In case of disagreement with a party decision or policy, to make reservations and present their views to party organizations at higher levels up to and including the Central Committee, provided that they resolutely carry out the decision or policy while it is in force.
(8) To put forward any request, appeal or complaint to a higher party organization up to and including the Central Committee, and ask the organization concerned for a responsible reply.

No party organization, up to and including the Central

Committee, has the right to deprive any party member of the above-mentioned rights.

Article 5. New party members must be admitted through a party branch and the principle of individual admission must be adhered to.

An applicant for party membership must fill in an application form and must be recommended by two full party members. The application must be accepted by a general membership meeting of the party branch concerned and approved by the next higher party organization; and the applicant should undergo observation for a probationary period before being transferred to full membership.

Party members who recommended an applicant must make genuine efforts to acquaint themselves with the latter's ideology, character, personal history, and work performance; must explain to each applicant the party's programme and Constitution, qualifications for membership and the duties and rights of members; and must make a responsible report to the party organization on the matter.

The party branch committee must canvass the opinions of persons concerned, inside and outside the party, about an applicant for party membership and, after establishing the latter's qualifications following a rigorous examination, submit the application to a general membership meeting for discussion.

Before approving the admission of applicants for party membership, the next higher party organization concerned must appoint people to take with them, so as to get to know them better and help deepen their understanding of the party.

In special circumstances, the Central Committee of the party or the party committee of a province, an autonomous region, or a municipality directly under the central government has the power to admit new party members directly.

Article 6. A probationary party member must take an admission oath in front of the party flag. The oath reads: It is my will to join the Chinese Communist Party, uphold the party's programme, observe the provisions of the party Constitution, fulfil a party member's duties, carry out the party's decisions, strictly observe party discipline, guard party secrets, be loyal to the party, work hard, fight for communism throughout my life, be ready at all times to sacrifice myself all for the party and the people, and never betray the party.

Article 7. The probationary period of a probationary member lasts one year. The party organization concerned should earnestly educate and observe probationary party members. Probationary members have the same duties as full members. They enjoy the right of full members except those of voting, electing, or standing for election.

When the probationary period of a probationary member has expired, the party branch concerned should promptly discuss whether he is qualified to be transferred to full membership. A probationary member who conscientiously performs his duties and is qualified for membership should be transferred to full membership as scheduled; if continued observation and education are needed, the probationary period may be prolonged, but by no more than one year; if a probationary member fails to perform his duties and is found to be unqualified for membership, his probationary membership shall be annulled. Any decision to transfer a probationary member to full membership, prolong a probationary period, or annul a probationary membership must be made through discussion by the general membership meeting of the party branch concerned and approved by the next higher party organization.

The probationary period of probationary member begins from the day of the general membership meeting of the party branch, which admits him as a probationary member. The party standing of a member begins from the day he is transferred to full membership on the expiration of the probationary period.

Article 8. Every party member, irrespective of position, must be organized into a branch, cell, or other specific unit of the party to participate in the regular activities of the party organization and accept supervision by the masses inside and outside the party. Leading cadres of the party must also participate in democratic discussions at meetings of party committees or units. There shall be no privileged party members who do not participate in the regular activities of the party organization, and do not accept supervision by the masses inside and outside the party.

Article 9. Party members are free to withdraw from the party. When a party member asks to withdraw, the party branch concerned shall, after discussion by its general membership meeting, remove his name from the party rolls, make the removal publicly known, and report it to the next higher party organization for the record.
    The party branch concerned should educate a party member who lacks revolutionary will, fails to fulfil the duties of a party member, and is not qualified for membership, and should set a time limit by which the member must correct his mistakes; and if he remains incorrigible after repeated education, he should be persuaded to withdraw from the party. The case shall be discussed and decided by the general membership meeting of the party branch concerned and submitted to the next hither party organization for approval. If the party member being persuaded to withdraw refuses to do so, the case shall be submitted to the general membership meeting of the party branch concerned for discussion and decision on the removal of his name from party rolls, and the decision shall be submitted to the next higher party organization for approval.
    A party member who fails to take part in regular party activities, pay membership dues or do work assigned by the party for six

successive months without proper reason is regarded as having given up membership. The general membership meeting of the party branch concerned shall decide on the removal of such a person's name from the party roll and report the removal to the next higher party organization for approval.

Chapter II: Organizational system of the party

Article 10. The party is an integral body organized under its programme and Constitution, and on the principle of democratic centralism. The basic principles of democratic centralism as practised by the party are as follows:

(1) Individual party members are subordinate to the party organization, the minority is subordinate to the majority, the lower party organizations are subordinate to the higher party organizations, and members of the party are subordinate to the National Congress and the Central Committee of the party.

(2) The party's leading bodies of all levels are elected except for the representative organs dispatched by them and the leading party members' groups in non-party organizations.

(3) The highest leading body of the party is the National Congress and the Central Committee elected by it. The leading bodies of local party organizations are the party congresses at their respective levels and the party committees elected by them. Party committees are responsible, and report their work to the party congresses at their respective levels.

(4) Higher party organizations shall pay constant attention to the views of the lower organizations and the rank-and-file party members and solve in good time the problems they raise. Lower party organizations shall report on their work to and request instructions from higher party organizations;

at the same time, they shall handle, independently and in a responsible manner, matters within their jurisdiction. Higher and lower party organizations should exchange information and support and supervise each other. Party organizations at all levels shall make it possible for party members to have a better understanding of and more participation in the party's affairs.
(5) Party committees at all levels function on the principle of combining collective leadership with individual responsibility based on division of labour. All major issues shall be decided upon by the party committee after collective discussion. Members of the party committee shall effectively perform their duties according to collective decisions and division of labour.
(6) The party forbids all forms of personality cult. It is necessary to ensure that the activities of party leaders be subject to supervision by the party and the people, while at the same time to uphold the prestige of all leaders who represent the interests of the party and the people.

Article 11. The election of delegates to party congresses and of members of party committees at all levels should reflect the will of the voters. Elections shall be held by secret ballot. The lists of candidates shall be submitted to party organizations and voters for full deliberation and discussion. The election procedure of nominating a larger number of candidates than the number of persons to be elected may be used in a formal election. Or this procedure may be used first in a preliminary election in order to draw up a list of candidates for the formal election. The voters have the right to inquire about the candidates, demand a change or reject one in favour of another. No organization or individual shall in any way compel voters to elect or not elect any candidate.

If any violation of the party Constitution occurs in the election of delegates to a local party congress, the party committee at the next higher level shall, after investigation and verification, decide to invalidate the election and take appropriate measures. The decision shall be reported to the party committee at the next higher level for checking and approval before it is formally announced and implemented.

Article 12. When necessary, party committees at the central and local levels may convene conferences of delegates to discuss and decide on major problems that require timely solutions. The number of delegates to such conferences and the procedure governing their election shall be determined by the party committees convening them.

Article 13. The formation of a new party organization or the dissolution of an existing one shall be decided upon by the higher party organizations.

Party committees at the central and local levels may send out their representative organs.

When the congress of a local party organization at any level, including the grass-roots level, is not in session, the next higher party organization may, when it deems it necessary, transfer or appoint responsible members of that organization.

Article 14. When making decisions on important questions affecting the lower organizations, the leading bodies of the party at all levels should, in ordinary circumstances, solicit the opinions of the lower organizations. Measures should be taken to ensure that the lower organizations can exercise their functions and powers normally. Except in special circumstances, higher leading bodies should not interfere with matters that ought to be handled by lower organizations.

Article 15. Only the Central Committee of the party has the power to make decisions on major policies of a nationwide character.

Party organizations of various departments and localities may make suggestions with regard to such policies to the Central Committee, but shall not make any decisions or publicize their views outside the party without authorization.

Lower party organizations must firmly implement the decisions of higher party organizations. If lower organizations consider that any decisions of higher organizations do not suit actual conditions in their localities or department, they may request modification. If the higher organizations insist on their original decisions, the lower organizations must carry out such decisions and refrain from publicly voicing their differences, but have the right to report it to the next higher party organization.

Newspapers, journals, and other means of publicity run by party organizations at all levels must propagate the line, principles, policies, and resolutions of the party.

Article 16. When discussing and making decisions on any matter, party organizations must keep to the principle of subordination of the minority to the majority. A vote must be taken when major issues are decided on. Serious consideration should be given to the differing views of a minority. In case of controversy over major issues in which supporters of two opposing views are nearly equal in number - except in emergencies where action must be taken in accordance with the majority view - the decision should be put off to allow for further investigation, study, and exchange of opinions followed by another vote. Under special circumstances, the controversy may be reported to the next higher party organization for ruling.

When, on behalf of the party organization, an individual party member is to express views on major issues beyond the scope of existing decisions of the party organization, the content must be referred to the party organization to which the party member is affiliated to, for prior discussion and decision; or must be referred to the next higher party organization for instructions. No party member, whatever his position, is allowed to make decisions on major issues on his own. In an emergency, when a decision by an individual is unavoidable, the matter must be reported to the party organization immediately afterward. No leader is allowed to decide matters arbitrarily on his own or to place himself above the party organization.

Article 17. The central, local, and primary organizations of the party must all pay great attention to party building. They shall regularly discuss and check up on the party's work in propaganda, education, organization, discipline inspection, mass work, and united front work. They must carefully study ideological and political developments inside and outside the party.

Chapter III: Central organizations of the party

Article 18. The National Congress of the party is held once every five years and convened by the Central Committee. It may be convened before the due date if the Central Committee deems it necessary or if more than one-third of the organizations at the provincial level so request. Except under extraordinary circumstances, the congress may not be postponed.

The number of delegates to a National Congress of the party and the procedure governing their election shall be determined by the Central Committee.

Article 19. The functions and powers of the National Congress of the party are as follows:

(1) To hear and examine the report of the Central Committee;
(2) To hear and examine the report of the Central Commission for Discipline Inspection;
(3) To discuss and decide on major questions concerning the party;

(4) To revise the Constitution of the party;
(5) To elect the Central Committee; and
(6) To elect the Central Commission for Discipline Inspection.

Article 20. The authority and functions of the national conference of party delegates are to discuss and decide on major issues; and to readjust and elect through by-election some members of the Central Committee and Central Discipline Inspection Commission. The number of members and alternate members of the Central Committee adjusted or elected through by-election must not exceed one-fifth of the total number of Central Committee members and alternate members elected at the National Party Congress.

Article 21. Each term of the party's Central Committee is five years. In case of the advancement or postponement of the convening of the National Party Congress, the Central Committee's term shall be correspondingly shortened or extended. Members and alternate members of the Central Committee must have a party standing of five years or more. The number of members and alternate members of the Central Committee shall be determined by the National Congress. Vacancies on the Central Committee shall be filled by its alternate members in the order of the number of votes by which they were elected.

The Central Committee meets in plenary session at least once a year, and such sessions are convened by its Political Bureau.

When the National Congress is not in session, the Central Committee carries out its decisions, directs the entire work of the party and represent the CCP in its external relations.

Article 22. The Political Bureau, the Standing Committee of the Political Bureau, and the General Secretary of the Central Committee are elected by the Central Committee in plenary session. The General Secretary of the Central Committee must be a member of the Standing Committee of the Political Bureau.

When the plenary session of the Central Committee is not in session, the Political Bureau of the Central Committee and its Standing Committee exercise the functions and powers of the Central Committee.

The Secretariat of the Central Committee is an organization that runs day-to-day work for the Political Bureau of the Central Committee and its Standing Committee. Members of the secretariat are nominated by the Standing Committee of the Political Bureau of the Central Committee and approved by the Central Committee in plenary session.

The General Secretary of the Central Committee is responsible for convening the meetings of the Political Bureau and its Standing Committee, and presides over the work of the Secretariat.

Members of the Military Commission of the Central Committee are decided on by the Central Committee.

The central leading bodies and leaders elected by each Central Commission shall, when the next National Congress is in session, continue to preside over the party's day-to-day work until the new central leading bodies and leaders are elected by the next Central Committee.

Article 23. Party organizations in the Chinese PLA [People's Liberation Army] carry on their work in accordance with the instructions of the Central Committee. The General Political Department of the Chinese PLA is the political work organ of the Military Commission; it directs party and political work in the army. The organizational system and organs of the party in the armed forces will be prescribed by the Military Commission.

Chapter IV: Local organizations of the party

Article 24. A party congress of a province, autonomous region, municipality directly under the central government, city divided into districts, or autonomous prefecture is held once every five years.

A party congress of a county (banner), autonomous county, city not divided into districts, or municipal district is held once every five years.

Local party congresses are convened by the party committees at the corresponding levels. Under extraordinary circumstances, they may be held before or after their due dates upon approval by the next higher party committees.

The number of delegates to the local party congresses at any level and the procedure governing their election are determined by the party committees at the corresponding levels and should be reported to the next higher party committees for approval.

Article 25. The functions and powers of the local party congresses at all levels are as follows:

(1) To hear and examine the reports of the party committees at the corresponding levels;
(2) To hear and examine the reports of the Commissions for discipline inspection at the corresponding levels;
(3) To discuss and decide on major issues in the given areas; and
(4) To elect the party committees and Commissions for discipline inspection at the corresponding levels.

Article 26. The party committee of the province, autonomous region, municipality directly under the central government, city divided into districts, or autonomous prefecture is elected for a term of five years. The members and alternative members of such a committee must have a party standing of five years or more.

The party committee of a county (banner), autonomous county, city not divided into districts, or municipal district is elected for a term of five years. The members and alternate members of such a committee must have a party standing of three years or more.

When local party congresses at various levels are convened before or after their due dates, the terms of the committees elected by the previous congresses shall be correspondingly shortened or extended.

The number of members and alternate members of the local party committees at various levels shall be determined by the next higher committees. Vacancies on the local party committees at various levels shall be filled by their alternate members in the order of the number of votes by which they were elected.

The local party committees at various levels meet in plenary session at least twice a year.

Local party committees at various levels shall, when the party congresses of the given areas are not in session, carry out the directives of the next higher party organizations and the decisions of the party congresses at the corresponding levels, direct work in their own areas, and report on it to the next higher party committees at regular intervals.

Article 27. Local party committees at various levels elect, at their plenary sessions, their Standing Committees, secretaries, and deputy secretaries, and report the results to the higher party committees for approval. The Standing Committees at various levels exercise the powers and functions of local party committees when the latter are not in session. They continue to handle the day-to-day work when the next party congresses at their levels are in session, until the new Standing Committees are elected.

Article 28. A prefectural party committee, or an organization analogous to it, is the representative organ dispatched by a provincial or an autonomous regional party committee to a prefecture embracing several counties, autonomous counties or cities. It exercises leadership over the work in the given region as authorized by the provincial or autonomous regional party committee.

Chapter V: Primary organizations of the party

Article 29. Primary party organizations are formed in enterprises, rural villages, offices, schools, scientific research institutions, city neighbourhoods, PLA companies, and other basic units, where there are three or more full party members.

In primary party organizations, the primary party committees, or committees of general party branches and party branches are set up as the work requires and according to the number of party members, subject to approval by the higher party organizations. A primary party committee is elected by a general membership meeting or a meeting of delegates. The committee of a general party branch or a party branch is elected by a general membership meeting.

Article 30. A primary party committee is elected for a term of three or four years, while a general party branch committee or a party branch committee is elected for a term of two or three years. Results of the election of a secretary and deputy secretaries by a primary party committee, general party branch committee, or party branch committee shall be reported to the higher party organization for approval.

Article 31. The primary party organizations are militant bastions of the party in the basic units of society. They are the basis of the party's entire work and fighting capacity. Their main tasks are:

(1) to propagate and carry out the party's line, principles, and policies, and decisions of the party Central Committee and other higher party organizations, and their own party organizations; to give full play to the exemplary vanguard role of party members; and to unite and organize the cadres

and the rank and file inside and outside the party in fulfilling the tasks of their own units.

(2) To organize party members to conscientiously study Marxism-Leninism and Mao Zedong Thought; study Deng Xiaoping Theory and the party's line, principles, policies, and decisions; study essential knowledge concerning the party; and study scientific, cultural, and professional knowledge.

(3) To educate, manage and supervise party members, improve their quality, enhance their party spirit, ensure their regular participation in the activities of the party organization, promote criticism and self-criticism, safeguard and enforce party discipline, see that party members truly fulfil their duties, and protect their rights from encroachment.

(4) To maintain close ties with the masses, constantly seek their criticisms and opinions regarding party members and the party's work, protect their legitimate rights and interests, and ensure good ideological and political work among them.

(5) To give full scope to the initiate and creativeness of party members and the masses; discover, train, and make recommendations for talented people; encourage them to contribute their wisdom and talent to reform, opening up, and modernization drive; and support them in these efforts.

(6) To educate and train activists asking to be admitted into the party, recruit party members on a regular basis, and attach importance to recruiting outstanding workers, peasants, and intellectuals working on the forefront of production and other fields of endeavour.

(7) To see that party and other non-party functionaries strictly observe the state laws and administration discipline, and the financial and economic regulations and personnel system; and that none of them infringe the interests of the State, the collective, and the masses.

(8) To educate party members and the masses to conscientiously resist unhealthy tendencies and wage resolute struggles against various lawbreaking activities.

Article 32. Neighbourhood, township and town primary party organizations, and village party branches lead the work of their areas; support administrative, economic, and mass self-management organizations; and ensure that such organizations fully exercise their functions and powers.

In a State-owned enterprise, the primary party organization shall give full play to its role as the political nucleus, and perform its work around enterprise production and management. It shall ensure and supervise the implementation of party and State principles and policies in the enterprise; support the factory director (or manager) in performing his duties according to the law, and uphold and improve the system of full responsibility for factory directors (or managers); rely wholeheartedly on the masses of workers and staff members, and support the workers congress in performing its work; participate in making major decisions for the enterprise; strengthen itself; and lead ideological and political work as well as trade union and Communist Youth League organizations.

In an institution implementing the system of full responsibility for administrative leaders, the primary party organization shall give full play to its role as the political nucleus. In an institution where the system of full responsibility for administrative leaders is implemented under the leadership of the party committee, the primary party organization shall discuss major issues and decide on them, and ensure that the administrative leader fully exercises his functions and powers.

In party or State offices at all levels, the primary party organizations shall assist the head of these offices in fulfilling their tasks, improving their work, and in exercising supervision over all party members, including the heads of these offices who are party members. However, they shall not lead the work of these offices.

Chapter VI: Party cadres

Article 33. Party cadres are the backbone of the party's cause and public servants of the people. The party selects its cadres according to the principle that they should possess both political integrity and professional competence, persists in the practice of appointing people on their merits and opposes favouritism; it calls for genuine efforts to make the ranks of the cadres more revolutionary, younger in average age, better educated, and more professionally competent.

The party should attach importance to the education, training, promotion, and appraisal of cadres, especially the training and promotion of outstanding young cadres. Vigorous efforts should be made to reform the cadre system.

The party should attach importance to the training and promotion of women cadres and cadres from among the minority nationalities.

Article 34. Leading party cadres at all levels must perform in an exemplary way their duties as party members prescribed in Article 3 of this Constitution and must meet the following basic requirements:

(1) To have a knowledge of Marxism-Leninism-Mao Zedong Thought and Deng Xiaoping Theory needed to perform their duties, and to strive to use the Marxist stand, viewpoint, and method to solve practical problems.
(2) To resolutely implement the party's basic line, principles, and policies, be determined to carry out reform and opening to the outside world, devote themselves to the cause of modernization, and work hard to blaze new trails

and make actual achievements in socialist construction.
(3) To persevere in seeking truth from facts, conscientiously conduct investigations and study, integrate the party's principles and policies with the realities of their areas or departments, tell the truth, do practical work, work for actual results, and oppose formalism.
(4) To be fervently dedicated to the revolutionary cause and imbued with a strong sense of political responsibility and be qualified for their leading posts in organizational ability, general education, and professional knowledge.
(5) To correctly exercise the powers entrusted to them by the people, be honest and upright, work hard for the people, make themselves an example, carry forward the style of hard work and plain living, forge close ties with the masses, uphold the party's mass line, conscientiously accept criticism and supervision by the masses, oppose bureaucracy, and oppose the unhealthy trend of abusing one's power for personal gain.
(6) To uphold the party's democratic centralism, have a democratic work style, take the overall situation into account, and be good at uniting and working with comrades, including those holding differing opinions.

Article 35. Party cadres should be able to co-operate with non-party cadres, respect them, and learn from their strong points with an open mind.

Party organizations at all levels must be good at discovering and recommending talented and knowledgeable non-party cadres for leading posts, and ensure that the latter enjoy authority commensurate with their post and can play their roles to the full.

Article 36. Leading party cadres at all levels, whether elected through democratic procedure or appointed by a leading body, are not entitled to lifelong tenure, and they all can be transferred from or relieved of their posts.

Cadres no longer fit to continue work due to old age or poor health should retire according to the State regulations.

Chapter VII: Party discipline

Article 37. Party discipline is the code of conduct that party organizations at all levels and all party members must observe; it is a guarantee for safeguarding the party's solidarity and unity and the accomplishment of the party's tasks. Party organizations shall strictly enforce and safeguard party discipline. A Communist Party member must consciously act within the bounds of party discipline.

Article 38. Party organizations shall criticize, educate, or take disciplinary measures against members who violate party discipline, depending on the nature and seriousness of their mistakes and in the spirit of learning from past mistakes to avoid future ones, and curing the sickness to save the patient.

Party members who have seriously violated the criminal law shall be expelled from the party.

It is strictly forbidden, within the party, to take any measures against a member that contravene the party Constitution or the laws of the State, or to retaliate against or frame up a member. Any offending organization or individual must be dealt with according to party discipline or the laws of the State.

Article 39. There are five measures of party discipline: Warning, serious warning, removal from party posts, placing on probation within the party, and expulsion from the party.

The period for which a party member is placed on probation shall not exceed two years. During this period, the party member concerned has no right to vote, elect or stand for election. A party member who during this time proves to have corrected his mistake shall have his rights as a party member restored. Party members who refuse to mend their ways shall be expelled from the party.

Expulsion is the ultimate party disciplinary measure. In deciding on or approving an expulsion, party organizations at all levels should study all the relevant facts and opinions, and exercise extreme caution.

Article 40. Any disciplinary measure against a party member must be discussed and decided on at a general membership meeting of the party branch concerned, and reported to the primary party committee concerned for approval. If the case is relatively important or complicated, or involves the expulsion of a member, it shall be reported, on the merit of that case, to a party Commission for discipline inspection at or above the county level for examination and approval. Under special circumstances, a party committee or a Commission for discipline inspection at or above the county level has the authority to decide directly on disciplinary measures against a party member.

Any decision to remove a member or alternate member of the Central Committee or a local committee at any level from posts within the party, to place such a person on probation within the party or to expel him from the party, must be taken by a two-thirds majority vote at a plenary meeting of the party committee to which he belongs. Under special circumstances, the Political Bureau of the CCP Central Committee or the standing committees of local party committees at all levels may adopt a decision on disciplinary measures, which has to be confirmed when the committees meet in plenary session. Such a disciplinary measure against a member or alternate member of local committees at all levels is subject to approval by the higher party committees.

Members or alternate members of the Central Committee who have seriously violated criminal law shall be expelled from the party on the decision of the Political Bureau of the Central

Committee; members and alternate members of local party committees who have seriously violated criminal law shall be expelled from the party on the decision of the Standing Committees of the party committees at the corresponding levels.

Article 41. When a party organization decides on a disciplinary measure against a party member, it should investigate and verify the facts in an objective way. The party member in question must be informed of the decision to be made and of the facts on which it is based. He must be given a chance to account for himself and speak in his own defence. If the member does not accept the decision that has been adopted, he can appeal; the party organization concerned must promptly deal with or forward his appeal and must not withhold or suppress it. Those who cling to erroneous views and unjustifiable demands shall be educated by criticism.

Article 42. Failure of a party organization to uphold party discipline must be investigated. In case a party organization seriously violates party discipline and is unable to rectify the mistake on its own, the next higher party committee should, after verifying the facts and considering the seriousness of the case, decide on the reorganization or dissolution of the organization, report the decision to the party committee higher up for examination and approval; and then formally announce and carry out the decision.

Chapter VIII: Party organs for discipline inspection

Article 43. The party's Central Commission for Discipline Inspection functions under the leadership of the Central Committee of the party. Local Commissions for discipline inspection at all levels function under the dual leadership of the party committees at the corresponding levels and the next higher Commissions for discipline inspection.

The local Commissions for discipline inspection serve a term of the same duration as the party committees at the corresponding levels.

The Central Commission for Discipline Inspection elects, in plenary session, its Standing Committee and secretary and deputy secretaries, and reports the results to the Central Committee for approval. Local Commissions for discipline inspection at all levels elect, at their plenary sessions, their respective Standing Committees, and secretaries and deputy secretaries. The results of the elections are subject to endorsement by the party committees at the corresponding levels and should be reported to the higher party committees for approval. The question of whether a grass-roots party committee should set up a Commission for discipline inspection or simply appoint a discipline inspection Commissioner shall be determined by the next higher party organization in the light of the specific circumstances. The committees of general party branches and party branches shall have discipline inspection Commissioners.

The party's Central Commission for Discipline Inspection shall, when its work so requires, accredit discipline inspection groups or commissioners to party or State organs at the central level. Leaders of the discipline inspection groups or discipline inspection Commissioners may attend relevant meetings of the leading party organizations in the said organs as non-voting participants. The leading party organizations in the organs concerned must support their work.

Article 44. The main tasks of the central and local Commissions for discipline inspection are as follows: To uphold the Constitution and the other important rules and regulations of the party, to assist the respective party committees in rectifying party style, and to check up on the implementation of the line, principles, policies, and decisions of the party.

The central and local Commissions for discipline inspection shall carry out constant education among party members on their duty to observe party discipline. They shall adopt decisions for the upholding of party discipline; examine and deal with relatively important or complicated cases of violation of the Constitution and other laws and regulations of the party by party organizations or party members; decide on or cancel disciplinary measures against party members involved in such cases; and deal with complaints and appeals made by party members.

The central and local Commissions for discipline inspection should report to the party committees at the corresponding levels on the results of their handling of cases of special importance or complexity, as well as on the problems encountered. Local Commissions for discipline inspection or such a Commission at the basic level should also present such reports to the higher Commissions.

If a discipline inspection Commission discovers violation of party discipline by any member of a party committee at the corresponding levels, it may conduct an initial verification of facts; if the case requires the setting up of a file for investigation, it should report to the party committee at the corresponding level for approval; if the case involves a Standing Committee member of the party committee, the Commission should report such an offence to the party committee at the corresponding level and to the higher discipline inspection Commission for approval.

Article 45. Higher Commissions for discipline inspection have the power to check up on the work of the lower Commissions and to approve or modify their decisions on any case. If decisions so modified have already been ratified by the party committee at the corresponding level, the modification must be approved by the next higher party committee.

If a local Commission for discipline inspection or such a

Commission at the basic level does not agree with a decision made by the party committee at the corresponding level in dealing with a case, it may request the Commission at the next higher level to re-examine the case; if a local Commission discovers cases of violation of party discipline by the party committee at the corresponding level or by its members, and if that party committee fails to deal with them properly or at all, it has the right to appeal to the higher Commissions for assistance in dealing with such cases.

Chapter IX: Leading party members' groups

Article 46. A leading party members' group shall be formed in the leading body of a central or local State organ, people's organization, economic or cultural institution or other non-party unit. The main tasks of such a group are: To see to it that the party's line, principles, and policies are implemented; discuss and make decisions on major issues in their respective units; to unite with the non-party cadres and masses in fulfilling the tasks assigned by the party and the State; and to guide the work of the party organizations of the department and those in the units directly under it.

Article 47. The members of a leading party members' group are appointed by the party committee that approves its establishment. The group shall have a secretary and deputy secretaries.

The leading party members' group shall subject itself to the leadership of the party committee that approves its establishment.

Article 48. Party committees may be set up in those government departments which need to exercise centralized and unified leadership over subordinate units. Procedures for electing such a committee and its functions, powers, and tasks shall be provided separately by the Central Committee of the party.

Chapter X: Relationship between the party and the Communist Youth League

Article 49. The Communist Youth League of China (CYL) is a mass organization of advanced young people under the leadership of the CCP; it is a school where large numbers of young people will learn about communism through practice; it is the party's assistant and reserve force. The CYL Central Committee functions under the leadership of the Central Committee of the party. Local CYL organizations are under the leadership of the party committees at the corresponding levels and of the higher organizations of the League itself.

Article 50. Party committees at all levels must strengthen their leadership over the CYL organizations, and pay attention to the selection and training of league cadres. The party must firmly support the CYL in the lively and creative performance of its work to suit the characteristics and needs of young people, and give full play to the league's role as a shock force and as a bridge linking the party with the broad masses of young people.

Those secretaries of league committees, at or below the county level or in enterprises and institutions, who are party members may attend meetings of party committees at the corresponding levels, and of their Standing Committees as non-voting participants.

DOCUMENT 18

United States
Foreign Relation Authorization Act
Fiscal Years 1996 and 1997

H. R. 1561
(Excerpt)

SECTION 1303. SPECIAL ENVOY FOR TIBET.

(a) UNITED STATES SPECIAL ENVOY FOR TIBET - The President should appoint within the Department of State a United States Special Envoy for Tibet, who shall hold office at the pleasure of the President.

(b) RANK - A United States Special Envoy for Tibet appointed under subsection (a) shall have the personal rank of ambassador and shall be appointed by and with the advice and consent of the Senate.

(c) SPECIAL FUNCTIONS - The United States Special Envoy for Tibet should be authorized and encouraged -

(1) to promote substantive negotiations between the Dalai Lama or his representatives and senior members of the governments of the People's Republic of China;

(2) to promote good relations between the Dalai Lama or his representatives and the United States Government, including meeting with members of the Tibetan Government-in-exile; and

(3) to travel regularly throughout Tibet and Tibetan refugee settlements.

(d) DUTIES AND RESPONSIBILITIES - The United States Special Envoy for Tibet should -

(1) consult with the congress on policies relevant to Tibet and the future and welfare of all Tibetan people;

(2) coordinate United States Government policies, programs, and projects concerning Tibet; and

(3) report to the Secretary of State regarding the matters described in section 536(a)(2) of the Foreign Relations Authorization Act, Fiscal Years 1994 and 1995 (Public Law 103-236).

SECTION 1410. EDUCATIONAL AND CULTURAL EXCHANGES AND SCHOLARSHIPS FOR TIBETANS AND BURMESE.

(a) ESTABLISHMENT OF EDUCATIONAL AND CULTURAL EXCHANGE FOR TIBETANS.

The Director of the United States Information Agency shall establish programs of educational and cultural exchange between the United States and the people of Tibet. Such programmes shall include opportunities for training and, as the Director considers appropriate, may include the assignment of personnel and resources abroad.

(b) SCHOLARSHIPS FOR TIBETANS AND BURMESE -

(1) For each of the fiscal years 1996 and 1997, at least 30 scholarships shall be made available to Tibetan students and professionals who are outside Tibet, and at least 15 scholarships shall be made available to Burmese students and professionals who are outside Burma.

(2) WAIVER - Paragraph (1) shall not apply to the extent that the Director of the United States Information Agency determines that there are not enough qualified students to fulfil such allocation

requirement.

(3) SCHOLARSHIP DEFINED - For the purpose of this section, the term `scholarship' means an amount to be used for full or partial support of tuition and fees to attend an educational institution, and may include fees, books and supplies, equipment required for courses at an educational institution, living expenses at an educational institution, and travel expenses to and from, and within, the United States.

SECTION 1411. INITIATION OF BROADCASTS BY RADIO FREE ASIA

Section 309 of the United States International Broadcasting Act of 1994 (22 U.S.C. 6208) is amended by adding at the end of the following new subsection:

(j) Not later than 180 days after the date of the enactment of the Foreign Relations Authorization Act, Fiscal Years 1996 and 1997, Radio Free Asia shall initiate regular broadcasts to the People's Republics of China, Burma, Cambodia, Laos, North Korea, Tibet, and Vietnam. Such broadcasts shall be conducted under the name `Radio Free Asia' and shall provide accurate and timely information, news, and commentary about the events in the respective countries of Asia and elsewhere, and shall be a forum for a variety of opinions and voices from within Asian Nations whose people do not fully enjoy freedom of expression.

DOCUMENT 19

House of Commons Debate on Tibet

April 1, 1998

Mr Harry Cohen (Leyton and Wanstead): I am delighted to have obtained this debate on Tibet. I am a member of the all-party parliamentary Tibet group, and I pay tribute to its members and officers, such as Lord Weatherill, a former Speaker of the House; my hon. Friend the Member for Stoke-on-Trent, South (Mr. Stevenson), the Chairman; the hon. Member for Ruislip-Northwood (Mr. Wilkinson), Lord Avebury and Lord Willoughby de Broke, the vice-chairs; my hon. Friend the Member for Sunderland, South (Mr. Mullin), the secretary; and the hon. Member for Belfast, South (Rev. Martin Smyth).

Last month, my colleagues and I attended a wreath-laying ceremony at the monument to innocent victims of violence at Westminster Abbey. Many Tibetans are innocent victims of violence, and the debate takes place at a good time, because the Asian leaders summit is taking place in London this week. China, one of the great powers in Asia, will be represented.

I have great respect for the progress that China has made, especially economic and social progress, but it should not expect to flout long-accepted international standards without serious criticism. It has flouted those established standards to a major extent in Tibet. I hope that the government will tell the Foreign Minister that colonisation, imperialism - a word that they will understand - attempts to extinguish a unique cultural heritage and the denial of proper human rights in Tibet are unacceptable.

If China is to be a truly great player in the world and respected throughout the world, it now has to adopt internationally accepted norms of democracy, human rights and the tolerant acceptance of diversity, especially of cultures of long standing and of religious beliefs. China is not meeting those norms in Tibet.

The legal status of Tibet has a long history, but was a *de facto* independent state between 1913 and 1950. Central Tibet was ruled from Lhasa. It demonstrated all the conditions of statehood generally accepted under international law. It was a people, a territory, and it had a government who conducted their domestic affairs free from any outside authority. Then came the Chinese invasion. In 1951, a 17-point Agreement between Mao Tse-Tung and the Dalai Lama was signed. The Dalai Lama had no choice but to sign it in the wake of the Chinese takeover. It was a *fait accompli*.

Even the 1951 agreement has been violated in main part by the Chinese. They undertook to maintain the existing political system in Tibet, to maintain the status and functions of the Dalai Lama, to protect freedom of religion and the monasteries, and to refrain from compulsory reform. They have not done so. They have proceeded with a policy of absorption of Tibet into China. That has been recognized and objected to by the United Nations in its resolutions of 1959, 1961 and 1965.

A report was published in December last year by the International Commission of Jurists, which has consultative status with the United Nations. The report is a 390 page indictment of Chinese rule in Tibet. It focuses not only on the entire period since the Chinese invasion of central Tibet in 1950, but on events in recent years. It finds that repression in Tibet has increased steadily since 1994. It refers to the third national forum on work in Tibet, a key Chinese grouping of senior officials. The forum has embarked on a campaign to curtail the influence of the Dalai Lama and to crack down on dissent.

The ICJ report says that, from the beginning of 1996, there has been further escalation of repression in Tibet, with a re-education drive in monasteries, and intimidation of monks and nuns. It says that, in 1997, the forum labelled Buddhism a foreign culture. That is in Tibet, the home of Tibetan Buddhism.

The report is damning in many regards. On autonomy, it says that there is a centralized dominance of the Chinese communist party, and that Tibetans are excluded from meaningful participation in regional and local administration. Where Tibetans are in positions of nominal authority, they are shadowed by much more powerful Chinese officials. The ICJ says that that is not in keeping with the concept of autonomy.

The report refers to threats to Tibetan identity, and quotes the United Nations resolution, which talks about the suppression of the distinctive cultural and religious life of the Tibetan people. The report refers to the 1991 sub-commission on prevention of discrimination and protection of minorities of the United Nations Commission on Human Rights, which expressed continuing concern at the reports of violations of fundamental human rights and freedoms which threaten the distinctive cultural and religious national identity of the Tibetan people.

The ICJ report refers to population transfers. Since 1950, there has been a large influx of Chinese into Tibet. Tibetan urban centres have been sinicized. It is estimated that Chinese people now account for one third of the total population of all areas within the Tibetan autonomous area.

Tibet's cultural heritage is also referred to in the CIJ report. It says that, in the early years of Chinese rule, there was a destruction of the monastic system, and that that was carried on in the cultural revolution. Few of Tibet's thousands of monasteries have survived. Traditional Tibetan architecture has been demolished, and entire neighbourhoods of Tibetan houses have been razed to the ground.

The report says that the Chinese language dominates in every walk of life, and that the Tibetan language has been marginalized. Even subjects such as Tibetan art are taught in Chinese. The report recognizes that the Chinese have brought in modern technologies of health care, transport and communication, but says that development has marginalized Tibetans, excluding them from effective participation. The livelihood of most Tibetans has been neglected, receiving little of the Chinese investment.

The report says that, in the 40 years since the Chinese takeover, most Tibetan wildlife has been destroyed, and much of the forest has been cut. Watersheds and hill slopes have been eroded, and downstream flooding has heightened. Degradation of the rangelands has resulted in the desertification of large areas capable of sustaining both wild and domestic herds. The extent of the grassland deterioration threatens the long-term viability of nomadic Tibetan civilisation.

The report says that a primary stated goal of the justice system of the Chinese in Tibet is the repression of Tibetan opposition to Chinese rule. Many Tibetans, especially political detainees, are deprived of even elementary safeguards of due process.

The report refers to the low quality of educational facilities and teachers for Tibetans, and their difficulties in access to education. Their rate of illiteracy, which is triple the national average, is indicative of a discriminatory structure. Education in Tibet serves to convey a sense of inferiority in comparison with the dominant Chinese culture and values.

The report refers to discrimination and false evictions of Tibetans, and the demolition of their homes. On the right to health, the report acknowledges that important improvement have been introduced by the Chinese, but says that there are signs of discrimination in their application. The infant mortality rate of Tibetans is three times the national average, and there is a serious problem of child malnutrition. There is a shortage of trained village-level health professionals to help Tibetans in villages.

The ICJ report refers to arbitrary detections. Tibetans are detained for long periods without charge, or are sentenced to imprisonment for peacefully advocating Tibetan independence or maintaining links with the Dalai Lama. It quotes the number of political prisoners as having risen in recent years to more than 600, and some Tibetan organizations put the figure at double that, which is an horrendous number.

The United Nations working group on arbitrary detention has criticized China and "called ... for the release of dozens of Tibetans detained in violation of international norms guaranteeing freedom of expression and freedom of religion."

However, there has been no response from China.

The report states:

> "Nuns account for between one-quarter and one-third of known political prisoners ... Torture and ill treatment in detention is widespread in Tibet",

involving the use of electric cattle prods and beatings with chains and sticks. The ICJ says:

> "Women, particularly nuns, appear to be subjected to some of the harshest, and gender-specific, torture, including rape using electric cattle-prods and ill treatment of the breasts."

On extra-judicial and arbitrary executions, the report states:

> "A number of unclarified deaths of political prisoners, including nuns, have occurred in Tibetan prisons in recent years, allegedly as a result of torture or negligence ... The imposition of the death penalty in Tibet - which was reportedly used 34 times ... in 1996 - is devoid of the guarantees of due process and fair trial."

The ICJ refers to freedom of expression being severely restricted, and says that the Buddhist religion is subject to "pervasive interference" by the authorities. What a damning report the ICJ's is.

The Panchen Lama is the second most important person in Tibetan Buddhism, and, by tradition, the Dalai Lama and the Panchen Lama verify one another's reincarnation. The Chinese decided to interfere with that process, and to draw lots for the choosing of the Panchen Lama.

A senior Tibetan abbot, Chadrel Rimpoche, sought a consensus between the Dalai Lama and the Chinese to get Gedhun Choekyi Nyima, the boy chosen by the traditional methods, accepted; but, for his pains and because he had consulted the Dalai Lama, he was imprisoned for six years. The Chinese returned to their system of drawing lots, and Gedhun Choekyi Nyima, his parents and all his family vanished, taken into so-called protective custody by the security forces in China.

In New Delhi, six members of the Tibetan Youth Congress are conducting a hunger strike. Their demands include that the UN resume its debate on Tibet based on its previous resolutions, and that a special rapporteur be set up to investigate the human rights situation in Tibet.

I pay tribute to the Dalai Lama and to his representatives and followers in this country - for example, the Tibet Society. The Dalai Lama is a Nobel peace prize winner, and anyone who has met him or heard him speak knows that he deserves that honour. He is a peace-loving, compassionate and wise man, who constantly opposes the use of violence in his people's struggle to regain their liberty. That non-violence is remarkable, in view of the suffering and injustice endured by the Tibetan people.

The Dalai Lama stresses the case for negotiation between him and his representatives and the Chinese Government to achieve a peaceful settlement, and, although that has not been taken up, it remains the way forward. The Chinese say that they moved in to get rid of feudalism, and that they were bringing Tibet forward. The Dalai Lama has moved away from feudal structures, toward a more modern democratic model. In that way, he has surpassed the Chinese in modernity.

The Foreign Secretary in 1947 wrote a memorandum that forms the basis of the United Kingdom Government's position on this matter. It states:

"Tibet has enjoyed *de facto* independence since 1911, and that the

British Government had always been prepared to recognize Chinese sovereignty over Tibet but only on the understanding that Tibet is regarded as autonomous."

Well, Tibet is not truly autonomous. In a letter sent to the hon. Member for Ruislip-Northwood (Mr. Wilkinson) the Vice-Chairman of the all-party group on Tibet, the government say that they believe that human rights improvements in China should best be achieved

> "through the EU's substantive human rights dialogue with China, supported by practical co-operation."

I asked the Minister to be specific about how and when he expects those discussions to result in human rights improvements in Tibet.

There should be a special co-ordinator for Tibetan affairs, either of the UK Government, or of the European Union. The US State Department has set up such a co-ordinator, and there is a European Parliament resolution calling for the EU to follow suit. I hope that the Minister will support such a move.

The special co-ordinator could argue for the human rights of the Tibetan people, and ensure that they were properly respected and monitored. He or she could press for human rights organizations such as Amnesty and the Red Cross to be allowed to operate freely in Tibet. It is shocking that even the Red Cross cannot work in Tibet. He or she could press for negotiations with the aim of achieving real autonomy for the Tibetan people.

The ICJ report's executive summary says:

> "These abuses of human rights and assaults on Tibetan culture flow from the denial of the Tibetan people's most fundamental right - to exercise self-determination."

It states that the Chinese currently operate an "alien and unpopular rule", and that self-determination should be established.

To call what is happening in Tibet repression is the kindest way of putting it; one might call it an inexorable cultural and religious genocide; but, whatever one calls it, it is not acceptable in a modern civilized world. It is Maoist fundamentalism - a form of nationalism that incorporates racism, insists that only Chinese standards are acceptable, and does not allow diversity or different cultural or religious beliefs.

That fundamentalism is not the modern way, and the Chinese need to be told as much. I hope that the government will tell China that it needs to move away from Maoism in respect of Tibet, as it has already done in other respects. I await the Minister's reply with interest, and I hope that he will speak up for greater autonomy and human rights for the Tibetan people.

The Minister of State, Foreign and Commonwealth Office (Mr. Derek Fatchett): I am grateful to my hon. Friend the Member for Leyton and Wanstead (Mr. Cohen) for raising the subject of Tibet and China and the related issues of human rights and the UK's relationship with China. I shall reply to his speech by making a few general points then turning to human rights and China, and finally making more specific points relating to Tibet. In that way, I should be able to answer the points he raises.

We as a government are deeply concerned about reports of human rights violations wherever they occur, not only in Tibet, but elsewhere in China and in other parts of the world. The House is fully aware of the government's commitment to the promotion of human rights - indeed, it is a centrepiece of our foreign and domestic policies. We are committed to the principle of the universality of human rights: human rights - economic, social, cultural, civil and political - are for all people, regardless of their sex, age, ethnic origin or where they live. All human rights are interrelated and interdependent: as my hon. Friend says, people cannot fully realise their economic rights in those countries where their civil rights are consistently violated. We share with my hon. Friend a strong commitment to the promotion of human rights.

My hon. Friend also mentioned the fact that the Asia-Europe conference takes place this week. Asian leaders will be visiting the United Kingdom, and the conference marks the first overseas visit as Prime Minister of the new Chinese Prime Minister, Zhu Ronghi.

My hon. Friend knows that, since the smooth transition in Hong Kong last year, the relationship between the United Kingdom and China has moved on to a new, more constructive footing. We hope that Premier Zhu's visit this week will strengthen that relationship.

We will continue to build upon that, but our desire for a better relationship with China does not mean that the government will turn a blind eye to the many serious concerns about the observance of human rights in China, including Tibet - far from it. We believe that, in the context of a broad, co-operative new relationship with China, we will be able to address those human rights issues directly and to work with China to bring about concrete improvements on the ground. That will be a long process, but I believe that we are already beginning to see the first fruits of the policy.

As my hon. Friend asked a direct question about it, I shall list the areas in which we believe that the United Kingdom-China and European Union-China dialogues have led to some action on the human rights agenda. I shall then give way to my hon. Friend the Member for Stoke-on-Trent, South (Mr. Stevenson).

First, as part of the dialogue, we have raised human rights issues directly with the Chinese Government. Since this government were elected on 1 May last year, Ministers have taken every opportunity to raise the subject of human rights with the Chinese Government. We have done so in eight separate Foreign Office meetings, and, most recently, my right hon. Friend the Foreign Secretary raised the matter during his visit to China in January. We shall continue to press the Chinese Government - as the Foreign Secretary and I have done - to live up to international standards. The Prime Minister and the President of the European Commission will address human rights issues in their meetings with the Chinese Premier tomorrow.

Secondly, in September last year, we established a bilateral human rights dialogue with China. In October last year, the EU resumed its human rights dialogue with China. There have already been a total of four rounds of talks, and three more are scheduled to take place this year.

Thirdly, in support of this dialogue, the European Union and China have agreed a package of practical assistance, which includes projects in the areas of civil and political as well as economic and social rights. Projects range from support for village-level democracy to help for orphans. Those projects are in addition to our own bilateral assistance programmes, such as the training of lawyers and judges, which are already in place. Before I talk about the results of that process, I give way to my hon. Friend.

Mr George Stevenson (Stoke on Trent, South): I am grateful to my hon. Friend for giving way. He will know that the troika of the European Union is due to visit Tibet in May this year. Given that it has requested to sight and make contact with the imprisoned Panchen Lama, and that the Chinese authorities have noted that request, will my hon. Friend take the opportunity presented by meetings with Premier Zhu to repeat that request on behalf of the troika with a view to obtaining a definitive answer?

Mr Fatchett: I shall come to the details of our relationship with China in terms of Tibet in a moment. My hon. Friend is correct to state that the troika wishes to see the Panchen Lama. We welcome the recent press reports that information about the child's whereabouts was given to the Austrian Foreign Minister when he visited Tibet in March. That is a step forward, and we hope to build on that move in terms of our relationship with China.

I shall briefly address the tangible results of the human rights dialogue and the approaches that we have made so far. I can cite nine positive results of that dialogue. That is not to say that that is the end of the story: we believe that it is a continuing process. However, it is important to recognize that there have been some results from the process so far. I shall list them for the benefit of the House.

First, the Chinese have signed the international covenant on economic, social and cultural rights. That is very much a step in the right direction. Secondly, the recent announcement by the Chinese that they are preparing to sign the international covenant on civil and political rights is a further step in an appropriate direction in the area of human rights.

Thirdly, we welcome the release of Wei Jingshen, who, as hon. Members will know, met me two months ago and my right hon. Friend the Foreign Secretary last month. Fourthly, the Chinese have greed to transmit Hong Kong reports under the United Nations covenants, which was one of our major objectives. That means that there will be separate reporting of Hong Kong human rights issues.

Fifthly, the European Union technical co-operation package has been agreed. I mentioned that earlier as part of the ongoing process. Sixthly, and very importantly, the Chinese have invited the United Nations High Commissioner for Human Rights, Mary Robinson, to visit China later this year. We welcome that move. Seventhly, the UN group on arbitrary detention visited China in October last year, as part of the process of more open relations.

Eighthly, as my hon. Friend the Member for Stoke-on-Trent, South said, an EU troika will visit Tibet in May. That is a good and positive sign regarding the on-going relationship with China. Finally, the EU-China seminar on the administration of justice and human rights, attended by legal experts, academics and government officials from both sides, took place in Beijing in February.

I make two points to my hon. Friend. First, we are addressing the human rights issue. Secondly, we have a strategy and a process that we believe are beginning to bear some fruit. I hope that I have set out that out for my hon. Friend.

I turn now to the issue of Tibet, about which my hon. Friend the Member for Leyton and Wanstead has expressed such knowledge and his understandable concern regarding the situation in that country. Tibet is, rightly, an issue of special concern to both the public and Parliament. I think that every hon. Member regularly receives letters from constituents about that issue. We in government share the deep concerns expressed by many inside and outside the House, and we are actively addressing those concerns with the Chinese through our human rights dialogue. The situation in Tibet features prominently in that dialogue.

My hon. Friend referred to the legal status of Tibet. I must remind the House that successive British Governments have regarded Tibet as autonomous, while recognizing the special position of China there. That continues to be the government's view. Tibet has never been internationally recognized as independent, and the government do not recognize the Dalai Lama's "government in exile". However, we strongly believe that Tibetans should have a greater say in running their own affairs in Tibet, and we have urged the Chinese authorities to respect the distinct cultural, religious and ethnic identity of the Tibetan people.

My hon. Friend referred at some length to the case of the Panchen Lama, Gedhun Choekyi Myima. My hon. Friend is correct to say that that issue raises particular worries, which not only he but other hon. Members have raised with me several times. The boy is now aged only eight, but he was detailed following his recognition in 1995 by the Dalai Lama as Panchen Lama, the second highest religious figure in Tibet.

The government cannot and will not hold a view about the child's religious candidacy as the Panchen Lama, which we believe is a matter for the Tibetans alone to decide. However, he is a child, and therefore we are deeply concerned about his welfare. His is one of the individual cases that we shall continue to raise with the Chinese at each and every opportunity.

My hon. Friend the Member for Stoke-on-Trent, South mentioned the EU troika visit. In view of the special nature of the situation in Tibet, the European Union suggested that a delegation of EU troika ambassadors in Beijing should visit Tibet as part of the EU-China human rights dialogue.

I am pleased to announce today that the Chinese have now agreed to that suggestion, and the ambassadors of the EU troika will make a week-long visit to Tibet in May in order to assess the situation there. We welcome that development. The troika programme is not yet finalized, but the ambassadors are expected to have a range of meetings not only with the government of the Tibet autonomous region but with religious leaders and ordinary Tibetans. I am sure that my hon. Friend the Member for Stoke-on-Trent, South will agree that that is very good news.

I hope that, in the brief time available to me, I have outlined the government's policy on human rights, our dialogue with China and the special importance that we attach to the question and status of Tibet. I am sure that I have persuaded the House that we take those issues seriously. There is an on-going process, and I am sure that my hon. Friend the Member for Leyton and Wanstead will be pleased to hear about the EU troika ambassador's visit. We look forward to that visit, and to their report.

It being Two o'clock, the motion for the Adjournment of the House lapsed, without Question put.

INDEX

Agreement on Measures for the Peaceful Liberation of Tibet
Agreement between the Chinese and the Tibetans 1912
   text
      translation from Nepalese   240-41
      translation from Tibetan   238-9
Agreement for the Restoration of Peaceful Relations
   and the Delimitation of a Provisional Frontier
   between China and Tibet 1918
   text   256-60
Agreement on Measures for the Peaceful Liberation
   of Tibet 1951(17-point Agreement)
   autonomy and   78
   International Commission of Jurists reports on   44-8
   ratification by Tibet   49
   repudiation by Tibet   49-51, 52
   Sino-British Joint Declaration on the question of
      Hong Kong 1985 compared   163-4, 165
   summary of Tibetan status under   28-31
   text   263-7
   Tibet's entitlement under Vienna Convention
      to repudiate   33-44
   violation by People's Republic of China   44, 48, 52
Albania   61, 65, 67
Alexandrowicz-Alexander, Professor   88
Altankhan   6
Andorra   94
Anglo-Egyptian Treaty of Alliance 1936   51-2
Anglo-Russian Convention 1907   13-14, 18, 77, 83
   text   227-9
Anglo-Tibetan Trade Regulations 1914   16
   text   251-5
arbitrary arrest   138-9
Arbitration Commission of the European Conference
   on Yugoslavia   98

Asia Relations Conference 1947	17, 91
Attlee, Clement Richard	183
Australia	65
Austria	191
autonomy	xviii
see also independence; status	
Hong Kong and	163-5
weasel word	78-9
Bailey, Colonel	18
Balfour, Arthur James	11
Bao Tong	176
Belgium	94, 190-91
Bell, Charles	17, 18
Bevin, Ernest	168, 173-4
Bhar-Khor demonstration	72
birth control and women's rights	137-8
Blair, Tony	176
Bogle, George	7
Bosnia-Herzegovina	100
Brabazon of Tara, Lord	171
Britain	
see also United Kingdom	
agreements between China and Tibet and	14
see also individually named Agreements	
conventions between China and	
see also individually named Conventions	
1890, relating to Sikkim and Tibet	8
text	211-13
1906, respecting Tibet	12, 13
suzerainty and	77, 83
text	223-6
independence of States and	93, 95
Indian independence from	17

policy on Tibet	xvii-xix, xxi, 167-9, 171-4, 183
Tibetan border disputes and	7-8
Brittan, Sir Leon	191
Broderick, Mr	171, 172
Brown, George	168
Bulgaria	61, 67, 94
cadre, weasel word	80-81
Cambodia	65
Carter, Jimmy (39th President of the United States)	180
Cassese, Antonio	112-13
CCP *see* Chinese Communist Party	
Chadrel Rinpoche	116
Chang Chub Gyaltsen	6
Chao Erh-feng	15
Chen Shui Bian	206
Chiang Kai-shek	20, 21, 178
child's rights	139-40
see also human rights; rights	
China	
see also People's Republic of China; Taiwan	
agreements between Britain and Tibet and	14
see also individually named Agreements	
conventions between Britain and	
see also individually named Conventions	
1890, relating to Sikkim and Tibet	8
text	211-13
1906, respecting Tibet	12, 13
suzerainty and	77, 83
text	223-6
destruction of Tibet by	3-4
invades Tibet 1906	15
revolution	
1911, led by Sun Yat-sen	15

1912 Communist	19-20, 21
status of Tibet and	83-5, 88-91
suzerainty over Tibet	11, 14
weakening influence over Tibet	8-9
Chinese Communist Party (CCP)	
Constitution 1982	158, 159, 160
cadre and	80-81
text	334-69
Chirol, Valentine	12
Choki Gyaltsen	6
Chu Hailan	141
Chvalkovsky, M	51
Clinton, Bill (42nd President of the United States)	185
Cohen, Harry	169-70
Conference of International Lawyers on Issues relating to Self-Determination and Independence for Tibet 1993	92
Congo (Brazzaville)	67
Convention *see individually named Conventions*	
Costa Rica	65
counter-revolutionary, weasel word	82
Croatia	100
Cuba	67
Curzon, Lord	7, 8, 9-10, 173
Cushing, Caleb	177
Czechoslovakia	51, 61, 67
Dalai Lama	6, 7
13th	15
asserts Tibet's independence	8-9
declaration of independence by	16, 89-90
visited by British political officers	17-18
14th	18, 28
appeal to United Nations 1959	53-4
appeal to United Nations 1960	56

establishes government in exile in India	53
Nobel Peace Prize lecture 1989	193-5
on need for free and democratic China	202-3
repudiation of 17-point Agreement by	49-51
wishes for future	204-5
Declaration of Independence 1913	93
text	242-4
democracy, weasel word	79-80
Deng Xiaoping	xvi, 202
Disraeli, Benjamin	167
documents, index to	209-10
Dolan, Lieutenant Brooke	181
Dorjie Ceiring	158
Dulles, John Foster	183
Eden, Sir Anthony	169
education	
patriotic re-, weasel word	82
right to	135-7
Edward VII, King of Great Britain and Ireland	11
El Salvador	
draft United Nations resolutions on Tibet	
1961	59-62
1965 and	65-7
Tibet question before United Nations 1964-65 and	64
Tibet's appeals to United Nations	
1950, motion on	25-6, 84
1960 and	57-8
election, weasel word	81-2
ethnic minorities, human rights abuses by China and	140-41
European Union,	xx, 98-9, 100, 187-92
fair trial, right to	139
Fatchett, Derek	170-71

Federation of Malaya *see* Malaysia
France   190
freedom of expression and opinion   134-5
freedom of religion, thought, conscience and association   131-2

Gedhun Choekyi Nyiama   116
genocide
   by People's Republic of China in Tibet   44-5, 126-7
   enforced birth control and   137-8
Genocide Convention 1948   44
Germany   51, 190
Gilbert, Sir Humphrey   167
Goldwater, Senator Barry   180
Gould, Basil   18
Great Britain *see* Britain
Greece   94
Guatemala   65
Guinea   65, 67
Gyaltsen Norbu   116, 136

Hacha, Emil, President of Czechoslovakia   51
Hamilton, Lord George   172-3
Harrer, Heinrich   99
Hastings, Warren   7
Hay, John   177
Hienstorfer, Dr   92
Ho Chi-Minh, Nguyen Van Thann   178-9
Hong Kong   78, 161-6
House of Commons
   debate on Tibet 1998   169-71
     text   373-85
human rights
  see also rights
   European Union and   187-90, 191

international enforcement of	xxii–xxiv
major United Nations agreements	121-4
People's Republic of China and	
Constitution 1982	86-7, 148, 153-4, 155-7
Law on Regional National Autonomy 1984	158-9
position	86-7, 196, 197-8
record	45-7, 114-16, 125-8
United Kingdom and	119-20
Hungary	64-5, 67
Hurd, Douglas Richard	169
Hyashi, General	178
independence	93-5
see also autonomy; status	
India	
draft United Nations resolution on Tibet 1965 and	65, 66
El Salvador's motion on Tibet's appeal to	
United Nations and	26
independence from Britain	17
People's Republic of China's note to government on	
Tibet's status	85-6
regrets Chinese invasion of Tibet	21-2
Indonesia	57
International Commission of Jurists	xvii, 44, 65-6, 197-8
see also Legal Inquiry Committee on Tibet	
International Court of Justice	31-2, 33
International Covenant on Civil and Political Rights	118-19
International Covenant on Economic, Social and	
Cultural Rights	118, 119-20
International Law Commission	32-3
Ireland	54, 57-62, 65-7
Israel	95
Italy	191

Jampa Chung	116
Jebtsundamba Hutuktu	142
Jiang Zemin, President of the People's Republic Of China	xvii, 176, 185, 206
Jigme Sangpo	115-16
Jokhang massacre	73-4
Kooijmans, P	129-30
Kublai Khan, Emperor of China	5
Labouchere, Mr	171-2
Lansdowne, Lord	174
Lantos, Tom	184
Lauterpacht, Sir Hersch	101-2
Leahy, Senator Patrick	184
Lee Teng-hui, President of Taiwan	196-7
Legal Inquiry Committee on Tibet	44, 48, 60, 91-2, 97
see also International Commission of Jurists	
Lhasa Convention 1904	11-12, 102
declaration appended to	13-14
text	222
suzerainty and	77
text	218-21
Li Peng	151
Liang Guoqing	130
Liechtenstein	191
Lin Hai	135
Lithuania	100
Lodi Gyari	78
Lukhangwa	49
Luxembourg	191
Macartney, Lord	7
Macdonald, Brigadier-General James	10

Malaysia	54, 56, 58-62, 65-7
Malta	65-7
Mao Zedong	20, 21, 178
Marshall, George Catlett	183
McMahon, Sir Henry	89
Minot, Lord	15
Mirsky, Jonathan	73
Mongolia	142-4
Montevideo Convention on the Rights and Duties of States 1933	97
Moore, Professor John Bassett	75
Motherland, weasel word	80
Munich Agreement 1938	51
Nationalist China *see* Taiwan	
New Zealand	57-8, 65
Ngawang Kyonmey	134-5
Ngawang Phulchung	115
Ngawang Sangdrol	114-15
Nicaragua	64, 65-7
Norway	65
pacta sunt servanda principle	32-3
Padmasambhava	5
Parker, Theodore	79
patriotic re-education, weasel word	82
Patten, Chris	169
People's Republic of China (PRC) *see also* China; Taiwan	
Communist Party Constitution 1982	158, 159, 160
cadre and	80-81
text	334-69
Constitution 1982	145-8, 149-53, 155, 159-60
human rights and	86-7, 148, 153-4, 155-7

text	268-311
defies United Nations over human rights	xvi-xvii, xx, xxiv, 197-8
El Salvador's motion on Tibe'sn appeal to United Nations and	26
future of Tibet and	xv-xvi, 203-5, 206-7
genocide	44-5
human rights abuses	45-7
invades Lhasa 1951	49
invades Tibet 1950	21-2
Law on Regional National Autonomy 1984	145, 157-8, 160
autonomy and	78
cadre and	81
human rights and	158-9
text	312-33
living standards	xvi, 198-202
status of Tibet and	85-6
Tibetan civil unrest and	72-4
Philippines	64, 65-7
Poland	64-5, 67
PRC *see* People's Republic of China	
Public Security Bureau, demonstration outside	72-3
Quianlong, Emperor of China	7, 8
Qin Yongmin	160
Reagan, Ronald (40th President of the United States)	183
recognition	96-103
Rhodesia	101
Richardson, Hugh	17, 18, 19
rights	
see also human rights	
child's	139-40
international covenants on	118-20

subsistence, violation of	135-7
women's	137-8
Romania	57, 67
Roosevelt, Franklin Delano (32nd President of the United States)	181-2
Roosevelt, Theodore (26th President of the United States)	177-8
Russia	
see also Soviet Union	
Bolshevik revolution	18
Britain's policy on Tibet and	xvii, 7, 10, 13-14, 167
Buddhism in	10
Samdrup	116
Santarakshita	5
self-determination	104-9, 110-13
Serbia	100
Shaw, Professor	102
Simla Convention 1914	16
Chinese proposals to renegotiate	17
suzerainty and	77, 83
text	245-50
Sino-British Joint Declaration on the question of Hong Kong 1985	163-4, 165
slavery and forced labour, protection from	132-4
Slovenia	100
Songtsen Gampo, King of Tibet	5
South Africa	99-100
Soviet Union	
see also Russia	
draft United Nations resolutions on Tibet and	61, 67
El Salvador's motion on Tibet's appeal to United Nations and	26
independence of states and	100, 103
Mongolia and	143

Tibet question before United Nations 1964-65 and	64-5
Tibet's appeal to United Nations 1960 and	57
splittism, weasel word	80
statehood	97-8
status	xvii, xviii, xxi-xx
see also autonomy; independence	
17-point Agreement summary	28-31
before 1913	6-14, 15-16
between 1913 and 1950	14, 16-19, 20, 99, 102
China's position	83-6
International Commission of Jurists on	48
Ireland on	58
People's Republic of China and	21-2, 85-6
Soviet Union on	57
Tibet's position	89-92
Stimson doctrine	96
strike hard	
campaign	131, 196
weasel word	82
subsistence rights	
see also human rights; rights	
violation of	133-4
Sun Yat-sen	15, 19
Supplementary Agreement regarding Mutual Withdrawal of Troops and Cessation of Hostilities between the Chinese and the Tibetans 1918	
text	261-2
suzerainty, weasel word	75-8
Taiwan	65, 66, 202
see also China; People's Republic of China	
unification with People's Republic of China	196-7, 206
United Nations membership	23-4, 95
Taktra Rimpoche	183

Tenzin Tsedup	139-40
territorial integrity, self-determination and	111
Thailand	56, 58-62, 65-7
Thisong Detsen, King of Tibet	5
Tiananmen Square massacre	127-8
Tibet	
agreements between Britain and China and	14
see also individually named Agreements	
civil unrest	72-4
climate	3
destruction by China	3-4
early history	5-6
ethnic structure	3
factors leading to present situation	xv
future	206-7
geography	1-2, 3
modernization attempts	18
population	2-3
Tirsong Detsen, King of Tibet	5
Tolstoy, Captain Ilin	181
torture	128-31
Trade Regulations	
1893	8
1908 agreement between Britain, China and	
Tibet amending	14
text	230-37
text	214-17
1914 Anglo-Tibetan	16
text	251-5
treaty	
see also individually named treaties; Vienna	
Convention on the Law of Treaties	
establishing German protectorate over Bohemia	
and Moravia	51

obligations in international law for making	31-3
Treaty of Bucharest 1812	94
Treaty of Khykhta 1915	143
Treaty of Nanking 1842	161
Treaty of Sterfano	94
Treaty of Urga 1912	89, 143
trial, right to fair	139
Truman, Harry S (33rd President of the United States)	179
Tsepan W D Shakabpa	30-31
Turkey	93-4
Turner, Captain Samuel	7
Tweedsmuir, Baroness	174
U Thant	xxiii
United Kingdom	
see also Britain	
future of Tibet and	207
House of Commons debate 1998	169-71
text	373-85
human rights and	119-20
policy on Tibet	xix, 174-6
United Nations	17
Charter	
principles	23, 24-5
void treaty and	31
China and	198, 203
Declaration of Human Rights	44, 45
failure to discuss Tibet since 1965	71
human rights and	70-71, 116-18, 119-21
major agreements	121-4
people, defined	109-10
resolutions on Tibet	
1961	58-64
1965	65-9

self-determination and	104-9
Tibet's appeals to	
1950	22-3, 26-7
El Salvador's motion	25-6, 84
1959	53-6
1960	56-8
vote on Palestine	95
United States	26, 65, 66-7
Foreign Relations Authorization Act 1996-97	183, 184-5
text	370-72
policy on Tibet	xx-xxi, 177-83, 186
recognition and	97-8
USSR *see* Soviet Union	
Van Dyke, Vernon	110-11
Vgajen, Kazi	9
Vienna Convention on the Law of Treaties 1969	52
grounds for invalidating, terminating, withdrawing	
from or suspending operation of treaty	34-5, 40
consent invalidated	35-7, 40-41, 42
fundamental change of circumstances	39-40
impossibility of performance	39
material breach	37-9
void	37, 41-2, 42-3
International Law Commission commentary	32-3
right to denounce, withdraw from or suspend	
operation of treaty	34, 42-4
Tibet's entitlement under to repudiate 17-point	
Agreement	33-44
validity of treaty	34
Vienna Convention on the Law of Treaties 1969	
void treaty and	31-2
Wang Youcai	160

Wavell, Lord	183
Wei, Jingsheng	xxiv-xxv
Weir, Colonel	18
Wenli	160
Williamson, Harry	18
women's rights	
see also human rights; rights	
enforced birth control and	137-8
Wu, Harry	133
Wu Xuequian	148-9
Younghusband, Sir Francis	10-11, 12, 90
Yuan Shih-Kai	19
Zemin, Jiang *see* Jiang Zemin	
Zhao Ziyang	176